THE FEMALE HERO
IN FOLKLORE AND LEGEND

THE FEMALE HERO IN FOLKLORE AND LEGEND

TRISTRAM POTTER COFFIN

A CONTINUUM BOOK
THE SEABURY PRESS · NEW YORK

The Seabury Press, Inc.
815 Second Avenue
New York, N.Y. 10017

Printed in the United States of America

Library of Congress Cataloging in Publication Data

Coffin, Tristram Potter, 1922-
  The female hero in folklore and legend.

  (A Continuum book)
  1. Folk-lore of woman. 2. Women in literature.
I. Title.
GR470.C63   398'.352   75-14412
ISBN O-8164-9263-8

Passage from *The Forgotten Language* by Erich Fromm. Copyright © 1951 by
Erich Fromm. Reprinted by permission of Holt, Rinehart and Winston, Publishers.

This book is dedicated, in general, to all those women who, given another chance in some Barrie-like magic forest, would choose to be female again; and, in particular (and so in paradox), to my mother:

E. P. R. C.

CONTENTS

LIST OF ILLUSTRATIONS

ACKNOWLEDGMENTS

No one writes a book entirely by himself. I would like to thank certain publishers for materials I have included and certain people for aiding me along the way. Reprinted with permission are the description of a Court of Love from Curtis Howe Walker's *Eleanor of Aquitaine,* University of North Carolina Press, Chapel Hill, 1950, 121-122; "Dula's Own Song" from the *Frank C. Brown Collection of North Carolina Folklore,* Duke University Press, Durham, 1952-1964, Vol. II, 713; the exposition of the "Little Red-Cap" story from Erich Fromm's *The Forgotten Language,* Holt, Rinehart and Winston, New York, 1951, 235-241; and the anecdote about Annie Oakley in Frank Seidel's *The Ohio Story,* World Publishing Co., New York and Cleveland, 1950, 18-21. Other passages, either brief enough for "fair use" or in public domain, have been included. Most important are from Hans Volkmann's *Cleopatra* (as translated by T. J. Cadoux), Elek Books, London, 1958; the "Introduction" to James L. Rosenberg's translation of *Sir Gawain and the Green Knight,* Holt, Rinehart and Winston, New York, 1967, *lxix-lxxi;* Roger Loomis' *The Development of Arthurian Romance,* Hutchinson, London, 1963, 52-53; Anne B. Cohen's *Poor Girl, Poor Pearl* (Memoir # 58, American Folklore Society), University of Texas Press, Austin, 1973, 5; Ruth Beitz's "The Rochester Legend" as printed in the *Annals of Iowa,* Third Series, 1966, 181-185; and John Greenway's remarks in the "Memorial Issue to Aunt Molly Jackson" of the *Kentucky Folklore Record,* Oct.-Dec., 1961. References to these and other sources are also made in the text in passing.

The traditional ballads reprinted are as follows: the #156A text of "Queen Eleanor's Confession" from Francis James Child's *The English and Scottish Popular Ballads,* Boston, 1882-1898; the text of "Burns and His Highland Mary" from Gavin Greig's *Folk-song of the North-East,* Peterhead, 1909; the text of "Frankie and Albert" as collected in North Carolina and previously published with full notes by Mellinger Henry in the *Journal of American Folklore,* XLV, 142; the broadside of "The Lexington Miller" from the Harvard College Library holdings and also previously published by Mellinger Henry in the *Journal of American Folklore,* XLII, 249-250; the same text of "Dreadful Memories" sung by Aunt Molly Jackson and printed by John Greenway in his *American Folksongs of Protest,* Philadelphia, 1953; and a variant of "Grace Brown and Chester Gillette" as sung by Robert Seager II ("The Singing Dean"), now of Baltimore, Maryland. Seager learned the song from a farmer in Pataskala, Ohio.

I would also like to thank the following persons for various services: Eve M. and Elizabeth Bachman, Kenneth S. Goldstein, Albert Harkness, Jr., William Miller, Arthur H. Scouten, Christiane and Harold M. Thewlis; in addition to Justus George Lawler, my editor, whose advice was as usual shrewd. This is not to forget either my wife, Ruth Anne, who read the manuscript, or my daughter, Priscilla, who typed it and encouraged me.

THE FEMALE HERO
IN FOLKLORE AND LEGEND

1

OF LADIES AND LEGENDS

. . . Of Ladies:

We don't split in half like amoebae—and peoples in every time
and every clime have marked the fact. Shrewdly, they have embraced *la différence,* with the result that uni-sex has always been
out, while "his and hers" has always been in.

Generally matters have been handled pragmatically. Up until
the later portions of the Paleolithic period, sex-roles amounted to
little more than assigned occupations, the division of labor being
based on mobility more than anything else. As Mother Nature
had blessed her own sex with the privilege of carrying and nursing infants, and as the men enjoyed no such blessing, it made
sense not to assign tasks that involved raid, escape, fisticuffs and
the like to those members of society who were often too swollen
to handle them.

Thus, men tended to "count coup" or run "off to the highlands a-chasing the deer" while women tended to pound corn,
poke fires, feed starving youngsters from their breasts, or do anything else that they could do efficiently. From this hard-headed,
survival-oriented cooperation emerged sexually identified skills.
But there seems to have been no comparative evaluation of the
work. The fact that there may be more glamor and excitement in

grabbing a tiger by the tail or slitting a sleeping throat than there is in plucking a duck or chewing leather did not give men ownership of anything women couldn't own. Women were not harmless, second-class drudges; they simply did what benefited the community in one way, while their unimpeded brothers did what benefited it in another.

Persons lived this way for thousands of years. It was only when some got more advanced, when property entered the picture and people began to measure status by means of possessions, that man began to capitalize on the biological fact that he doesn't have to worry about pregnancy and nursing. It was this freedom to swoop down upon, wrest, and ward off, much more than his superior strength or speed, that enabled him "to have and to hold." It resulted in his role as possessor, protector, and provider, while his mate, almost always vulnerable, found herself being possessed, protected, and provided for. As a matter of course women came to be looked upon as property, not markedly different from cattle, slaves, land and the other measurements of wealth. The patriarchies developed, while she (raided, raped, and maintained) assumed her position below as inevitably as he assumed his above.

For, simplified, the plot of the human comedy has always turned on two motifs: reproduction and food. And for most of history the female has had not only her hands, but her whole body full. It isn't until health and population growth make the need for "replacements" less crucial, until machines and steady meals offer her contraception, as well as mobility and strength if *enceinte,* and until the mind becomes more important than the body that she can do what a man does—or be, as we say, "liberated."

Moreover, it is a fact that responsible anthropologists, grouchy enough to each other on most matters, are quite in harmony on one point: there is no evidence that there ever was a "halcyon era in the past" during which women were matriarchs, the rulers of the roost, the carriers of culture. The matriarchal theory, which was popular in the nineteenth century when Western Europeans were "rediscovering" the ladies, argued that the world lost "a certain something" when She dropped the scepter and He grabbed it. Charming as it may seem to one's dinner partner, this romantic hope now lies wheels up in the junkyard of ideas, along with the Second Law of Thermodynamics, Ptolemaic astronomy, and the search for the Northwest Passage.

On the other hand, women's status in the Western world did hit an all-time low during those long years that spread between the Bronze Age and the Iron Age of classic times. It was not to rise again until the development of the bourgeois class, with its steady progress toward science, machinery, and rights. And it was between the two eras, the Paleolithic and the Modern, that our Western European culture evolved, most of our present attitudes were shaped, and our legends were made. This was an era when women, though generally freed from worry over the fruits of the field, still had her problems with the fruits of the womb—in fact, it was an era when her natural ability to foster and engender was not only institutionalized and idealized, but defined pretty much to the exclusion of other skills. The "weaker sex," she also became the "fairer."

Thus, the book at hand might well be entitled "Legends from the Doll House," for almost all the tales in it derive from Western societies in which men held property, in which women were purchasable, and in which phrases like "don't bother your silly little head about it" seemed scientifically sound. Both the heroic and the every-day women that people the stories are by necessity skilled at working obliquely, know how to attain success through another, and are willing to wait, if they must, to see their own dreams realized in a son. Still, it would be preposterous to think the mothers of the Hampdens and the "little Hampdens" didn't find ways to grasp the tiller for themselves, to sight their own stars, to acquire dominion over palm and pine. They did. And when they did, the rest, all the rest, sang their song. Yes, they left a host of "ballads," these dead ladies, and it is time we moved along to them.

Shall we, then, join the . . . legends?

. . . Of Legends:

Legends are historical stories telling about man's adventures in a world made for him by his gods. They differ from myths which are the religious stories telling how those gods created, regulated, and ordered that world; and they differ from marchen which are never-never stories taking place in a half-real, half-imaginary world in a time called "once upon." For there is an atmosphere of belief present when legends are told. Historical figures like Helen of Troy, Caesar, Cleopatra, and Abe Lincoln left footprints on our planet just as we do. And while the gods left their footprints too, they were of "another time and another place." But no one believes in Jack the Giant-killer or Cinder Ella at all. Märchen are make-believe, narrator and listener both knowing quite well that the White family had no daughter called Snow and there were no babes in the woods with either goldy locks or little red hoods.

Nonetheless, one can't forget that stories do continually shift definition as they wander from mind to mind and group to group. Legends can turn into myths, myths can become marchen, and so forth. Gods of discarded religions are not necessarily forgotten. They may become historical figures who supposedly lived in the distant past. Or they may develop into fanciful characters acting out never-never plots. Actual people may be deified, and once in a while a completely fictional character takes on historical reality. Scholars learn it is what the tale-teller and his audience consider a story to be that defines it. They can only label it as it flourishes or flourished at one time, in one place. So Hercules, an Asia Minor lion-god, becomes a misty historical figure to the fifth-century Greeks. So Juan Oso, of Spanish fairy-tale fame, was once a primitive bear-god and Uncle Remus' Br'er Rabbit once a mythological West African trickster. So Christ is a mortal prophet to the Jew, but God Himself to a Roman Catholic neighbor. So the medieval chronicler thought Aeneas to have founded Rome and his grandson, Felix Brutus, to have been the first King of Britain. Nor does this facility of stories to shift classification disappear in learned societies such as ours. The modern American is willing to travel to Hannibal, Missouri to see "the very fence" that Tom Sawyer's pals were conned into whitewashing, and the movie producer gladly hires some "scholar" to tell him what King Arthur's Round Table looked like. And what about the housewife who not only mails a letter to Sherlock Holmes at #221B Baker St., London, England, but receives an answer? And how many juvenile hearts have stood still before visions of Rhett Butler or Eustacia Vye or a dead Marilyn Monroe?

Most legends, however, are born from kernels of historical fact and remain legends as long as they are told. They spring like plants from a culture, feed on fragments of actuality, hardening and rooting firmly as they flourish. It is worth reviewing Barbara Frietchie's story, a classic, laboratory case.

BARBARA FRIETCHIE

Up from the meadows rich with corn,
Clear in the cool September morn,

The clustered spires of Frederick stand
Green-walled by the hills of Maryland.

Round about them orchards sweep,
Apple and peach tree fruited deep,

Fair as the garden of the Lord
To the eyes of the famished rebel horde,

On that pleasant morn of the early fall
When Lee marched over the mountain-wall,—

Over the mountains winding down,
Horse and foot, into Frederick town.

Forty flags with their silver stars,
Forty flags with their crimson bars,

Flapped in the morning wind: the sun
Of noon looked down, and saw not one.

Up rose old Barbara Frietchie then,
Bowed with her fourscore years and ten;

Bravest of all in Frederick town,
She took up the flag the men hauled down;

In her attic window the staff she set,
To show that one heart was loyal yet.

Up the street came the rebel tread,
Stonewall Jackson riding ahead.

Under his slouched hat left and right
He glanced: the old flag met his sight.

"Halt!"—the dust-brown ranks stood fast.
"Fire!"—out blazed the rifle-blast.

It shivered the window, pane and sash;
It rent the banner with seam and gash.

Quick, as it fell, from the broken staff
Dame Barbara snatched the silken scarf.

She leaned far out on the window-sill,
And shook it forth with a royal will.

"Shoot, if you must, this old gray head,
But spare your country's flag," she said.

A shade of sadness, a blush of shame,
Over the face of the leader came;

The nobler nature within him stirred
To life at that woman's deed and word:

"Who touches a hair of yon gray head
Dies like a dog! March on!" he said.

All day long through Frederick street
Sounded the tread of marching feet:

All day long that free flag tost
Over the heads of the rebel host.

Ever its torn folds rose and fell
On the loyal winds that loved it well;

And through the hill-gaps sunset light
Shone over it with a warm good-night.

Barbara Frietchie's work is o'er,
And the Rebel rides on his raids no more.

Honor to her! and let a tear
Fall, for her sake, on Stonewall's bier.

Over Barbara Frietchie's grave,
Flag of Freedom and Union, wave!

Peace and order and beauty draw
Round thy symbol of light and law;

And ever the stars above look down
On thy stars below in Frederick town!

John Greenleaf Whittier's ballad, which appeared in the October 1863 pages of the *Atlantic Monthly,* was part of the burst of Civil War nationalism that gave us classics like "The Midnight Ride of Paul Revere" by Henry Wadsworth Longfellow and "Sheridan's Ride" by Thomas Buchanan Read. Along with those potboilers, it was memorized and fondled by thousands of schoolchildren until its heroine became as familiar as Molly Pitcher, Nathan Hale, and the U. S. S. *Constitution.* Mrs. Frietchie's legend had another force propelling it: it stirred up a tempest which still rages over certain local teacups, and once was a matter of national scholarly concern.

The controversy turns on three things. Was there really a woman whose name was Barbara Frietchie? If there was, did she actually wave the Union flag in defiance of the Confederate troops in Frederick? And was Stonewall Jackson the general who "called off" his men and let "the old gray head" be? The answers, which turn out to be: "yes," "no," and "no," explain the legendary process.

A Barbara Hauer Frietsche (also spelled Frietschie, Fritsche, Frietche, Fritchee, and Fritchie) was born to Palatine German parents, Catherine and Johann Niklaus Hauer, who emigrated to

America in 1754. The date seems to have been December 3, 1766, and she was the fourth in a line of eight children. The place was probably Lancaster, Pennsylvania, as her name is listed in the baptismal records of the First Reformed Church there and her obituary read that she had "removed" to Frederick "as a child."

She undoubtedly lived in Frederick all her life, for though information on her is sparse, it is known she was confirmed there in February, 1782, and married John Casper Frietsche there on May 18, 1806. The bridegroom was fourteen years younger than his wife, and Barbara was only nine years younger than her mother-in-law. Frietsche was an undistinguished soul, the youngest in a family whose main claim to fame was the father who was accused, then hanged, drawn, and quartered in August, 1781, as the result of Loyalist plotting during the Revolution. William and Dorothy Quynn, descendants of the Hauers, who have done the sensible research on the whole subject, suspect that some or all of the Frietsche children were brought up in the Hauer family after this execution and that Barbara and John may well have known each other as "younger brother and older sister" long before their marriage.

All evidence points to the fact that Barbara Hauer Frietsche was a markedly ignorant woman, and one student of her life claims that her father knew her and was amazed when he found out that she could actually sign her name. The other facts about her are sparse. The census of 1850 lists her as "head of her family" and the Evangelical Reformed Church of Frederick records her participation in communion from 1858 till her death in 1862. The question of her health in her last years has absorbed "scholars" who have questioned whether she could have made it to the window—much less waved a flag. Theories run from "very active for her age" to "bed-ridden." As she died at the age of ninety-six, both descriptions, as well as a number in between, may be accurate.

But there is no doubt a Barbara Frietsche lived in Frederick, Maryland, during the Civil War. What doubt there is centers on whether she did any flag-waving, and, if so, when and at whom. The Quynns really go into the problem, perhaps farther than most of us who aren't quite sure which side was blue and which was gray care to go. Like bloodhounds, they trace Stonewall Jackson's every move from September 2, 1862, when the Battle of Bull Run ended and Lee's army encamped south of Frederick, to early morning September 10, when the Confederate troops left the immediate area travelling west along the streets toward Hagerstown. Without lingering on such interesting events as Jackson's sleeping through a Reformed Church service in which a hymn condemning the Rebels was sung and a prayer for the President of the Union offered, one can summarize the Quynns' conclusions in this sentence from their booklet: "Perhaps the only glimpse that Barbara Frietsche ever had of General Jackson was in the Reformed Church that Sunday night, providing she was well enough to go to Church at that time." Oddly, they seem sure that just about all the Southern troops went right past the Frietsche house on Patrick Street—excepting Stonewall Jackson and a handful of his men, who had stopped to see the Reverend Dr. Ross, an old friend of Mrs. Jackson's family, on the way out of town. "Just why," ponder the Quynns, "the Barbara Frietsche story has attached itself to Jackson, the only Confederate infantry officer who did not pass the house, it is impossible to say."

Actually, it is not impossible to say. Stonewall Jackson was a distinguished general and he had been in town at church. He not only knew a minister in the community, but had taken the trouble to "visit" him, establishing his presence quite clearly in the local consciousness. There had been, during the Confederate "occupation," a great many flag-waving incidents: things like Confederate soldiers tying Union colors to their horses' tails and dragging them about town; like Union women holding their noses when the Rebels passed, waving Union flags, or, if more discreeet, taking down their flags and wrapping them about their bodies or folding them into their Bibles to keep them from being confiscated. None of the newspaper articles about such goings-on mention Barbara Frietsche's name.

The closest contemporary report comes is in a letter left by a friend of the Frietsches', Lewis Steiner, M.D., who wrote in his diary that a "clergyman" once told him that "he saw an aged crone come out of her house as certain rebels passed by, trailing the American flag in the dust. She shook her long, skinny hands at the traitors and screamed at the top of her voice: 'My curses be upon you and your officers for degrading your country's flag.' " But, as the Quynns point out, it is not likely that Steiner would have chosen to describe his friend Barbara as "an aged crone"— even though that is exactly what she was. There is also a note in the Whittier correspondence in which an unidentified Confederate officer recalls talk of a woman who held or displayed a Federal flag during the march through the town and that the officer in command, Colonel Stark, "let it alone." And there were many union colors on display when the Federal troops under General Jesse Lee Reno entered the town three days later. The Washington *Daily National Intelligencer* commented that: "The loyalty of Frederick is most determined. It flutters out in hundreds of flags from all parts of the sky."

Barbara Frietsche was one of those people who waved banners. Her obituary even mentions it, and there is a strong chance that she owned a local reputation for being a bit "dotty" on the subject. There is no doubt that Reno rode by her house, saw a large flag flying from her window and, impressed by her age and possibly her reputation for loyalty, stopped to speak to her. She gave him that flag, and he took it along. His brother, who was present, recorded the incident and stated that this made the cloth that covered his coffin after his death at Antietam.

Anyone who has been about legends and legend-making can understand quite easily how the Barbara Frietchie legend which Whittier consecrated built itself from such loosely related fragments. One need only to recall three truisms: that legend tends to seek out the most distinguished figures available; that once these figures are placed in the plot, adjacent facts and incidents tend to rearrange themselves appropriately; and that time and place distortions are easily effected in those things man recalls without written record.

It's most simple. 1) Women with Union sympathies waved Federal flags at Confederate troops during the occupation of Frederick. 2) One of the most dramatic of these incidents in-volved "an old crone." 3) Colonel Stark "let alone" a flag-waving woman while his troops marched by her. 4) Old crone Barbara Frietsche was singled out by General Reno for waving a Federal flag when the Union troops came to town a few days later. 5) Stonewall Jackson was prominently "in Frederick" during the occupation period. Q.E.D., according to the logic of legend, gossip, and rumor, Colonel Stark must have been the more distinguished Stonewall Jackson and Barbara Frietsche must have been the "old crone" Jackson/Stark "let alone." Of course, Barbara's flag becomes the only one that was displayed as Lee's forces marched away; of course the troops are made to fire at the banner; of course Barbara is given the spunk and vocabulary to tell them off; of course Stonewall Jackson is given the "greatness" to "understand." Later, local minds recall her and the affair quite well. Later, the very flag she waved turns up. Later, anecdotes revealing other facets of this unusual personality begin to circulate.

So at twenty-four Miss Hauer was present at an afternoon quilting party in Kimball's Tavern when George Washington himself arrived. As the flustered "girls" had nothing suitable in which to serve the great man coffee, Barbara hurried home and returned with a "Staffordshire pot" her parents had brought from Germany. Washington was so pleased with such ingenuity, alertness, and charm, he produced a Lowestoft china bowl and gave it to her. Dismissed are certain details: that Washington stopped at Brother's, and not Kimball's, when he visited Frederick in 1790; that his papers do not mention his being entertained by anyone on this particular occasion; that he would not have customarily coffeed with "the girls" in such a situation; that there is no way of proving Barbara ever had a treasured Lowestoft bowl; that it is most unlikely the Father of Our Nation traveled with a couple of breakable items in his luggage ready for distribution to "local lovelies"; that the Staffordshire coffee pot, which still survives, almost surely did not come from Germany in 1754, but is clearly an early nineteenth-century piece.

And who would be so heartless as to point out that the building which bears the inscription "Barbara Frietsche's House" was constructed in 1926, sixty-four years after Lee's troops "marched by it"; fifty-eight years after the waters of Carroll Creek rose so high they carried away a large chunk of the original Patrick Street home; fifty-seven years after the real Frietsche house was razed because the town corporation voted to widen the creek in order to avoid future floods. Nor is it relevant that research has shown the present "replica" to bear little resemblance to the original. Filled with "relics," it *must* exist, like King Arthur's birthplace Tintagel, Juliet Capulet's garden, the false Betsy Ross House in Philadelphia. For legends survive best when identified concretely. It makes them tangible. And what people can see and touch and feel has to be true.

It isn't, ventures the cynic, so much that "those who cannot remember the past are condemned to repeat it" as "those who do not distort the past may be condemned to learn what they don't want to learn from it!"

A "legend" for our book thus established, let us return now . . . to the ladies.

2

ANCIENT SEX

The mortal who conceives of the sun as a handsome chap gallop-
ing along a road in the sky or who is mystified by the fact that
fermented vegetation gets him drunk is certain to be in awe of the
womb. So it matters little how dominant male is over female, she
remains a mystery to him (and to herself), in some ways nearer
to the gods than anything either knows. Neither male nor female
is ever psychologically free of the fact that life issues from her,
depends upon her in infancy, and can be manipulated by her
glances, motions, and smiles. Ruler enthralled, enthraller ruled—
it is small wonder so many legends center on sex, on the way, not
only "of a man with a maid," but of a maid with a man.

Had some hostess suddenly challenged Sigmund Freud himself
with the word "sex," even his response might well have been
"Cleopatra." For nowhere has the "way of a maid with a man"
been more crassly and persistently exploited than in the case of
this quite distinguished politician. In spite of a diplomatic and
military career that compares favorably with that of any ancient
ruler, Cleopatra has been popularly remembered as the queen of
ancient sex, keeper of a hedonistic court, before whose couch
emperors such as Julius Caesar and Mark Antony surrendered.
This "world view" of her, which was developed while she ruled,
has been touched up and colored by the best imaginations—by

saints, historians, hucksters, musicians, dramatists, and movie producers—so that today there are few among us who don't equate classic seduction with the Nile as matter-of-factly as we equate current seduction with the Seine.

Like most political stories, Cleopatra's story had its origins in the economics and power politics of the time. In the century before Christ's birth, the outstanding fact of the Mediterranean world was that Egypt had an established refinement and lots of money, while Rome had military force. Cleopatra's Alexandria was the intellectual center of its era, a Vienna, a Paris. Behind its rulers lay centuries of aristocracy, art and cultural stability; under them was a country as industrially and economically advanced as any of the time. In contrast, Rome was simply *parvenue,* and what's more "strapped for cash." True, it had great armies, developed and perfected under a series of rulers and generals who had carved out its vast sphere of influence, but the naive agrarian economy of the early Republic was simply not able to support the military. With a high percentage of its citizens farmers, living on what they grew, Rome had developed little trade and had a limited base for taxation. The government continually needed "walking around money." The two main methods of gaining such money—conscripting a wealthy citizen's real estate or proscribing his life and possessing his fortune—both had obvious limitations. Nor did the method of paying centurions and other soldiers by giving them plots of land when the varied hostilities came to an intermission always work. Sometimes there wasn't enough land to go around, and sometimes the results of hostilities were not decisive enough to warrant seizure. Always in the wings stood other generals and other politicians who were ready to offer promises of greener plots and future spoils to "the cheated" and the discontent. The result was continual turmoil beside the Tiber and a marked lack of economic, political, and cultural stability upon the Seven Hills. The situation gave Rome a sense of inferiority where Egypt was concerned. They needed to control it, could control it, but were uneasy before its steady sophistication.

It is easy to see that an alliance between Egypt and Rome had great advantages. The idea occurred to Julius Caesar, Mark Antony, Cleopatra, Octavius Caesar and almost everyone else who thought about such things 2,000 years ago.   One immediate advantage of the union would be control of Asia Minor.   A disadvantage, from the Roman point of view, was the fact that the new political center of such an Egypto-Roman Empire might well have to be to the East, probably at Byzantium, and there were a good many Romans whose vested interests made them violently opposed to any such move.   In fact, the chances are excellent that this was the major motivation for the liquidation of Julius Caesar.

That alliance was Cleopatra's life ambition.   Descended from Ptolemaios, a trusted Macedonian general in the armies of Alexander the Great and the founder of the Ptolemaic succession, she was the seventh of her name to rule Egypt.   She was well trained for her role, probably as well trained as any woman in history.   Plutarch admits she knew six languages, at least well enough to converse with foreign emissaries.   "She spake," he says, "unto few barbarous people by interpreter, but made them answer herself . . . whose languages she had learned."   Sensible and pragmatic, she played the roles life gave her with acumen.   She was a good public wife for her two brothers whom she married according to Ptolemaic custom, and a good private mistress and wife to both Julius Caesar and Antony.   She was a good mother to her children.   But she moved with poise, harshness, and finality when power politics demanded it.   That she used feminine charms to persuade, influence, and ally herself with the Romans who "swam into her ken" is scarcely surprising.   Charm is always a device.   But her purposes went well beyond "a relationship."   They were unwaveringly political, "unsexed," designed to secure the future of her people, her royal line, and her own rule.   That she lost the game was due largely to her inability to persuade the Romans in Rome that their future lay in the East, to the fact that Antony's alliance with her looked "treacherous" in the West and that this encouraged many Roman soldiers to desert when the showdown with Octavius Caesar finally came.

It is a bit strange, but posterity is not certain who Cleopatra VII (*the* Cleopatra)'s mother was.   Speculation has centered on Cleopatra V who was married in 78 B.C. to her brother Ptolemy XII, *the* Cleopatra's father, derisively known as "The Flute-

The death of Cleopatra, 19th century lithograph by August von Heckel.
(NEW YORK PUBLIC LIBRARY PICTURE COLLECTION)

player." This incest, not only approved but traditionally required, resulted in two girls, Berenice and Cleopatra VI. Cleopatra VII may have been the third child of the relationship. However, Ptolemy XII is thought to have married again, to a lady whose name has been lost, and *the* Cleopatra likely was the first child of this new marriage, which also produced a younger sister Arsinoe IV and the two little Ptolemies, XIII and XIV, later to become *the* Cleopatra's husbands. She has even been reported to be the offspring of one of the court concubines, though if such were the case the scandal-mongers of history have done little with it. Of all the charges leveled at her, this one has seldom been fired.

Cleopatra's legendary life begins in 48 B.C., when she was twenty or twenty-one years old and met Julius Caesar who, in one of those typical struggles by which a triumvirate is reduced to one, was pursuing Pompey in Egypt. Cleopatra's father had died a few years before, and she was involved in a power struggle with her brother-consort, Ptolemy XIII. When Caesar, then over 50, came to Alexandria, where Pompey had been treacherously killed, he might have supported either side. Not surprisingly, when one examines his track record with the fillies (he felt Venus to be his special angel), the woman won out. Cleopatra's "trick to catch the old one" is almost as famous as her death by asp-bite. She slipped into Alexandria by boat at night, had herself rolled into a carpet and delivered to the Roman armed only with her femininity. This was, however, no small armament.

Exactly how beautiful she was is a matter of dispute, especially as taste in such matters changes rapidly. According to an imprint of her features on coins struck in her honor by her contemporaries, we see a rather puffy face, pouting lips, teeth that need orthodontistry, and a prominent nose. Her figure, short and fleshy by modern standards, (*bouffie, peut-être*), was probably more sinuous than those of the Roman beauties Caesar and Antony had become accustomed to. Roman women tended to be dumpy. No matter, she had a lot going for her besides her looks and was quite capable of conquest by means other than surrender. Particularly she seems to have had a reputation for "chic" and an ability with cosmetics. In addition, she was a mistress of conversation, charm, and manners, with a wonderful voice—"a lyre," as it has been called, "of many strings." To paraphrase William Whitehead's poem, there was "a provoking charm of Cleopatra altogether."

So Caesar was undone, and "every woman's man" as he was called in Rome, became this woman's man. He put aside his own problems for awhile, crushed Ptolemy XIII and set Cleopatra on the throne, making her youngest brother, then eleven, her husband and co-regent. The whole Cleopatra affair was unpopular at home, and Romans in general were irritated that the Queen had been able to distract their leader on what seemed a provincial matter. It didn't help that Cleopatra followed Caesar to Rome where he set her up in a villa and dedicated a statue in the Temple of Venus to her. In Rome, she had a son who she said was Caesar's and whom she named, Ptolemy Caesar—certainly not after her Egyptian consort.

Today we are apt to think of this Cleopatra in terms of George

Bernard Shaw's dramatization of her early life. Because Shaw was anxious to debunk the legendary (i.e. romantic) concept of Cleopatra, he shows her as a pert ingénue waiting for some Caesar to mold her into a ruler. And it makes good theater, this relationship between a patient, avuncular hero and an impudent, untutored "campus queen." But it is nonsensical historically. Any woman maturing in the "Ptolemy eat Ptolemy" world of ancient Egypt knew the royal score quite well by the time she was sixteen—and Cleopatra was an exceptional creature. Brooks Atkinson once wrote that "Shaw's account of the relations between Caesar and Cleopatra is not reliable, for it omits sex—an element in human relations that is more popular with most people than it ever was with Shaw." More important, it omits her training in diplomatic procedure, military matters, the six languages, and survival. This is not to say Caesar taught her nothing. When they met, he was a man of real genius, and she a brilliant young woman. But surely she never pestered him with "juke-box questions" about lost cats, kittenish ancestors, and "scary Romans" as Shaw has her do. Cleopatra must have been far closer to a Henry James heroine, an Isabel Archer or a Daisy Miller, than to Shaw's "spunky little thing," who is told at the final curtain she will get "a beautiful present from Rome" to replace "her Caesar" who must leave her in Egypt "all alone."

When Caesar was "rubbed out" in 44 B.C. (and that is exactly what happened to him), Cleopatra returned to Alexandria. Almost at once her co-regent Ptolemy XIV died; "by poison or the art of the Queen" was the murmur. Because she couldn't rule without a consort, she made her three-year-old son, Ptolemy Caesar, co-regent and went about her business. She had been frustrated in her efforts to use "the grandeur that was Rome" to enhance Egyptian glory, but she was going to get a second chance.

The Triumvirate that formed after Caesar's death was made up of Octavian, the eighteen-year-old great-nephew and adopted son of Caesar; Lepidus, a politically ineffectual "master of horse"; and Mark Antony, whose stirring speech over Caesar's coffin was made famous by an Elizabethan playwright who had probably never seen Rome. These gentlemen divided the Republic between them, and then set about the lobsterish task of fighting each other until one was left.

Antony, who had the most prestige, received the whole East as his share. He immediately set out for his demesne, happy in the belief he could sift enough cash from Egypt to pay off his quite considerable war debts. Forty at the time, he was a "fine figure of a man." He thought he resembled local Roman portraits of Hercules, so he affected carefully insouciant dress and demeanor "the way that ancient warrior would have done." Particularly he liked to strut about in his military cloak, wearing a large sword, sporting a curly beard, and showing off his powerful, masculine frame. He seems to have had an ego problem. It is thus not surprising to learn he drank heavily (once he threw up just as he was about to deliver a speech in the Forum), demanded attention (he did things like putting an "actress-friend" in a chariot pulled by two lions and speeding her about the streets), and had a penchant for ladies who would bother to flatter him. But he was basically likable, in a locker room way, if coarse and blunt, generous and ready for whatever laughs were available. Supposedly he gave one friend of his a million *sestertii,* and when his cashier poured the amount on a table to show what a foolishly extravagant gift it was, he ordered the sum doubled. His wife, Fulvia, who was as near a "women's libber" as you could be in Rome, had him under control—in Plutarch's words "fully tamed." And if he wasn't the faithful type, he was so broken to bridle that almost any female could lead him about by his prominent nose. In short, he was "born and bred" for Cleopatra who saw in him the chance to re-dream all those plans from which she had been awakened by Caesar's death.

The story of her conquest of Antony is the most famous of all the Cleopatra tales. He awaited their encounter of state at Tarsus where the River Cydnus flows into the Mediterranean Sea. Everyone knows she came to him, floating down the Nile in what one no-nonsense scholar has termed "a masterpiece of diplomacy." Plutarch was somewhat more sensitive to the scene, calculated as it may have been, and his description, put into English by Thomas North and into blank verse by William Shakespeare, has become a classic.

ENOBARBUS   I will tell you.
              The barge she sat in, like a burnish'd throne,

AGRIPPA / ENOBARBUS ·

Burn'd on the water. The poop was beaten gold;
Purple the sails, and so perfumed that
The winds were lovesick with them; the oars were silver,
Which to the tune of flutes kept stroke, and made
The water which they beat to follow faster,
As amorous of their strokes. For her own person,
It beggar'd all description. She did lie
In her pavilion, cloth-of-gold of tissue,
O'erpicturing that Venus where we see
The fancy outwork nature. On each side her
Stood pretty dimpled boys, like smiling Cupids,
With divers-colour'd fans, whose wind did seem
To glow the delicate cheeks which they did cool,
And what they undid did.

AGRIPPA   O, rare for Antony!
ENOBARBUS   Her gentlewomen, like the Nereides,
So many mermaids, tended her i' th' eyes,
And made their bends adornings. At the helm
A seeming mermaid steers. The silken tackle
Swell with the touches of those flower-soft hands
That yarely frame the office. From the barge
A strange invisible perfume hits the sense
Of the adjacent wharfs. The city cast
Her people out upon her; and Antony,
Enthron'd i' th' market place, did sit alone,
Whistling to th' air; which, but for vacancy,
Had gone to gaze on Cleopatra too,
And made a gap in nature.

AGRIPPA   Rare Egyptian!
ENOBARBUS   Upon her landing, Antony sent to her,
Invited her to supper. She replied,
It should be better he became her guest;
Which she entreated. Our courteous Antony,
Whom ne'er the word of "no" woman heard speak,
Being barber'd ten times o'er, goes to the feast,
And for his ordinary pays his heart
For what his eyes eat only.

For the rough soldier from the austere world of Rome, a boy from
the backroom, the display was enchanting. Hans Volkmann adds
details on pages 98-99 of his *Cleopatra:*

Cleopatra went to meet Antony with the dignity that befitted an exalted goddess. She rejected his invitation to dinner, and summoned him to eat with her on board her ship. He went: and the soldier, habituated to coarse pleasures, saw displayed for his benefit the tasteful and refined table-luxury of the royal court.

Light streamed from all sides, reflected by an array of mirrors. All the table-ware was of gold studded with jewels and adorned with exquisite work by the best artists. Purple tapestries, embroidered with gold, covered the walls. Twelve dining-couches stood ready to receive the triumvir and his retinue. Antony expressed his surprise at the magical speed with which this splendid reception had been prepared. The Queen replied with a smile that he must make shift with what had been done, and pardon the deficiencies due to the haste of her arrival. She would know how to make them good if he would consent to dine again with her on the morrow. She also invited him to accept from her as a gift, everything he saw. On the following day he was welcomed to a repast still more splendidly appointed, utterly eclipsing the first one; at the end of which everything was again presented to him as a gift. Nor were his followers forgotten. Each of his officers received from her the sofa on which he had reclined at table and the goblet and fine table-ware that had stood before him, and, finally, was made to keep the litter in which he was taken home and the slaves who bore it. The other members of his retinue received horses with valuable silver trappings and torch-bearing slaves from Ethiopia. On the fourth day of the celebrations Cleopatra expended one talent per guest on roses, with which she had the floor covered to a depth of a cubit.

Antony, overpowered by this style of living, invited Cleopatra in his turn and poured scorn himself on the paltry entertainment he offered. He was utterly carried away by this enchanting queen of twenty-eight years.

Of course, Antony became her lover, and they spent the winter of 41 B.C. in dalliance in Alexandria. Actually, "dalliance" may be too gentle a word, for they ate, drank, and made merry with an energy and insouciance that might well have startled Zelda and Scott Fitzgerald. They even formed a society whose sole purpose was to throw parties, each member pledged to outdo the other. Antony shirked his state duties. Pressing political problems in Judea and Syria were ignored or handled "out of hand." He even gave up being Hercules and entered his "Graecian period,"

Actress Elizabeth Taylor in the title role of the 1961 movie, "Cleopatra."

wearing white Attic sandals. Cleopatra played along, biding her time, binding Antony to her and to her cause. One of the bonds turned out to be twins, Alexander Helios (Sun) and Cleopatra Selene (Moon).

Meanwhile back by the Tiber, forces which had organized about Antony's power-conscious wife Fulvia began to wage civil war. The situation became heated enough and Fulvia's (really Antony's) position shaky enough that he roused himself, left Alexandria, and began to tend to his business. To make a power struggle short, Fulvia died. Octavian and Antony, under some real pressure from the public which was tired of power struggles, decided to let bygones be bygones. Octavian trotted out his mild, lovely sister Octavia and Antony married her as an indication of good faith. For about two years, Octavia ruled Antony. They had a child, and Cleopatra was eclipsed. Then, in 37 B.C., an Eastern rendezvous occurred while Antony was in Antioch. The idea seems to have been his, but one can't be sure when dealing with the Cleopatras of the world. At any rate, the lovers were married, Octavia be damned, and the old game began anew. Within three years, Antony and Cleopatra had persuaded each other to set up an Eastern Empire with her children as rulers of the varied parts and Cleopatra as a sort of chancellor, "The Queen of Kings."

War with Octavian was now inevitable. The details are not important, except that in four years the lovers would be dead. Cleopatra stood by Antony to the end, frequenting his successive war camps. Both Antony's officers and his men resented her female presence in the field, though one is said to have remarked that she was footing the bills and had more brains than the whole pack put together. When morale failed at Actium and desertions swept the ranks, she realized that the jig was over and that she had once again failed to grasp the Dream. She fled back to Alexandria and, well or not, "the world was lost."

Literature and legend would have one think this happened overnight. Actually, Octavian took almost a year to consolidate things. During this time, the defeated lovers quibbled, planned, and hoped that their fortunes might turn for the better. Cleopatra even made efforts to revive the court gaiety that had characterized the winter of 41 B.C., hoping to rouse Antony from "the blues." But in the summer of 30 B.C., when Octavian inevitably returned to conquer Egypt itself, Antony was to commit suicide. He ran on his sword after the battle for Alexandria, thinking Cleopatra had deserted him in his desperate moment and believing a report that she had already killed herself. Just before he died, Cleopatra's private scribe is supposed to have told him that the Queen was alive and barricaded in a mausoleum. It is hard to imagine, but we are told that he was hoisted, bloody and half-conscious, through the upper windows of the building where he died in her arms.

Cleopatra killed herself a few days later. Practical to the end, she arranged a private meeting with Octavian. The "sexualists" have tried to see this as an effort by the nymph of the Nile to form a relationship with the victor similar to those she enjoyed with Caesar and Antony. In this theory, Octavian's chastity is too much for her sensuality. The idea is unlikely. At the time she was thirty-eight, not young in those days, and even with her gift for cosmetics, she was probably too spent physically and psychologically to vamp a younger man. What she really wanted to do was to secure the future of her children. Octavian, who couldn't have cared less about her children, probably consented to the conference because he didn't want her to commit suicide before he could display her in a triumphal procession in Rome. Plutarch thinks that Octavian left the meeting certain he had lulled her for the nonce. But she must have suspected her fate. When a Roman nobleman in Octavian's following let leak that she and her children would be sent to Rome in three days, she acted, for she had no intention of being displayed in the streets as her sister Arsinoe had been. She got permission to visit Antony's tomb, bathed, and sent Octavian a letter requesting she be buried by Antony's side. When Octavian received the letter, he knew what she was about but by the time his men arrived, she was dead, lying on a golden couch, her waiting-woman Charmion dying by her side.

No one has ever known for sure exactly how Cleopatra killed herself. On her left arm were found two tiny pricks. It was speculated that they had been caused by an asp brought in with a basket of figs delivered by a peasant. Whether she arranged to have the peasant come or whether the snake was in the figs by chance, no one knows. Though "death by snake-bite" was the official verdict, the asp was never found. Still, it is likely the official verdict is correct. In Egyptian belief, the asp was an animal sacred to Amon-Ra, the Sun-God. Egyptian kings bore the effigy on their diadems. To die from the bite of this snake was to be welcomed into the company of the gods. It would be a most appropriate (if not particularly Macedonian) method for Cleopatra to choose. Legend, at least, has entertained no doubts. The asp was brought to her on purpose. She placed it against her full breast, not arm, and it realized "her immortal longings."

Octavian, who well understood the power of the press, ably established that his struggle with Antony and Cleopatra was not a political conflict between ambitious statesmen, but was a near-ethical conflict between two parts of the world with very different life-views: the sturdy, straightforward, vigorous Roman homeland and the pleasure-loving, decadent East. He placed the fulcrum of his comparisons on the personality of Cleopatra, who he stressed was an outlander married to and attempting to control a Roman leader, not for the first, but now for the second time! So crucial is Octavian's technique in understanding later views of

Cleopatra that Hans Volkmann introduced his study by reference to it:

We have seen quite enough, in our lifetime, of the mischievous inter-weaving of politics and propaganda. We are in fact inclined, in this age of the radio, the cinema and the press, to think that political propaganda is a weapon peculiar to our own times. But there has always been propaganda, both in politics and out of it: the only changes have been in the media it employs. Often it went unrecognized and its effects were not appreciated. Hence there has been no comprehensive survey of propaganda as it was conducted in the ancient world.

In any such survey Cleopatra, the last queen of the Ptolemaic dynasty, would merit a special place. For it was her name that Octavian—the later Emperor Augustus—employed to kindle a spirit of battle in the united forces of the western Mediterranean when he summoned them to a 'national war' against the East. 'Cleopatra' was the keyword in a masterly campaign of political propaganda which, developed in detail, enabled him to raise his personal struggle for power with Antony to a national and ideal level, and in the course of it to grow to the stature of an arbiter of world history.

Octavian, of course, emphasized the disgraceful immorality of Antony's Eastern life, telling tales of the Queen's taking a pearl worth millions and dissolving it in a glass of vinegar for no other purpose than to quaff off a toast to Antony's health. It was broadly suggested that Ptolemy Caesar was not Cleopatra's son by Julius Caesar, but the kit of some straying tom. It was adver-tised that Antony had confiscated all sorts of art treasures, even statues of the gods themselves, as well as 200,000 manuscript rolls from the library at Pergamon and had taken them to Alexandria (not Rome) simply to please Cleopatra. Naturally, his political and military moves were criticized, usually with the implication that dalliance and immorality were clouding his judgment or that Cleopatra was using the old lever of sex to get Antony to make decisions favorable to her and not to his homeland.

That this propaganda was largely successful, especially with the Roman senators, who were well-known for their ability to change allegiance frequently and subjectively, is not so signifi-cant as the fact that it shaped the image of Cleopatra in ways that were to become too hardened ever to change. Octavian's theme echoes again and again throughout literary and popular history, drowning out chroniclers who were sophisticated enough to see that Octavian had his own vulnerabilities and that it takes two, a willing Antony as well as a scheming Cleopatra, to tango. In fact, some of the historians, like Livy and Paterculus, stressed Antony's fatal passion, not the Queen's maneuverings, as the cause of it all, but the moral note has never been absent for long. Plutarch saw to that, and no historian has had more influence on this particular legend than Plutarch.

A Theban rhetorician, Plutarch produced his *Parallel Lives,* in which famous Greeks are compared to famous Romans, in the second century A.D. Antony's life is paralleled to that of the Macedonian Demetrius, who ironically was beaten in his battle with Cleopatra's progenitor, Ptolemaios. Most of the findings are based on Dellius' notes of the Parthian War; on the memoirs of Cleopatra's personal doctor, Olympus; and on a mass of oral testimony. Plutarch was a good scholar-writer and his work became a classic, especially for the Renaissance. For years all views of Antony and Cleopatra, as well as of Julius Caesar and Octavian, were either copied from or derived from translations of his books.

It is quite clear how Plutarch saw Cleopatra. She was a *femme fatale,* with grace, charm, and unusual appeal. ". . . so sweet," he says, "was her company and conversation, that a man could not possibly but be taken." The "age cannot wither her nor custom stale her infinite variety" woman Enobarbus describes in Shakespeare's play is Plutarch's Queen. The step from the picture of a beauty whose charm is such that she can entrance any man to a hussy who boldly vamps any male within range is not great. To Florus, writing shortly after Plutarch, Cleopatra is a Circe amid enswined lovers. One of the swine, Antony, whirls through life perpetually drunk, steeped in pleasure and vice. Cleopatra offers herself to him "on one condition only"—he give her the Roman Empire. Octavian, in contrast, has no interest in such entanglements, except to see them eliminated. Chaste, he saves the day, while the thwarted Circe places herself in the dead Antony's coffin and applies a serpent to her veins.

It was natural that the medieval Christian moralists would be attracted to Florus' variant, and the clerics were quick to turn the old tale into an exemplum warning everyman against five-sevenths of the worldly Sins: pride, covetousness, lust, gluttony and sloth. Cleopatra becomes an animal in some sort of perpetual heat, as Scarus describes her in Shakespeare's play: "a ribaudred nag of Egypt" with "the breeze upon her, like a cow in June." Antony, the sodden, prodigal fool, trapped by her Satanic duplicity, responds to her scent and discards his duties to follow her to damnation. In this view of things, it is important that Cleopatra be black, the color of the Devil and Hell. Her Egyptian nature is stressed, and she becomes a tawny harlot, a blackamoor nymph, hot as the African sun.

At the medieval courts, writers could afford to be more sentimental than the clerics. There the idea that Cleopatra was "Love's martyr" became popular. Quite contrary to Plutarch's *femme fatale* and the Church's Satanic harlot, Cleopatra was seen as a woman so smitten with love for Antony that she supported him blindly, even to disaster, and followed him into the other world when it became obvious that she could not have him in this. Chaucer, who had bruised the tender sentiments of the court ladies with his quizzical view of Criseyde in love (he claims the God of Love charged him with the offense), decided to make amends by writing *The Legend of Good Women* to show that all sweethearts are not wanton. He led off with Cleopatra's story, describing that oft-maligned Queen as fidelity itself. He titles the passage *"Legenda Cleopatre martiris"*. ". . . Was never unto hir love a trewer quene," he writes, ". . . And she hir deeth receyveth with good chere, For love of Anthony that was hir so dere."

When one considers the inconsistencies of character that run through these three views of Cleopatra it becomes easy to see why the character of the legendary Cleopatra has proved as troublesome to writers in more recent times as the character of the real lady proved to statesmen in ancient times. Moreover, quite unlike the story of Cleopatra and Julius Caesar, the story of Cleopatra and Antony has a conflict in it that is not easy to resolve. Caesar, a middle-aged wencher of great reputation, might well have been amused by and attracted to a charming twenty-one-year-old Egyptian queen no matter how the writer decides to

Bust of Cleopatra, from a drawing by Michaelangelo.

characterize him or her. The situation is sound. But the relationship of Cleopatra and Antony is not "sound" in that sense. In the first place, the affair lasted twelve years, while the woman was in her thirties and the man in his forties. Even in modern times, when people stay young a lot longer, the lovers would be mature and well beyond the age in which they can, sensibly, toss over the affairs of state for a giddy Romeo-and-Juliet passion. As Alexander is supposed to have said when he gave his Campaspe to the youth she loved, "It were a shame Alexander should desire to command the world, if he could not command himself." What kind of man, after all, throws his entire career away for an affaire? And what kind of woman lets him? The story of Antony and Cleopatra is the tale of "all for love" and "a world well lost"— and yet, given their ages, how can it be? If it's about two old fools, a sot and a faded flirt, it is farce. If it's "a trip to the moon on gossamer wings," both parties are too old.

To be sure, such inconsistencies don't bother legend-makers or movie producers. The Cleopatra of the advertisements and the "Great White Ways" needs no anchor to reality; and she can be played as the greatest stateswoman in history, a *femme fatale,* a tawny harlot, love's martyr, and honeysuckle rose all at once—easily. But things like this did bother Shakespeare, who in spite of his commercial nature couldn't help being a perceptive student of people as they really are.

Critics have always bayed a bit at Shakespeare's picture of Cleopatra, calling it "inconsistent" and "hard to act." Given the fact that the Elizabethan public, like the modern public, knew only the legendary Queen and wanted to see just that, he had to deal with a paradoxical character. But he was the world's greatest writer, too, and I, for one, have always felt he never proved it more convincingly than he did in re-creating Cleopatra. He simply poured all the themes together, offering his Cleopatra as womanhood personified, making her the very paradox her legend has created: "the way of a maid with a man." And "age cannot wither . . . her infinite variety." And "she makes hungry where most she satisfies." And "vilest things become themselves in her." And "the holy priests bless her when she is riggish."

The role is best interpreted when it is given to an actress who sets out to show the audience how a woman, her physical charms dulled by time, can still hold and fascinate a man. The actress should have chic, charm, a voice that is "a lyre of many strings," and a way with cosmetics (if you will), but it is best she be not too young and lovely so that she, like the thirtyish Cleopatra, cannot rely on those things. Shakespeare develops the appeal of his Cleopatra by centering the role on two feminine techniques, both every bit as important as youth and beauty: the Queen must remain one jump ahead of Antony at all times; and she must be continually interesting. Shakespeare's Cleopatra does these things, understanding her man fully, aware the bland Octavia is no real threat (even after Antony marries her) and using such ploys as asking her servants to determine Antony's mood so she can assume a different one when they meet. Her egocentrism is immense, and she demands stage-center from all, Antony included. Even when he is dying, she interrupts him continually, so that during his death speech he actually has to say to her,

> I am dying Egypt, dying.
> Give me some wine, and let me speak a little.

Even then, as she listens, her thoughts are on her effect upon him, not on his death. And when she prepares her own suicide, she thinks again only of the effect her marvelously staged ending will have on him when he hears of it in the after-world. "Methinks," she says, "I hear Antony call. I can see him rouse himself to praise my noble act." Shakespeare knew instinctively what any student of the Cleopatra legend quickly learns: that the Queen is no longer a person whose character can be re-created. She is the stateswoman, the fatal lady, the harlot, the martyr, a "dream walking" all at once, a heroine who long before 1607 had assumed a thousand faces, a thousand complexions, a thousand personalities. We can't see her, we can't describe her, we can't label her—because she has dwelled too long in too many minds. But we all know what Cleopatra is. Cleopatra is ancient sex, *la différence*—and it was for this then that worlds as great as the Eastern Mediterranean have been lost, that "Usna's children died," that "Troy passed away."

Nevertheless, Egypt's legend has never gravitated completely free from the notes of sinfulness that Octavian and later Plutarch sounded across it. Whatever she was, Cleopatra cannot be "innocent beauty." There has always been "something wrong" in loving her. And, of course "the maid's way" doesn't have to be like this. "Helen's beauty" need not exist in the "brow of Egypt."

3

GOLDEN GIRL

In Scene xiii of Dr. Faustus, Christopher Marlowe meets and responds to a real dramatic challenge. Faust, given anything he wishes by Mephistopheles in exchange for a lien on his soul, requests that Helen of Troy, the most beautiful woman who ever lived, be reincarnated for him. The request is granted. All eyes turn toward the tiring-house doors. Out steps a boy actor, probably with apples for breasts, and the playwright must make the onlookers believe that this really is "the beauty which called when glory led the way." Marlowe came through. The speech he wrote for Faust is the best poetry he ever wrote, and it makes you believe. "Was this the face that launched a thousand ships, and burnt the topless towers of Ilium? Sweet Helen, make me immortal with a kiss." Faust kisses her, and her lips "suck forth" his soul: "Come, Helen," he pleads, "come, give me my soul again."

Sweet Helen, "She" holds his soul, but Sweet Helen is no Egypt. Her very name means beauty, beauty beyond sex, and she symbolizes exactly what men have built and protected "doll houses" for, age after age—the girl described by James Stephens in his *Irish Fairy Tales:*

Indeed, Fionn loved her as he had not loved a woman before and would never love one again. He loved her as he had never loved anything before. He could not bear to be away from her . . . . She filled him with wonder and surmise. There was magic in the tips of her fingers. Her thin palm ravished him. Her slender foot set his heart beating, and whatever way her head moved there came a new shape of beauty to her face.

"She is always new," said Fionn. "She is always better than any other woman; she is always better than herself."

She is a heroine inspiring devotion, the golden girl of mankind's märchen. It can't be wrong, loving her.

Helen (the symbol)'s beauty is divine, anyhow. She was the daughter of Zeus and Leda, the mortal wife of the Spartan King Tyndareus, though exactly how she was conceived and born is subject to some confusion. One theory holds that Helen resulted from Zeus' pursuits of the goddess of Retributive Justice, Nemesis, who fled him "down the nights and down the days" through a whole list of animal, fish, and fowl forms hoping to avoid outright rape. She failed. Zeus, as a swan, caught up with her in duck form and fertilized a hyacynthine egg that Nemesis finally deposited in Sparta, where Leda picked it up and put it in a chair. There a succession of warm bodies encouraged Helen to hatch. A second theory holds that Zeus was, true enough, in the form of a swan, but was not raping anybody. He was being chased by an eagle and dove into Nemesis' arms for sanctuary. Never one to miss an opportunity, he impregnated her while she protected him and the fertile egg developed. Leda ends up with the egg in that story also. Unladylike, she is reclining on a couch with her legs spread, and the egg is slipped between her thighs where it hatches. According to Pausanius this very egg was hanging from the ceiling of a Spartan temple in the second century A.D.

Pausanius to the contrary, neither of these is the most widely accepted thesis on Helen's birth. Both seem afterthoughts in which Nemesis, Retributive Justice, is introduced to further explain the whole Trojan disaster. The widely accepted version is that Zeus, without giving Nemesis a thought, is smitten with Leda's beauty. Taking the form of a swan, he simply paddles up to her while she is bathing and attacks. "A sudden blow," Yeats called it. And the result is the egg. The egg is most remarkable.

Not only is it laid by a mortal woman, but it contains four yolks from which spring two sets of twins: Castor and Pollux, Helen and Clytemnestra. Who is father of whom in all this gets confused because of the old folk belief that twins are the product of two men having had intercourse with the same woman during her period of conception. Time has definitely concluded that Zeus fathered Helen while Tyndareus, who evidently slept with his wife about the time of the rape, fathered Clytemnestra. Zeus is said to be the parent of Castor, Tyndareus of Pollux; but things get mixed up and sometimes, contrary to the folk belief about twins, Zeus is supposed to have begotten both future stars.

No matter, the half-divine Helen was so beautiful that any man who laid eyes on her fell hopelessly in love with her. Theseus was one. He and his blood-brother, Pirithous, had decided they would both marry daughters of Zeus, and Theseus wanted Helen. With his friend's help he was able to carry her off. Pirithous then selected Persephone, wife to the King of the Underworld, and true to his bond Theseus left Helen to accompany him to Hades. There they were both captured and held on an enchanted rock by Dis, who didn't think highly of their plans. Later Hercules rescued Theseus (by simply yanking him loose), but left Pirithous, who, as far as we know, is still stuck there. While Theseus was imprisoned, he lost Helen. Castor and Pollux recaptured their lovely sister, dragging Theseus' mother along to serve as a handmaiden.

Helen's beauty continued to cause unrest. Every man desired her, and it was obvious if someone claimed her she would be abducted back and forth, hither and yon, at least until age itself came to the rescue. Thus a plan was devised, by none other than Odysseus, that once Helen chose a husband, all her former suitors (which was everyone who had seen her) were honor-bound to protect the winner's rights. The pledge was taken, and Helen married Menelaus.

The couple were living happily together, when (unbeknownst to them) another marriage took place that was to change their lives and all history. Thetis, a goddess nearly as lovely as Helen, was won by the mortal Peleus. A wedding was scheduled, and all the gods were invited to this high point of the Olympian social season—all except one, Eris, the irritating Goddess of Discord. Enraged at the snub, Eris threw an apple among the guests. On it was the baffling inscription. "For the fairest." To make a long story short, Hera (Zeus' wife), Aphrodite, and Athene all claimed it, and Zeus was asked to decide which one should get it. Zeus, who had made a career of pursuing lovely ladies, knew better than to mix himself up in that one (especially since his wife was involved), so he sent the three aspirants to Mount Ida where Paris, the youngest and handsomest of the 100 sons of King Priam of Troy, was besporting himself with his girl friend, the nymph Oenone.

Paris had become a shepherd by means of an old folk motif. It seems that his parents, Priam and Hecuba, were warned during the pregnancy that the forthcoming child was to be a firebrand: i.e., the cause of the burning of Troy. Priam decided to rid himself of the threat by hiring a man to kill the baby. The man couldn't bring himself to do this and left little Paris on a hillside where he was found by a shepherd and brought up to raise sheep. Paris was neither as experienced as Zeus nor in a position to stand up to a triumvirate of goddesses, so he agreed to make the delicate choice. In the most Mediterranean of ways, each lady offered a bribe: all the riches and power he might want if he chose Hera; all the wisdom he might want if he chose Athene; the most beautiful woman in the world as his own if he chose Aphrodite. With all the sagacity of the average college sophomore, Paris gave the apple to Aphrodite (who actually was the "fairest" of the three), and she, good to her word, arranged that he might carry off Helen. Oenone was forgotten, and Paris stole Helen from Menelaus taking her to Troy, where Priam and Hecuba (dismissing the prophecy) welcomed them. Hera and Athene were furious, and together vowed to make bitter enemies. Athene, in particular, was anxious to show Paris, his family, and his homeland that hell truly has no fury like a goddess scorned. In Homer, one learns she succeeded.

I won't review the ten epic years which chronicle the "delights" of the battle fought "far on the ringing plains of windy Troy" (to say nothing of the ensuing odysseys), but the results of not asking Eris to Thetis' wedding are quite literally cosmic.

Aphrodite persuading Helen to love Paris, from a relief in the Naples National Museum.

Though not the root of all the motivation in this ancient "arthuriad," that *faux pas* resulted in the death of Agamemnon (murderer of his own daughter) at the hands of Helen's mortal sister Clytemnestra; in the death of Clytemnestra at the hands of her own children; in Oenone's suicide on Paris' funeral pyre; in Athene's devotion to Odysseus as she helps that "weary, wayworn traveller" home; to say nothing of the carnage of a decade of fighting. It is the child of Peleus and Thetis, Achilles, who leads the Greeks in battle against Trojans under the command of Paris' older brother Hector. It is Paris who fires the arrow that strikes Achilles' heel where his mother had held him as she dipped him in the River Styx to make him wound-resistant. And it is Hermione, the daughter of Helen and Menelaus, who finally marries Neoptolemus, Achilles' son. By the Middle Ages, the whole matter involved Troilus, unhappy lover of the careless Cressida, and Aeneas, lover of Dido and founder of Rome, who were listed as Paris' brothers and sons of Priam. Aeneas even became the ancestor of all the British kings (of Lear, Old King Cole, and Cymbeline) through his descendant Felix Brutus who left Italy and settled the British Isles. Eris' apple caused as much discord as Eve's.

Sweet Helen's role in all this has been hard for subsequent generations to evaluate, because they keep treating her as a person rather than as a symbol. What bothers "behaviorists" is that she can marry Menelaus, go off with Paris, and return happily to Menelaus after Troy falls. Egypt might do such things, but nice girls don't. And if they do, the men in their lives aren't going to like it. As a result, attempts to reconstruct Helen's personality have run the gamut: she has been seen as everything from Dendritis, a tree-goddess on Rhodes, to a slut. In the *Iliad,* Homer makes her repentant for her actions. In Euripides' *The Trojan Women,* Menelaus is hurt and angry, claiming "he doesn't care" and fights only to vent his spleen on Paris. Helen wiggles around his wrath using methods evidently standardized long before her time. She simply focuses her beauty on her husband and tells him Hecuba, Priam, and the gods are to blame for the whole mess, summarizing her defense with that unassailable comment: "Exactly what was I supposed to do?" Nevertheless, many have found it hard to avoid remarks about her apparently "easy" ways. Shakespeare has Hector say, "She is not worth what she dothe cost." Stories have grown up about her relationship with Paris' brother, Deiphobus, before she returns to Menelaus. And Virgil even has her taking up with the Shade of Achilles after her death. Not that she hasn't had her defenders. One standard excuse is that Aphrodite had been forced to bewitch her into infidelity so that Paris could get her to leave Menelaus, and the curse lingered on. Another states categorically that she was "repelled by Deiphobus' approaches" and even tried to escape Troy and flee to the Greek camp. The most elaborate notes that on the way to Troy, Paris and Helen stopped to spend the night in Egypt. There Proteus, the clairvoyant son of Neptune, hid Helen in a cave and sent "a shade in her shape" along with Paris. After the war, Menelaus, who had been apprised of the trick, stopped off in Egypt and reclaimed his unblemished wife. Thus, all the "bad things" were done by the "alter Helen."

The fact of the matter is that Helen, if she is to be thought of as actual at all, has to be thought of as a woman of the times in which her legend formed, not as a nineteenth-century, medieval, or even Roman lady. The original plot makes it clear she was property—lovely, valuable property, but property nonetheless, like a handsome horse or a living doll. The plot gives her no moral decisions to make. She went with whoever could take her and hold her: Theseus, Menelaus, Paris, Deiphobus, Menelaus again, Achilles' ghost. To accuse her of immorality or to wonder, as one "biographer" (John Erskine) did, how she could reconcile her behavior with her conscience is to re-cast the tale, to demand that Greek ships run by steam, that Trojan solders drink 3.2 beer from Dixie cups instead of blood from bladders, that Achilles not love Patroklos quite as ardently as he did.

But there is no point in worrying about an historical Helen anyhow—when she was born (scholars have said 1200 B.C.), who she was, or if her famous war was just a reprisal for piracy. If there ever was a real Helen, and there undoubtedly was some reasonably attractive queen whose abduction touched off an inevitable trade war centuries ago, her actuality has faded behind the clouds of time. The only Helen that exists now is "Sweet Helen," Shakespeare's "pearl whose price hath launch'd above a thousand ships, and turn'd crown'd kings to merchants." A Helen whose only purpose is to be "divinely tall and most divinely fair."

There's a lot of literature in the world where the feminine lead has no more complex role than Helen's; where gotten, lost, and re-gotten, she need have no personality, no goals, and no motivations other than the willingness to mate. Nor are such simplistic plots out of keeping with life itself, for the animal which mates has, if nothing else, done its bit to counter extinction.

However, survival is not the only important thing. It is also important that the best females be mated to the best males, for the improvement of the breed. Stubbornly, for generations, people have insisted that their stories be about golden lads and golden girls, that their heroes settle for no less than a Helen. And so the "Andromeda theme," with its thousands of variations, has developed.

The "Andromeda theme" involves beauty courted by the beast, but rescued from that plight and its disastrous biological potential by a "white knight." The name comes from the classical tale of Perseus. In that story Cassiopeia boasts that she is decidedly better-looking than the Nereids, a group of lovely sea-nymphs.

Thetis, almost as lovely as Helen, was a Nereid. Such mortal impudence irritates these demi-goddesses, and they persuade Neptune, who is married to one, to have Ethiopia ravaged by a monster. In an effort to get rid of the dragon, Andromeda, Cassiopeia's lovely daughter, is tied to a rock as a sacrifice. There she is spied by Perseus who is flying home after his fight with the Gorgon. He falls in love with her beauty on sight, swoops down to kill the approaching monster, and is rewarded by being given Andromeda in marriage. Their grandchild, Alcmene, was to be Hercules' mother—a further proof of the biological benefits of the plot.

Naturally the Andromeda theme doesn't have to involve dragons and heroes with magic powers. The theme works in medieval England, nineteenth-century Wyoming, or twentieth-century Paris, and it does as well using a farmer's daughter, landlord, and local lad; a schoolmarm, outlaw, and cowhand; or a Restoration flirt, old husband, and rake as it does with Andromeda, the monster, and Perseus. The only really important thing is that the girl be divinely fair, the villain intent on destroying her or unsuitable to mate with her, and the hero the top stud available. Of course, she can't get "uppity" once saved. She must give herself to him, doe to stag, without question.

At the folk and popular levels of fiction, the fact that Andromeda has almost no mind of her own and a limited personality is not important. But the better writers have always been quite aware that beauty may lie "skin deep" over an active brain, and that reality's Andromeda, once freed from the rock, is likely to have second thoughts about Perseus, no matter how obligated she may feel to him. Furthermore, just because he looks good with a dragon wheezing its life away at her feet does not mean that he will be "so nice to come home to" after the blood has dried. Thus, the great writer has to consider "divorce" as a possible future for Jason and Medea, death as a way of preserving the "endless honeymoon" for Romeo and Juliet, infidelity as part of the make-up of Arthur his Guinevere.

Moreover, great writers are in the habit of walking around the pedestal, looking at Helen and Andromeda from all angles, loving them for their "flaws of perfection" as well as their virtues. One of Henry James' notes to his brother William shows this. It was written from Italy just after he heard of the death of his young cousin, Mary ("Minnie") Temple, the lovely girl whose freshness, potential, and beauty haunted James for the rest of his life. He modeled Daisy Miller, Isabel Archer, and to some extent all his "American" heroines after her and wrote *The Wings of the Dove* as a sort of "biography" of the life she might have led. Had he written about Helen or Andromeda or Juliet somehow or another each would have been Minnie. Yet there is something almost humorous in his inability to be blinded by her. Even just shocked by news of her death, he feels compelled to examine her.

. . . . So it seems, at least, on reflection: to the eye of feeling there is something immensely moving in the sudden and complete extinction of a vitality so exquisite and so apparently infinite as Minny's. But what most occupies me, as it will have done all of you at home, is the thought of how her whole life seemed to tend and hasten, visibly, audibly, sensibly, to this consummation. Her character may be almost literally said to have been without practical application to life. She seems a sort of experiment of nature—an attempt, a specimen or example—a mere subject without an object. She was at any rate the helpless victim and toy of her own intelligence—so that there is positive relief in thinking of her being removed from her own heroic treatment and placed in kinder hands. . . .

Upon her limitations, now, it seems idle to dwell; the list of her virtues is so much longer than her life. My own personal relations with her were always of the happiest. Every one was supposed, I believe, to be more or less in love with her: others may answer for themselves: I never was, and yet I had the great satisfaction that I enjoyed *pleasing* her almost as much as if I had been. I cared more to please her perhaps then she ever cared to be pleased. Looking back upon the past half-dozen years, it seems as if she *represented*, in a manner, in my life several of the elements or phases of life at large—her own sex, to begin with, but even more *Youth*, with which owing to my invalidism, I always felt in rather indirect relation.

But if the golden girl proves difficult when she steps out of the dream, she is adept at adjusting to newer times and different places. In the bourgeois world, for instance, her appeal may have to involve more than just beauty, and since the Middle Ages she has often been identified so closely with the socio-economic advantages of marrying her that it is sometimes hard to know which glister the hero is after. Shylock, rushing out into the street after his Jessica has eloped, calling alternately for his daughter and the ducats she has carried away, knows quite well what two-fold riches his new son-in-law has attained. The more modern golden girl engineers her own mating, stoops in order to conquer, works out her Life Force, or remains the constant wife while conducting an affair. Today Andromeda will help take on the dragon, perhaps even saving Perseus in the bargain.

But the refrain doesn't die, and as long as "slender feet" set man's "heart beating" there will be Sweet Helens for whom the boats must be launched, Jessicas worth "twice their weight" in gold, and Minnie Temples "without practical application to life." For "She" has not yet ceased to fill him with "wonder and surmise."

About 800 years ago, this "wonder and surmise" became institutionalized in the Courts of Love, which were promulgated by Eleanor of Aquitaine and which created a code that has dominated man-woman relationships in the Western World to the present. It is a lot easier to describe this medieval cult of courtly love than it is to trace the origin of its blend. Certainly the popularity of Ovid's *Ars Amatoria* had something to do with it. Ovid, who was an exact contemporary of Christ's mother Mary, wrote his poem as a guide for worldly men and women who wish a bedmate. The instruction is consistently coarse and based on the principle that "all women" can be had. In fact, says Ovid, if the man fails to ask first, the woman, who by her very nature is already won, will become aggressive. Ovid's idea of love is sensual, "all's fair" extra-marital lust in which ploys and deceits that would be unfair in war are sanctioned. When ploys and deceits fail, force, actually outright rape, is suggested. What's more, lovers should have more than one partner, using duplicity to prevent any of the favored knowing there are rivals. What moral notes there are center on the fact that the male must suffer for his privileges. Love will make him pale and wan, forcing him to tremble, feel nauseous, moan, groan, and faint. He may even go mad or die from his passion—and "there is nothing he can take to relieve that pleasant ache," either. "If any," Ovid writes, "be here ignorant of love, let him read this book and he shall a lover prove."

Ovid's blunt ideas are only a start. Also important was the undemocratic, feudal relationship of the vassal and his lord. The vassal owes obedience, veneration, and loyalty to his master and has but one duty in this world, to serve him. The master in turn rewards this devotion with benefits, virtues, and what other fruits ripen in *noblesse oblige*. The vassal-lord relationship was embraced by the entire culture, much the way the concept of "égalité" has been embraced by ours. You encounter it everywhere. Not only does master care for his obedient peasant, but Christ cares for His servant, Pope for bishop, bishop for cleric, knight for squire, hunter for hound. Husband cared for wife, too. However, when one realizes that by the end of the twelfth century, civilization had developed sufficiently that women were able, particularly in France, to inherit large fiefs, one can also see that the master-servant relationship might sometimes become that of mistress-man. The poets of Provence, in southern France, were among the first to capitalize on this "new" juxtaposition. In order to gain favor with the wives and daughters of the great landowners, many of whom inherited their husband's or father's power, singers began to idealize important women, developing the master-servant relationship along amorous lines designed to please the Lady.

Originally, there must have been little more in their poetic effusions than there were in the incredible efforts of the sixteenth-century court climbers to compliment the vanity of Elizabeth R.— Edmund Spenser's "faerie queen," the "lovliest woman of them all" to whom George Peele awarded the "Apple of Discord." But such poetry was not difficult for composers to extend or for broader audiences to enjoy. Southern France had long known books like the *Dove's Neck-Ring* of Andalusian Ibn Hazm. Moorish, such works stressed the sovereignty of the beloved woman; the feverish, sleepless role of the lover; his obligations to her; the secrecy in which all of this best flowers; and the power love has to make the cowardly brave, the testy tractable, the doltish clever, even the ugly beautiful. And if the Moors did not argue for adultery or outright lust, their ideas mixed nicely with those of Ovid, mellowing the blend into a religion of love. Called *fin amor,* the courtly love creed stressed extra-marital passion—sublimated, all-absorbing, enduring, often unrequited. It exalted the lady far above her lover-vassal, ennobling her by giving her obligations to men that the daughters of Eve had seldom known, ennobling him by demanding aspiration, renunciation, and devotion.

Roger Loomis describes the whole matter in his *The Development of Arthurian Romance:*

> This . . . woman-worship was revolutionary in two respects. It defied the teachings of the Church and the conventions of society by rejecting marriage, as then determined by property and pedigree, and substituting a relationship based on free choice. It defied Church and society by giving woman a higher worth and a superior status to man's. This was a very natural revolt. There is no blinking the fact that most feudal marriages represented a financial or political bargain, and often the bargain was made when the bridegroom and the bride were twelve years old or under. As Benjamin Franklin observed: "Where there is marriage without love, there will be love without marriage." Both Church and society were agreed that the female sex was inferior to the male. Made of Adam's rib, Eve brought about his fall and so the fall of all mankind; and Eve's daughters were notorious for following the example of their mother. So spake the Church, though making exception for virgin martyrs and holy women. . . . It must have given a profound joy to women of spirit when, instead of being reminded continually of their sins and their subject state, they were adored by their poet lovers and credited with every virtue.

In spite of Church stodginess, 12th century Christianity was a particularly good place for the blend to age. Veneration for Mary, the Immaculate Mother of the Savior, was developing with the mystic movements that swept the Church between the First and Second Crusades (1095 and 1145) and the end of the century. Woman worship was the enthusiasm of the time. And while scholars are pretty well agreed that the cult of the Virgin flowered later than courtly love, surely we have to note, as Henry Adams noted, ". . . the coincidence that while the Virgin was miraculously using the power of spiritual love to elevate and purify the people, Eleanor and her daughters were using the power of earthly love to discipline and refine the courts." But however things worked, the veneration of Mary in its turn did its share to establish the astrophel-stella relationship between lover and his woman. And by the time a few generations passed, it mattered little which came first, the egg or the womb.

All this gave *fin amor* a religious atmosphere which greatly helped it permeate Christian culture. With a Virgin at the center of the religion who shone, as St. Anselm said, "with a purity so great that nothing greater under God can be imagined" and with prayers continually begged of a "tender Queen of mercy", as St. Bernard conceived her, it was quite natural for the earthly to idealize and beg favors of a touchable lady. In short, the literary, philosophical, religious, and even political atmosphere was right. Moreover, *fin amor* had a champion, in Eleanor of Aquitaine who, through her marriages with Louis VII of France and Henry II of England and through her daughters and niece, spread the doctrine far and north. Ultimately this fashion for treating women mystically and ideally passed from Provence, central France, and England into Italian literature where it was developed and given stature by Roman Catholic poets like Guinizelli and Dante. And as Italy became the fountainhead of literary and courtly matters, it was respread across Europe through the Renaissance. So it has come down to us, coloring practically all the polite relationships between men and women until today.

The doctrine of courtly love as it was thought of in the late twelfth century in southern France is published in a three-book treatise by Andreas Capellanus called *De Amore Libri Tres*. Andreas, who wrote under the tutelage, if not the actual guidance, of Eleanor of Aquitaine's daughter, Marie de Champagne, directs his remarks to a friend Walter. Of questionable altruism, they are offered with the express purpose of telling Walter all about love so he can avoid it and be rewarded in Heaven for abstaining from an earthly pleasure he knew perfectly well how to obtain. Book I concentrates on the techniques and complications of the man-woman business. It is very conscious of the medieval class system and devotes a good bit of space to the distinctions associated with social status and love-making. Book II is the most famous.

It features information on acquiring, consummating, increasing, and even decreasing love. In it is given the list which is so frequently reproduced today as a kind of rule-book for the courtly love game.

THE RULES

    I. Marriage is no real excuse for not loving.

    II. He who is not jealous cannot love.

    III. No one can be bound by a double love.

    IV. It is well known that love is always increasing or decreasing.

    V. That which a lover takes against the will of his beloved has no relish.

    VI. Boys do not love until they arrive at the age of maturity.

    VII. When one lover dies, a widowhood of two years is required of the survivor.

    VIII. No one should be deprived of love without the very best of reasons.

    IX. No one can love unless he is impelled by the persuasion of love.

    X. Love is always a stranger in the home of avarice.

    XI. It is not proper to love any woman whom one would be ashamed to seek to marry.

    XII. A true lover does not desire to embrace in love anyone except his beloved.

    XIII. When made public love rarely endures.

    XIV. The easy attainment of love makes it of little value; difficulty of attainment makes it prized.

    XV. Every lover regularly turns pale in the presence of his beloved.

    XVI. When a lover suddenly catches sight of his beloved his heart palpitates.

    XVII. A new love puts to flight an old one.

    XVIII. Good character alone makes any man worthy of love.

    XIX. If love diminishes, it quickly fails and rarely revives.

    XX. A man in love is always apprehensive.

    XXI. Real jealousy always increases the feeling of love.

    XXII. Jealousy, and therefore love, are increased when one suspects his beloved.

    XXIII. He whom the thought of love vexes eats and sleeps very little.

    XXIV. Every act of a lover ends in the thought of his beloved.

XXV. A true lover considers nothing good except what he thinks will please his beloved.

XXVI. Love can deny nothing to love.

XXVII. A lover can never have enough of the solaces of his beloved.

XXVIII. A slight presumption causes a lover to suspect his beloved.

XXIX. A man who is vexed by too much passion usually does not love.

XXX. A true lover is constantly and without intermission possessed by the thought of his beloved.

XXXI. Nothing forbids one woman being loved by two men or one man by two women.

By adhering to such rules, the reader, as well as Walter, can make himself into an expert.   Book III explains why Andreas wrote Books I and II, and informs Walter that true rewards await him if he never uses his fresh-gained knowledge. The tone of Book III is satiric, and most urbane in its rejection of everything that has just been so carefully explained. Needless to say, Book III has caused some confusion as to just how seriously Andreas took the whole matter.

But Marie seems to have taken it seriously. She was also sponsor to Chrétien de Troyes, a great poet, who did much to popular-

ize the relationships that Andreas codified. Chrétien's re-tellings
of the *Arthuriad* were "best-sellers" in their day. In them he re-
arranged Arthur's relationship with his wife Guinevere along
courtly lines, giving her the gallant Lancelot as lover and leaving
the King, like the husband in Scott's "Lochinvar," standing
around "dangling his plume." According to Geoffrey of Mon-
mouth (who pretty much invented the basic plot of the *Arthuriad)*
Guinevere or Guenhuvara was of Roman descent and the ward of
Cador of Cornwall. Arthur, who became king at fifteen after defeating a dozen rebellious princes, wins her as a reward for saving
Carmalide and lives with her happily for twelve years. However,
while he is on the Continent defeating enemies, marching on
Rome, and crossing the Alps, his nephew Mordred usurps his
throne and Guenhuvara along with it. Arthur returns, but receives
his death-wound during a tremendous battle in which Mordred is
slain. Miraculously, he is borne off to Avalon to be cared for by
Morgan le Fay. Guenhuvara then does what any red-blooded
girl of the time would do. She enters a nunnery.

It is obvious that Geoffrey and other narrators of Guinevere's
life gave Chrétien some grounds for interpreting her as unfaithful.
Like Helen before her, she had to go along with whoever pos-

*Lancelot and Guinevere, from a miniature
in 11th c. manuscript, National Library,
Paris.*

(NEW YORK PUBLIC LIBRARY
PICTURE COLLECTION)

sessed her: first Arthur, then Mordred, and surely if he hadn't
been wounded, Arthur again. And like Helen's, her subsequent
reputation suffered for it. Even today in some parts of Wales to
call a girl "a Guinevere" is to call her "indiscriminate." Of
course, Chrétien didn't see her that way. Following the rules of
fin amor, he idealized her infidelity in his tale, *Lancelot,* making
it of the highest sort and utterly respectable. And he gave her a
vassal-lover far superior to Mordred (for that matter to Arthur), a
champion whose "every act ends in the thought of his beloved."

In fact, so enthusiastic is he in developing the courtly love relationship, scholars are split as to whether he, like Andreas, may
have been making fun of the whole matter. It is hard to take some
of the scenes seriously. At one point Lancelot finds a comb in
which some strands of Guinevere's hair linger. He presses it to his
cheeks, eyes, and lips 100,000 times before secreting it under his
shirt next to his heart. At another time he is day-dreaming of
Guinevere so deeply he has to be challenged three times and
finally knocked off his horse before becoming aware another
knight wants to test him. Guinevere even commands him to act
like a coward during a tournament at Noauz. Dutifully, he obeys
and is chased around the field for two days to his great disgrace

and shame. When she relents and permits him to do his best on the third day, he sweeps the field in a scene that the author of the Baseball Joe books might interpret as unreal. And once, piqued over a display of "weakness" on his part, Guinevere scorns him although he fights an entire battle backwards so he won't lose sight of her as she watches from a tower.

Whatever Chrétien intended, his works were taken seriously by the public, and they were read and re-read over the years. Lancelot's response to Guinevere was accepted as the normal sort of thing that happens when normal lads fall in love. And actually, Lancelot's idiocies are not much more extreme than those of Romeo (our model lover) who leaps walls, climbs vines, and runs about so disconcertedly that neither Juliet nor Friar Laurence are really up to handling him. Nor are Guinevere's piques much more preposterous than those feminine whims that cause the "whole trouble" in a boy meets, loses, and gets girl movie or TV show. For Lancelot and Guinevere became the models for many lovers in much literature, and if their names change to Troilus and Cressida, Emily and Palomon, Astrophel and Stella, truck-driver and chorus girl; if a society judges that extra-marital love must give way to marital love; their way is still "the way"—the lover vassal to his lady, and the lady (secretly amused by her ability to evoke such devotion) withholding or bestowing mercy as it suits her fancy. It's a cliché we must all endure.

Of course, Andreas' three books and Chrétien's *Lancelot* are but two of a host, two morsels used to feed the appetite of the nobles for *fin amor*. So insatiable was this appetite that descriptions of actual courts of love are common. These were trials in which love problems were subjected to "scholastic debate" and at which decisions were handed down. Today it is hard to tell if such courts of love actually met or not—or if they did meet how big their vogue was. The whole thing may well have related to reality somewhat in the way our cowboy or detective shows relate to what actually happens on the plains or in the cities. However, if they did exist (and I think they did), they must have been conducted about the way that Curtis Howe Walker reproduces them on pages 121-122 in his *Eleanor of Aquitaine:*

The day of the court of love dawned auspiciously, with the sun glinting on the fresh verdure of grass and trees. At an early hour a gay procession headed by trumpeters and heralds moved slowly out of the courtyard and around the castle to a spot where there was a gentle slope. Here a semicircular amphitheatre had been built, consisting of a platform from which on either side several ranges of benches extended in a curve. The platform was sheltered by a green canvas awning, while varicolored banners fluttered from the window openings of Maubergeonne's Tower in the background. . . .

When all were seated, a blast on the trumpets silenced the buzz of conversation. A herald then stepped forward and declared that they were met under the aegis of the god of love, whose laws would govern the proceedings. By his edicts were to be decided all matters brought up for discussion before the president of the court, Her Highness Eleanor, Queen of England, Countess of Poitou, and Duchess of Aquitaine. All anxious lovers, vassals of the god of love, were invited to submit their problems and rest assured of just judgment.

Andreas the Chaplain submitted the first case. A knight had complained of his mistress' unjust treatment in extorting from him a promise not to speak a good word of her to others, on pain of losing her love. The lover faithfully kept his promise till one day, in the company of other knights and ladies, he heard them speaking shamefully about his lady. He endured this for a while with an ill grace, but when they continued to disparage his love, he at last burst out violently in her defense. When the affair came to his lady's ears, she condemned him to lose her love because he had violated her commands.

The honorable court lost no time in reaching a decision. Its unanimous opinion adjudged the arrogant mistress to be entirely in the wrong. It was deemed both unseemly and unfair for any woman to have laid such a command on a lover and then to blame him for not carrying it out. The gentleman, on the other hand, was commended for having defended the reputation of his mistress. . . .

Andreas now begged permission to present a problem involving the question of whether true love were possible between husband and wife. A certain knight, he said, was in love with a woman who had given her love to another man, but the suitor received from her this much hope—that if she should ever lose the love of her beloved, her love would go to this man. A little while later, the woman married her lover. The other knight then demanded that she give him the fruit of the hope she had granted, but this she refused to do, saying she had not lost the love of her lover. Eleanor, to whom the decision was again left, gave her response with evident reluctance: "We dare not oppose the opinion of the Countess of Champagne who once ruled in a lengthy letter that love can exert no power between husband and wife. Therefore, we recommend that the lady should grant the love which she has promised." Yet the tone in which she spoke, and the fact that she gave no command but only a recommendation, led some to suspect that her sympathies were with the woman.

And so it went, until the Queen, wearying, "signalled the heralds to proclaim the session over."

Obviously there are quite a number of possible trials. Andreas includes twenty-one examples which he claims to have been familiar with. These run a gamut any Hollywood writer could cherish: from the couple who have "united in love" unaware they are blood relatives to the lady who allows her lover to "enjoy" another's embrace and then repulses him as "no longer worthy" of her esteem when he comes back. In fact, Andreas' "21" is in effect a Barnes and Noble *Plot Outline of the World's Great Soap Operas.*

Such courts reflected, in lay fashion, two forces that were in collision in the ecclesiastical philosophy of the time. On one side, they feature scholastic emphasis on debate, where arguments, decision by council, and the dialectic method dominate. On the other, they feature the mystic relationship between man and his ideal, where enthusiasm, aspiration, and the spiritual are stressed. Perhaps the marriage of these two quite different approaches is most appropriately, if ironically, summed up in the life and legend of Pierre Abélard, a teacher in the Paris cathedral school in the years after 1113. Philosophers remember him as devoted to intellectual disputation and argument, a rebel who scorned his stuffy superiors, and a force in awakening the Church from its dogmatic slumbers. His works are frequently cited as "cases in point" of the early scholastic method. But popularly he is recalled as the impassioned worshipper of his pupil, the lovely Héloise, niece of the Canon of Fulbert. When the Canon, irate over their secret marriage, had Abélard castrated, there was little left for them to do but separate, she going to the nunnery at Argenteuil, he to the monastery at St. Denis. From then on they corresponded through beautiful love letters—while always there lingers the implication that his scholarly work was but a forgetting of a devotion Eleanor would have understood. Certainly the love of a free-thinking teacher for the beautiful niece of a canon is a case for any court of love, secret marriage or not.

The "tort" of Héloise and Abélard does make the disputations of *fin amor* seem much less preposterous than they might at first glance. For as James R. Kreuzer once wrote in an "Introduction" to *Sir Gawain and the Green Knight:*

. . . courtly love in its very artificialities, its excesses, its exaggerations is an externalizing, an acting out, of the complex feelings involved in one of the most complicated and powerful of human relationships. Though the institution of courtly love may have developed in an attempt to elevate the role of women in upper class society . . . it nevertheless gave opportunity for the expression in life and literature of much that medieval man—and modern man, too—knew as love. For the behavior of young people in love—since the Middle Ages and even in our own day—is not vastly different, in many ways, from that of the medieval knight. . . .

In our own day, Hollywood and television have portrayed scores of young lovers, sometimes seriously, sometimes humorously, suffering what Hamlet called the "pangs of despised love" or the fears that the girl in question may reject a proposal of marriage; we see a young lover giving up an honest but poorly paid job to commit crimes to meet the financial desires of a demanding wife or sweetheart—behavior that certainly may be as extreme as that of the knight going on a dangerous expedition to prove his worthiness of his lady. Even with the emancipation of women, our society still demands that men treat women with a courtesy and respect that would have pleased Eleanor of Aquitaine.

If the objection is made that love in our society normally has marriage as its goal and courtly love was extramarital, it is necessary to point out only that even before Chaucer's day many of the tenets of courtly love had found their way into married love. . . . In sum, then, much that characterizes courtly love remained through the centuries from Eleanor's to our own as acceptable—even natural—in the behavior of people in love.

While the voice of Faust becomes the plaintive voice of goodmen throughout the ages: Come Helen, come Andromeda, even Mary, "come, give me my soul again."

4

LA FILLE EN ROSE

The symbol for the Virgin was to be the Rose, replacing the lily with which artists had long associated Christ's Mother and upon which the Crucifixion had often been depicted. The Rose spoke of Mary's mercy, and so charity, and of Her ineffable beauty. Through its immaculate representation, the stained-glass window, the sunlight of God flowed and fell upon the altar of the medieval church. And if the church were a proper shrine, the builders constructed it so every vector of the architecture directed one's eye toward this reproduction of Christianity's Miracle. Nevertheless, the Rose was not only a religious flower. The very letters form an anagram of Eros, sexual Love itself, and the rose had long been associated with the interests of fleshly men in women. In fact, that is surely why Christianity adopted it, suggesting through it that spiritual devotions to the Virgin Mother are even more enthralling than everyday dreams of golden girls.

Originally, the rose was a Persian flower, and legend tells us that Alexander the Great introduced it to Greece and the West. This may or may not be true, but it is certain that Greek mythology associated it with Aphrodite and her son Eros, and so with the feminine force. The Greeks had a number of myths accounting for its origins. One says that it was a gift created by the gods to celebrate Aphrodite's birth from the sea.   Another says that when Aphrodite first cried her tears formed roses. There are also stories about its characteristics. Roses are red because Aphrodite, searching for her lover Adonis who lay gored to death by a boar, pricked her feet on their thorns, or because Eros whimsically emptied his cup of wine upon the petals. The thorns sprang from the plant after Eros, furious over being stung by a bee as he sniffed a rosebush, shot arrows at the plant. The thorns are also explained by the fact that Dionysius, lustily pursuing a terrified nymph, was stopped by a hedge of thorns which he promptly turned into a hedge of roses. In the confusion of his intended's dodgings, he ordered the roses to become thorns again. However, his powers (perhaps confused by a product of his vineyards) only worked in part. The thorns reappeared, but the flowers remained.

Hebraic myth tells us pink roses derive from the blushings of the white ones Eve kissed in the Garden, and the thorns are supposed to have appeared on the bushes after the Expulsion. It was only natural that Christ's crown of thorns was sometimes described as being made of roses, and that the red rose is the result of His Blood which spilled upon the petals during the Crucifixion.

The rose has traditionally had an aura of secrecy about it, a belief reflected in a phrase like "sub rosa" and the name of the Rosicrucian Society. Traditionally, if one places a rose over a conference or dining table or attaches it to the ceiling of a meeting room, this indicates that everything that takes place is to be confidential. The story goes that Eros had to bribe the God of Silence, Harpocrates, with a rose in order to cover up some indiscretions his mother had indulged in.

The rose also has the power of enchantment. People like Apulius and St. Denis of France were able to regain their human form after being transformed into animals by eating roses, and "pulling roses" in medieval times was an accepted way of "calling up" the fairies. Actually, the plant has a good many medicinal qualities. For instance, the hips are an excellent source of Vitamin C, while rose tea, rose powder, rose this, and rose that are reputed to cure everything from mad-dog bite to alcoholism. There's really no telling what a rose can do. In Transylvania (now Hungary) roses protected cattle against witches. In England a rose picked on Midsummer's Eve and worn to church at Christmas would be plucked from the girl's dress by the man she would marry.

It has also been a favorite funeral flower, its powerful odor working as a much-needed "room deodorant." The Greeks and Romans both used it this way, in addition to scattering petals in and about the grave. Supposedly it protected the deceased from evil. Even in late nineteenth-century Texas the "Dying Cowboy" requests not only that "six jolly maidens carry his coffin" but that it be covered with roses to "deaden the clods as they fall." In Switzerland a cemetery may be referred to as *ein rosengarten,* and in Wales a white rose is planted on the grave of a virgin and a red one on that of a respectable citizen. Anyone familiar with balladry knows that lovers who die before marriage will be remembered by a rose and a briar that are planted at the heads of their graves.

> Sweet William was buried in the old churchyard,
> Fair Eleanor in the choir.
> And out of the one grew a red, red rose
> And out of the other a briar.
>
> They grew and they grew to the steeple top
> Till they could grow no higher,
> And there they tied in a true lovers' knot,
> The rose around the briar.

Perhaps its funereal associations have made it a symbol of bad luck in some places. Falling rose petals indicate death in Germany. Roses that bloom out of season bode no good in England. Fading roses indicate fading love in the American South. And to scatter rose petals on the ground is to invite evil in most of Europe and the United States.

But all in all, the rose has been the most honored of flowers: not only among the Greeks, Romans, and Christians, but among the Arabs, where it is often a symbol of masculinity; among the Persians; and among many North American Indian tribes. Because of its associations with Aphrodite, magic, secrecy, death, and festival, it is no wonder time selected the rose to replace the lily as the symbol of the Virgin Mother, and through her to associate it with all that is ideally feminine. "Say it with flowers," we are told. Little does the high school senior dream what volumes he speaks when he buys his golden girl "one dozen roses, and puts his heart in beside them."

But little does the high school junior who receives them know what she is meant to be, for she is a real girl and the Virgin, Sweet Helen, and Juliet "scarcely dwell on her block." In fact, one of the real complications of her life will be the paradox she will have to act out, princess high in a white castle with four bedrooms upstairs, two baths, and 100 feet of frontage. And she will fail acting out the paradox, just as thousands of real girls have failed before her, simply because mortals "tumble short of dreams." Even Eleanor of Aquitaine, arbitrix of the love-courts, had no ready judgment for this paradox which haunted her own life. And it is ironic that the champion of *fin amor* should be remembered as much for her thorns as her petals, for conduct far more Ovidian than Provençal.

Eleanor of Aquitaine was golden, as golden as "girls who come to dust" are like to be. Make no mistake about that. Daughter of Duke William, a troubadour-poet himself, she was the great beauty of her time. Intimately involved in the cultural, political, and military affairs of France and England, she was Queen of one or the other for sixty-five years. She probably did more than anyone to upgrade the role of women in the western world. She bore two sons who were kings, went on a Crusade, and lived to an old age ripe enough that she could lead a defense of her besieged castle when she was nearly eighty. It is hard to believe anyone could live a fuller human life. Cleopatra, Elizabeth I and Victoria to the contrary, she probably had more to do with the world of her time than any woman who has ever lived.

Born in 1122, she came into prominence when, at fifteen, she married Louis VII of France. As with all marriages among people of her social class, this one had political overtones. It occurred about one month before he succeeded to the throne and just a year after he had become ruler of the huge duchy of Aquitaine. Louis not only won himself a beautiful bride, he gained con-

Effigy of Eleanor of Aquitaine (1122-1204).

trol of a crucial and powerful section of southern France. She, of course, gained military and economic security for her people. It seemed a veritable märchen: the Prince of France coming south to marry with the loveliest girl in the land, leading her home to rule by his side forever and a day. Forever and a day was actually fifteen years, until 1152. Then reality stepped in. Prince Charming had become tedious, his interest in religion quite usurping the "Molly and me, baby makes three" side of marriage. "More monk, than King," she called him. As he gave his time to ecclesiastical matters, her beauty and her brains made her restless. On the other hand, Queens were meant to produce sons, and Eleanor had had two girls. Divorce was inevitable.

It was accomplished by one of those tautological maneuvers that characterized medieval separation. The fact that Eleanor had failed to produce a male heir was attributed to God's irritation that King and Queen were related to each other "within the seven degrees of kinship" allowed by the Church. Louis, who seems to have remained devoted to Eleanor long after they had broken up, was unhappy about it all, but did what he felt he had to do. Eleanor was relieved. She had not conducted herself like a golden girl during her marriage anyhow. Boredom had worked its ways in the castle as effectively as it ever has in any suburb. Rumors about her indiscretions were widespread—their immorality magnified by the Satanic fact that a husband devoted to the church was being horned. Politicians certain to profit from the separation rejoiced.

The first "reports" seem to have developed during Louis' Crusade to the Holy Land, a difficult trip through hardship and luxury in which the King's religious fanaticism showed itself fully. Crusades, to be sure, were not designed for golden girls involved in "happily ever after." Eleanor probably shouldn't have been along, but she was—and she had put up with a lot. Letting her host seduce her in opulent Antioch probably seemed the most natural thing in the world. However, it was particularly unfortunate that her host was also her uncle, handsome Prince Raymond, who had invited Louis' entourage with the specific hope that Louis would help him in some local skirmishes before proceeding to the Holy Land. Amazed and angered when Louis refused, he began to try to get at the King through the Queen. Wining and dining her, showing her the sights, he fell in love with her and, perhaps partly out of revenge, entered into an affaire. Revenge may have occurred to her also. At the time, she was particularly irritated by Louis' singleness of religious purpose.

The affaire was shocking to the devout and the bill-payers in France, and as the scandal-mongers and political opportunists wagged their tongues, Eleanor's reputation took a turn along lines Cleopatra's had hundreds of years earlier. Other excitements were reported, some involving handsome slaves and even non-Christian lovers. Once, Louis was said to have snatched her from the very gangplank of a vessel that the Saracen Saladin had sent to fetch her after she had excited his infidel lust. Implying that she was to replace a whole harem, the gossips overlooked the fact that Saladin was a disinterested ten years old at the time.

Her reputation never fully recovered. Of course, her divorce from Louis and her marriage two months later to Henry, Duke of Normandy and Count of Anjou, did nothing to help. Walter Map accuses her of casting "glances of unholy love" at Henry well before she and Louis separated, and she probably did. But it is unlikely she flaunted herself before the barons right after the pronouncement ceremony, asking them if they didn't think she was a "delectable piece" and remarking that Louis, who had found her "a very devil," would miss what she had to offer. Her marriage to Henry, who was eleven years her junior, was certainly motivated by political opportunism more than passion. After all, she didn't have that many choices. She had to look after Aquitaine and Henry was a powerful consort. To his nineteen-year-old eyes, Eleanor must have seemed far more desirable as a symbol than as a woman.

During their long Lady December-Lord May marriage, it was he, not she, that "wandered." Already thirty when they wed, she had no chance of controlling his infidelities, even had the customs of the time been such that she expected to. Henry's lusts ranged wide. One resulted in an affair with a "street-girl" who persuaded the King to acknowledge her son as his. Another linked him with the French princess, Alais, who at nine was betrothed to his own son Richard (who incidentally never married her). Henry had been asked to bring Alais up, and he seems to have instructed her in his leisure time. But of all Henry's indiscretions, the one with Rosamund Clifford rankled Eleanor the most. As lovely as Eleanor had ever been, well-born, and above

An illustration depicting Eleanor of Aquitaine as Queen of England, taken from a turn-of-the-century romantic novel. Eleanor was actually over forty.

all young, "Fair Rosamund" is described in one ballad as having "a color in her cheeks as a drop of blood in snows" with "a waist, a waist, a waist like all my silver cane." She was kept by Henry near his manor at Woodstock. She seems to have been the "love of his life." When Eleanor was abroad, he "flaunted" Rosamund at court, and when she died he had her body honorably buried at Gadstow Abbey, where the resident nuns were richly rewarded for acquiescing to his wishes. Rosamund bore him a son, a lad of whom Henry was extraordinarily proud, and there is little doubt that Eleanor feared the chance that he might "leap into the father's seat."

Yet it was Eleanor who was considered wanton by the public. One medieval bard offered to "trade the world" if the Queen of England were "to lay in his arms." His wish was based on rumors telling how Henry's father, Geoffrey Plantagenet, had "known her" long before his son had even met her and on legends like the one preserved in the ballad, "Queen Eleanor's Confession."

> Queen Elenor was a sick woman,
> ˙ And afraid that she should dye;
> Then she sent for two fryars of France,
> For to speak with them speedily.
>
> The King called down his nobles all,
> By one, by two, and by three,
> And sent away for Earl Martial,
> For to speak with him speedily.
>
> When that he came before the King,
> He fell on his bended knee;
> "A boon, a boon! our gracious king,
> That you sent so hastily."
>
> "I'll pawn my living and my lands,
> My septer and my crown,
> That whatever Queen Elenor says,
> I will not write it down.
>
> "Do you put on one fryar's coat,
> And I'll put on another,

And we will to Queen Elenor go,
　　One fryar like another."

Thus both attired then they go;
　　When they came to Whitehall,
The bells they did ring, and the quirister's sing,
　　And the torches did light them all.

When that they came before the Queen,
　　They fell on their bended knee:
"A boon, a boon! our gracious queen,
　　That you sent so hastily."

"Are you two fryars of France?" she said,
　　"Which I suppose you be;
But if you are two English fryars,
　　Then hanged shall you be."

"We are two fryars of France," they said,
　　"As you suppose we be;
We have not been at any mass
　　Since we came from the sea."

"The first vile thing that ere I did
　　I will to you unfold;
Earl Martial had my maidenhead,
　　Underneath this cloath of gold."

"That is a vile sin," then said the king,
　　"God may forgive it thee!"
"Amen! Amen!" quoth Earl Martial,
　　With a heavy heart then spoke he.

"The next vile thing that ere I did
　　To you I'll not deny;
I made a box of poyson strong,
　　To poyson King Henery."

"That is a vile sin," then said the King,
　　"God may forgive it thee!"
"Amen! Amen!" quoth Earl Martial,
　　"And I wish it so may be."

"The next vile thing that ere I did
    To you I will discover;
I poysoned Fair Rosamond,
    All in fair Woodstock bower."

"That is a vile sin," then said the King,
    "God may forgive it thee!"
"Amen! Amen!" quoth Earl Martial,
    "And I wish it so may be."

"Do you see yonders little boy,
    A tossing of that ball?
That is Earl Martial eldest son,
    And I love him the best of all.

"Do you see yonders little boy,
    A catching of the ball?
That is King Henry's sone," she said,
    "And I love him the worst of all.

"His head is like unto a bull,
    His nose is like a boar."
"No matter for that," King Henry said,
    "I love him the better therefore."

The King pulld of his fryar's coat,
    And appeard all in red;
She shrieked and she cry'd, she wrong her hands,
    And said she was betrayd.

The King looked over his left shoulder,
    And a grim look looked he,
And said, "Earl Martial, but for my oath,
    Then hanged shouldst thou be."

Eleanor, there is little doubt, suffered from "the double standard."

Exactly how significant her husband's affaires were in her ultimate decision to support her sons (as well as her former husband Louis of France) in their rebellion against Henry is hard to say. With them, she fought him after the murder of Thomas à Becket

*Katharine Hepburn portrayed
Eleanor in the 1968 movie, "The
Lion in Winter."*

(PHOTO TRENDS)

in 1173—and lost. The result was almost ten years of genteel confinement, much of it at Salisbury Castle. That she and Henry were complete political realists in evidenced by the fact that in 1185 they were "on the same side" again, this time stressing to the new French King, Philip, their right to Aquitaine. In fact, she and Henry cooperated fully over the last five years of his life.

When Henry died in 1189 and their son Richard the Lion-Hearted became King, she again emerged as the power to be reckoned with in southwest France. Historians give her pivotal roles in blocking another son John's efforts to wrest Richard's crown from him while he was being held in Austria during the Third Crusade, in getting Richard ransomed, and in having this same son John, rather than her grandson Arthur of Brittany, made king when Richard died in 1199. It was during this struggle that, 79 years old, she resisted the siege of Mirabeau near Poitiers until John could hurry south and capture Arthur.

Still, her cultural power was even greater than her political power. It was Eleanor who brought the musical and literary culture of Poitiers and southern France to Paris and so to Europe. It was Eleanor who was as responsible as any one person can be for the code of polite behavior which has been practiced in Western nations since her time.   And it was Eleanor who fostered respect for women, bringing them dignity and power they had never dreamed of.   Her courts became schools of manners, and the lessons were passed on by her daughters, Marie of Champagne, Adèle of Blois, Eleanor of Castile, Matilde of Saxony, and by her niece, Isabella of England.   Her sons, too, felt her influence, particularly Richard, who shared his mother's interest in art, literature, and music.

Henry Adams, remember, saw her as the mortal parallel to the Virgin Mother, fostering at the fleshly level what Mary fostered at the spiritual.   In her own way, perhaps she was a rose—*la fille en rose* who had real virtues and just as real weaknesses.   Suffering what Oscar Wilde described as "the sordid perils of actual existence," she has not been enshrined.   She, like that high school junior, was not stained-glass.

Be that as it may, less deserving candidates than either have been enshrined by the force of the rose, and *fin amor* has deviated into some strange corners.   Yet it is hard to imagine its reaching a more unlikely vanity than it has in the so-called "mariology" surrounding the biography of Scotland's greatest poet, Robert Burns—a country lad whose attitude toward love was roughly that of a seasoned stallion among mares.   The flower *en rose* of the legend, Mary Campbell of Auchamore, "Burns' Highland Mary," plays her role as the "virgin vision" of the poet's fancy whose memory was ever clear before him as he wrote the verse which made him famous.   Or, as convert Alan Bayne put it in the *Burns Chronicle of 1906:*

Highland Mary for ever remains as the inspirer of Burns at his best, and so is linked to him eternally; and whoever seeks to defile this ideal maiden deserves the reprobation of all pure-minded men and women.

Believers worshipping at Mary Campbell's shrine are not, however, required to envision her the same way.   One qualifies if he sees Miss Campbell of Auchamore as the "one girl" Burns "ever really loved," a virgin throughout their relationship, snatched from him by typhus fever before they could marry.   He may also think that Burns never really knew Mary Campbell, but had gazed upon her beauty, and recalled her as a sort of "phantom of delight," thinking back on her through the years much the way the Judge recalled Maud Muller. Or he can believe that the Mary Campbell from Auchamore never really existed and that "Burns' Highland Mary" was a "vision of inspiration" which he turned to when the "girls of the world" disappointed him. And if the arguments between the three differing groups of adherents wax vicious, that's all right—the big thing is to believe!

The purpose behind the Burns "mariolatry" is clear enough. After all, Burns was a man with a penchant for what the Scots call "houghmagandie," a man who once advised his youngest brother "to try at once for intimacy." In the nineteenth century (when people were covering the bare legs of pianos with pantalettes) and even in the twentieth, it has been difficult for "good folk" to harmonize his obviously romantic lyrics with his equally obvious carnal aims. If, however, people "just realized" that Burns carried a "spiritual notion" about with him, a Beatrice who could lift him from his carnal self, then his "inexplicable" string of affairs can be rationalized as a forgetting, or at least as a disappointment when reality failed to measure up to his dreams. A sort of over-all morality can be established, bringing his lovely verse into sentimental harmony with the thoughts of the decent folk who enjoy his poems.

Sound scholarship, as usual, has offered the Burns mariolaters little succor. Even a peremptory survey of the Burns canon establishes quickly that he wrote and treasured a good many "carnal lyrics" (that is, outright dirty songs) to go with the "melodies sweetly played in tune" for which he is famous. In fact, some of his most famous lyrics have way-off-color variants. But even ignoring all that, the fact is that of the four (and that's all there are), of the four lyrics Burns supposedly wrote to his "ideal maiden," three ("The Highland Lassie O"; "Will ye go to the Indies, my Mary?"; and "To Mary in Heaven") are mediocre at best, and the fourth, telling the Sweet Afton to "disturb not her dreams" was probably inspired by someone other than Mary Campbell.

What's more, the story of Mary Campbell of Auchamore and Robert Burns has been rather carefully reconstructed, and it is not a pretty tale at all. The Mary Campbell Burns knew was the elder daughter of Archibald and Agnes Campbell who lived at Auchamore, near Duncan, then at Campbeltown and finally at Greenock. When this Mary got to the age of employment, she went to Ayrshire where she worked as nursemaid to one Alexander Hamilton (born on July 15, 1785). After that, she seems to have gone to Coilsfield as a dairymaid. Burns met her when he was having problems with the Armours over their pregnant daughter Jean. He had met Jean, a nineteen-year-old village girl, when he was writing and farming at Mossgiel in 1785. He had already become father of an illegitimate child by a servant-girl, Lizzie Paton, in May of that year. Regardless, and adhering to his brotherly advice, he tried "at once for intimacy" with Jean and was sufficiently successful that by winter she was pregnant. He planned to marry her. Under Scottish law (actually until as late as 1939), a couple who admitted sexual intercourse and who declared their intention to marry were in fact married. This is what Jean and Robert did, and to make the declaration more binding went so far as to put it in writing. However, when Jean broke the news to her father, that stonemason and contractor was so shocked he had to be revived with a cordial. Armour's fury was more because of Burns' reputation as a worthless rhymer, as a blasphemer against orthodox Calvinism, and as a fornicator in the area than it was because of his daughter's pregnancy, which was a "to-be-expected" stage in a farm girl's development. He persuaded Jean to go back on her promise, announced the marriage annulled (even though such marriages could not be annulled legally), refused to let Jean see Burns, and left the poet in the odd position of not really knowing whether he was joined or single.

So, for a while, Mary took Jean's place. In a note that "mariolaters" question, but which is generally accepted as authentic, Burns describes Mary as "a warm-hearted, charming young creature," saying she blessed him with "generous love" and telling of their "pretty long tract of the most ardent reciprocal attachment." Evidently he had learned "not enough and too much" from Lizzie and Jean, for the result of Mary's "generosity" and the "ardent reciprocal attachment" was another pregnancy. Burns, still not certain where he and Jean stood, promised to marry Mary. This

was in the spring of 1786. They met on the second Sunday of May
on the banks of the Ayr and exchanged Bibles, swore themselves
to each other, and planned to flee to Jamaica (the Indies) as soon
as she could straighten out a few affairs in the West Highlands.
The flight was logical, for the exchange of Bibles made it likely
that Burns was technically a bigamist under the Scottish law.

Mary's Bible still exists, presently in the Burns Monument at
Ayr, a copy of a 1782, two-volume Edinburgh edition. It found
its way into the possession of the family of Mary's younger sister,
the Andersons, and was carried to Caledon, near Toronto, where
it was rediscovered in 1840. The names on the flyleaves (Mary's
in Volume One and Robert's in Volume Two) have been deliber-
ately smudged so that only about half the letters are distinguish-
able. But Burns' mason's mark and quotations from *Leviticus*
and from *Matthew* in Burns' hand are clear. Undoubtedly the
stanza in "Will ye go to the Indies, my Mary?"

> I hae sworn by the Heavens to my Mary,
>   I hae sworn by the Heavens to be true;
> And sae may the Heavens forget me,
>   When I forget my vow!

refers to this matter.

Mary never did go to the Indies with Robert, nor did she ever
really claim him as husband. By October she was dead, though
no one is sure what happened between May and October or exactly what caused her death. The generally accepted theory runs
as follows. Mary left "the banks of Ayr" pregnant, thinking
Robert was her sworn husband, planning to go to Jamaica to start
a new life with him. She returned to her home where she spent
the summer. When her condition became obvious, she was either
cast out of her home or felt it was best to leave. She went to
Greenock where her mother had relatives. There, if she was indeed pregnant, she could bear her bairn out of the reach of gossipy home-folk. Unhappily, Greenock was being ravaged by a
typhus epidemic, and she contracted the disease and died. She
was buried at Greenock in the "lairs" of the old West Highland
church—another constant girl of sorrow.

Burns, nagged by the fact he was a bigamist, may well have used the Jamaica trip to put Mary off. No one seems to know. He later claimed Mary went to Greenock to rendezvous with him, where she died "a few days before I could even hear of her illness." An account persists that one day late in October 1786, a few weeks after Mary's death, a letter addressed in an unknown hand was delivered to Burns. Supposedly, Robert took it over to the window to get more light, and as he read his face turned pale. Immediately and without a word to anyone in the room, he turned on his heels and strode outdoors to be alone with his thoughts. Was the letter a more detailed account of Mary's death? Was it a harsh castigation from her father or brothers who refused to allow the name Robert Burns to be mentioned in their presence after the girl died? Or was it another matter, not related to Mary Campbell, who had unfortunately died, but whose death had the fortunate result of clarifying his muddled affairs?

Actually, his "muddled affairs" had clarified somewhat between the time of his parting with Mary and her misfortune. While Mary was at home in the highlands, he had been able to suffer public rebuke with Jean and so gain a certificate that he was a single man. By fall, his declaration with Jean was no longer a legal encumbrance, and when Mary went to Greenock, the whole idea of Jamaica had become less essential. When Mary died, it had no point at all, and freed of his bigamy problems, Burns lost all interest in it. What's more, in late November, his "Kilmanock poems," originally contracted to pay for the Jamaica trip, were published. He left for Edinburgh where he was to become immediately famous, lionized, and patronized. Of course, he had his conscience and Jean's family to cope with, for in September, but weeks before Mary died, Jean's condition resulted in twins, and the Armours notified Burns they would sue for their support.

Eventually, Burns married Jean Armour publicly. That was in August of 1788, after he had re-established his relationship with her and after she had borne him another set of twins. It is a little difficult to see exactly what this relationship was. Obviously, he was sleeping with her, but he had affairs and bastard children with a number of other women both before and after they were public man and wife. Jean even took one of the children, a girl by barmaid Anna Park, into her family. Burns, it appears, wanted to "settle down," needed a housekeeper, and, if not in love with Jean, was at least fond of her and still sexually attracted to her. Part of a letter he wrote in 1788, not many months before they were to be married, casts much light on their "love":

> Jean I found banished like a martyr—forlorn, destitute and friendless; all for the good old cause: I have reconciled her to her fate: I have reconciled her to her mother; I have taken her a room: I have taken her to my arms: I have given her a mahogany bed: I have given her a guinea; and I have f---d her till she rejoiced with joy unspeakable and full of glory. But—as I always am on every occasion—I have been prudent and cautious to an astounding degree; I swore her, privately and solemnly, never to attempt any claim on me as a husband, even though anybody should persuade her she had such a claim, which she has not, neither during my life, nor after my death. She did all this like a good girl, and I took the opportunity of some dry horselitter, and gave her such a thundering scalade that electrified the very marrow of her bones.

Patient Griselda—Jean's latter years were to be better than her first. She live until 1834, thirty-eight years after Robert died, her life made comfortable by three surviving sons (two of whom were Indian Army officers), able to bask in the ever-increasing fame of her lover-husband.

About fifteen years after Mary Campbell died and when her lover had become Scotland's most popular poet, a Burns Club was formed in Greenock—one of the first, incidentally, of over 800 that have existed. As a major project they planned to place a tablet on the grave of Mary Campbell. The gravesite was the lair of her mother's relation, Peter MacPherson, and though it took forty years for the project to be completed, the monument did go up. By then mariolatry was flourishing, and the monument and lair of the MacPhersons became crucial to arguments for, against, and within the cult.

The monument was, clearly, planned by citizens of Greenock to a Mary Campbell who they felt was Burns' Highland Mary. These were citizens who must have seen Mary, talked to her, been fully aware of her presence, and known of her death. Com-

bined with the findings of Burns' biographers, their identification
of the Mary Campbell who was buried in their town with Burns'
Highland Mary must make all arguments that Highland Mary
was "a spiritual notion existing only in the poet's imagination"
spurious. As Burns scholar Maurice Lindsey put it, "So much,
then, for those who would have us believe she never existed at
all." On the other hand, neither the monument nor the findings
of the scholars can be used to dismiss other mariolaters. It is
possible, no matter how unlikely, that Mary Campbell was a virgin bride snatched from the poet by death and not merely a duped
country wench. Consequently, there is no way to quash the idea
of Burns' lifelong devotion to his Highland lass. And one has to
admit it is hard to explain how Burns, married to Jean for over a
year, could in 1789 write a poem like "To Mary in Heaven"—

> O, Mary, dear departed shade!
> Where is thy place of blissful rest?
> See'st thou thy lover lowly laid?
> Or hear'st thou the groans that rend his breast?

a poem he sent off to his friend and patroness, Mrs. Dunlop, with
some sentences that tell how in Heaven he hopes to "again recognize my lost, my ever dear MARY! whose bosom was fraught
with Truth, Honor, Constancy, and Love—."
  Greenock became an industrial town. One hundred twenty-
four years after Mary died, the area in which she was buried was
needed for expansion of a shipyard and plans were made to move
the bodies in the old graveyard where Mary lay. This gave mariolaters a chance to open the MacPherson lair and prove or disprove
whatever one proves with such activities. Local officials, repre-
sentatives of the Burns Federation, and onlookers gathered: Robert Burns was now one of the world's great poets. What turned
up was the bottom board of a child's coffin, three skulls, a
thigh bone, part of a jaw bone, four teeth, some smaller bones,
and a few bits of black, hardened human flesh. So, as usually
happens in such matters, anyone could claim anything he wanted
—from the fact that there was no Mary and never had been one
because the grave was a "jumble," to the fact that Mary died

after giving birth to Burns' baby, to the fact that Mary couldn't have died in childbirth because if she had the infant would have been laid across her breast according to the custom of the time and not buried in a separate coffin. One citizen of Greenock, dedicated to the idea that there never was a real Mary, even brought forth the claim that the child in the grave was the baby of one of his ancestors buried there in 1827.

One thing, however, is sure, country hoyden, virgin, "spiritual notion," Mary Campbell's name is firmly and "for aye" associated with that of Robert Burns. Just as "people who know nothing else about William Shakespeare know he loved Mary Fitton," so people who know nothing else about Robert Burns know he harbored his love for Highland Mary in some secret corner of his heart. And their passion became legend, in Scotland and wher'er the Scots have wandered, forming the plot of a ballad about a bard and his country lass who swore to be true to each other, but who are parted by her untimely end. Originally, it was a "village news-sheet" composition, usually attributed to a country constable named Thomson, who emigrated to Canada. Often set to the tune "The Flowers of the Forest," the text makes no bones about the ideal nature of the love affair and has done its share to spread the doctrine of mariolatry abroad.

BURNS AND HIS HIGHLAND MARY

In green Caldeonia there ne'er were twa lovers
    Sae enraptured and happy in each ither's arms,
As Burns the sweet bard and his dear Highland Mary,
    And fondly and sweetly he sang o' her charms.

And lang will his sang sae enchanting and bonny,
    Be heard wi' delight on his ain native plains,
And lang will the name o' his dear Highland Mary
    Be sacred to love in his heart-melting strains.

'Twas on a May-day, and the flowers o' the Summer
    Were blooming in wildness a' lovely and fair,

When our twa lovers met in a grove o' green bowers,
    That grew on the banks o' the clear-winding Ayr.

"O Mary, dear Mary," exclaimed her fond lover,
    "Ye carry my heart to the Highlands with thee,
Every burnie and bank, every grove and green bower
    May talk of the love of my lassie and me.

"My life's sweetest treasure, my ain charming Mary
    To thee I'll be ever devoted and true;
For the heart that is beating so hard in this bosom
    Is a heart that can never love ony but you.

"Oh, dinna bide lang in the Highlands, my Mary,
    Oh, dinna bide lang in the Highlands frae me,
For I love thee sincerely, I love thee owre dearly,
    To be happy, sae far, my dear Mary, frae thee."

"I winna bide lang in the Highlands, dear laddie,
    I canna bide lang, for ye winna be there;
Although I hae freens I like weel in the Highlands,
    The ane I lo'e best's on the banks o' the Ayr."

Then he kissed her red lips, they were sweeter than roses,
    And her lily-white breast he did strain to his heart,
And his tears fell like dewdraps at e'en on her bosom,
    As she said, "My fond lover, alas, we maun part."

"Then farewell," he said, and he flew frae his Mary;
    "Oh, farewell," said she, for she could say nae mair
Little did they think they had parted for ever,
    When they parted that night on the banks of the Ayr.

Yet the green summer saw but a few sunny mornings,
    Till she, in the bloom of her beauty and pride,
Was laid in her grave like a bonnie young flower
    In Greenock Kirkyard, on the banks of the Clyde.

And Burns, the sweet bard o' his ain Caledonia,
    Lamented his Mary in mony a sad strain,

And sair did he weep for his dear Highland lassie,
    And ne'er did his heart love sae deeply again.

Then bring me the lilies, and bring me the roses,
    And bring me the daisies that grow in the vale,
And bring me the dew o' the mild summer's evening,
    And bring me the breath o' the sweet-scented gale.

And bring me the sigh of a fond lover's bosom,
    And bring me the tear of a fond lover's e'e,
And I'll pour them a' doon on thy grave, Highland Mary,
    For the sake o' thy Burns wha sae dearly lo'ed thee

It has, paradoxically, proved a wee bit more popular than the poet's own compositions to his Highland Mary rose.

But at least Burns knew Mary Campbell and "mariology" can be draped, one way or another, about the facts of his life. If a man "had no life," one would think this compulsion toward "phantoms of delight" and "spiritual notions" would be frustrated. However, such has not been the fate of W. Shakespeare. Because we know so little about the "mighty poet" (whose "works are not as those of other men") we have simply re-given him such things as an adventure-filled youth, an apprenticeship, a contented retirement, evenings in the Mermaid Tavern, and (to be sure) a "stained-glass passion" to haunt his mind. It matters little that scholars know as much about him as they expect to know about any dramatist of his day, that they know more about him than they do about Aeschylus, Sophocles, Euripides, Aristophanes, Plautus, or Terence, more than they know about his contemporaries Thomas Dekker and Thomas Heywood (to name two), more than they do about his editors John Hemmings and Henry Condell; there was, says curiosity, a day-to-day man behind the genius. And maybe the scholars can get along without details. But we can't! And what's more we aren't going to! The result has been that the volumes of fictional biography about the Bard take up a good many more pages than the "upstart crow" was able to scratch out in his whole career. For, as Logan Pearsall Smith once remarked, "Of the inhabitants of the insane asylums of Great Britain it has been calculated that, after religious maniacs, the next two largest classes consist of those who rave about the Royal Family or those who by thinking about Shakespeare have unhinged their minds."

The ingenuity of thinkers who would have a fuller Shakespeare biography has taken two forms, only one of which concerns *les filles en rose*.   The first is the "obvious conclusion" that if we know so little about Shakespeare when he is so famous, why then he probably didn't write the plays that his contemporaries knew he wrote. Let's skip that, dismissing the "twenty" candidates who have been trotted out by simply saying the whole question is about as sensible as speculating that Alexander Pope wrote *The Beggar's Opera* or that John Dos Passos wrote *The Sun Also Rises*. The other is the equally "obvious conclusion" that a man as famous as Shakespeare wouldn't have wanted the world to remain ignorant about his life and therefore must have left clues, tucked away as anagrams and secret symbols in his texts. This in spite of the fact that Shakespeare hadn't the foggiest notion that he was going to be famous; that he, like his contemporaries, thought drama of little more account than we think television; and that no clues satisfactory to an objective mind have ever showed up.

The great arena for those who would have Shakespeare leave posterity the secrets of his life is the sonnets. And logically so, for sonnets are personal, emotional expressions and are a place where a man will reveal himself if he is ever wont to. "With this key," said William Wordsworth, "Shakespeare unlocked his heart." Scholar after scholar has thus attempted to uncover a single connected story in those 154 poems, and over the years a consistent legend has developed about them. This legend embraces two steadily accepted "facts": 1) that Shakespeare wrote the bulk of the sonnets to a "young man" who was of higher social status than he; 2) that he wrote the other important ones to a "dark lady" who both fascinated and repelled him and who was unfaithful to him with, among others, the "young man."

Here, we are interested in the fabric that has been woven about Shakespeare's passion for the "dark lady." And it is an even queerer business than Burns' Highland Mary. Although the known facts about Shakespeare's love-life can be summed up in the statement: "He had to marry Anne Hathaway when she was twenty-six and he was nineteen," there is no denying he had some mistress whose "brows" were "raven black" in mind when he wrote Sonnets 127-154. That she fascinated him against his better judgment, that she was young enough so that he in his thirties could call himself old, that she was wanton and sensual, and that she involved herself with one of his friends are quite clear to anyone who reads the poems. That the same "woman colour'd ill" was used as a model for the Rosaline to whom Romeo is sensually attracted before he meets Juliet and for the Rosaline of *Love's Labour Lost* who is characterized by Berowne as "One that will do the deed, though Argus were her eunuch and her guard" is most likely. But who she actually was, whether she existed only in Shakespeare's imaginings, or what Anne Hathaway thought of all this, is just not going to be known short of revelation itself. Yet for many quite reputable students of the Bard it has become axiomatic that "the Dark Lady" not only drove the poet to distraction, melancholia, and foul abuse by her blend of beauty, disdain, and falsehood, but that she also affected his post-1600 playwriting, forcing him to look at the world far more cynically and scurrilously than he had before. With Anne Hathaway in the wings and with the poet telling himself that this woman "dark as night" woos "his purity with her foul pride," one might well dismiss the Dark Lady as a girl seen *en rose* by Shakespeare or anyone else. Certainly one would not be inclined to think of their relationship as *fin amor*. But that has not been the case. Identifications of the black seductress have been made, quite steadily, and with those identifications have come a series of romantic rationalizations that make Burns' "visionary Mary" seem sensible.

There are three major candidates for the role of Shakespeare's *grand passion:* a clerical error, a hostess who may never have laid eyes on the poet, and a court flirt who got pregnant trying to entrap an Earl. As Dark Ladies, one is as unlikely as the other. The "clerical error" is Anne Whately, who, if she existed at all, was the girl from Temple Grafton whom Shakespeare had hoped to marry in November of 1582, when he learned (to his dismay) that Anne Hathaway had prior claims through her pregnancy. It is a fact that the diocese records at Worcester, where marriage applications were recorded, indicate Shakespeare (spelled Shaxpere and Shagspere)'s intention of marrying Anne Whately on one day and his intention of marrying Anne Hathaway the next. It is also clear that two friends of the bride's family went over that way to make sure young Will made an honest girl of Miss Hathaway. But there are no details. Today, most scholars believe that the town clerk, probably having had a few nutbrowne ales, muddled the names Whately and Hathaway, as he seems to have done with a number of other facts, figures, and spellings in his records. But granting that possibility, it is hard to figure how many ales he would have had to quaff in order to mix up the towns Temple Grafton and Stratford. There may well have been an Anne Whately—and it is touching to think of the poet married-by-obligation dreaming of a dark-eyed fiancee he was ordered to desert. This would make his departure from Stratford for London, evidently without his wife and family, more understandable. William Ross, whose 1935 book *Anne Whately and William Shakespeare,* rallied about this desperate flag, even saw Anne Whately in a "what every woman knows" role, writing much of Shakespeare's work and composing the "young man" sonnets for her lost Will, while he worked out the dark lady pentameters for his wife who did attract him sensually in spite of the "pure love" he and Miss Whately shared.

Yet, unlikely a candidate as is Anne Whately, she looks good next to Mrs. Davenant, wife of the tenant of The Taverne (later the Crown Inn) at Oxford, and mother of the successful seventeenth-century dramatist, Sir William Davenant. Mrs. Davenant's claims rest on the gossipy pages of John Aubrey's *Brief Lives.* Aubrey, a biographer about as reliable as Parson Weems, knew William Davenant and attended his funeral in 1668. He states that Shakespeare used to stay at the Oxford tavern on his journeys between Stratford and London. Along with this "fact" he copied down two others which give Mrs. Davenant her claim as the "dark mistress." One, Mrs. Davenant is said to have been "very beautiful and of very good witt and of conversation extremely agreeable." Two, her son William "would sometimes, when he was pleasant over a glass of wine . . . say, that it seemed to him that he writ with the very spirit that Shakespeare . . .[word omitted] . . . and was seemed contentended [sic] enough to be thought his son." The implication is, of course, that Davenant was Shakespeare's bastard and that his mother "had very light report." What then can be more logical than the thesis that Shakespeare loved the innkeeper's lovely wife, that the fruit of the love was little William, called Davenant, who climbed through the dramatic rigging just as his daddy used to do? And who else, but this dark-eyed beauty, could possibly be the object of the appropriate sonnets?

Still, even if Shakespeare slept with Mrs. Davenant every time he went through Oxford and had a whole litter of illegitimate children by her, this does not guarantee that she was the dark lady of the sonnets. Her presence en route is but a first step. Her champions follow it with the incredible theory that Mrs. Davenant was the very innkeeper's wife pursued by a fellow named Henry Willobie in a second-rate poem of 1594 called "Willobie His Avisa." The poem tells how H. W. tries without success to cuckold an innkeeper, while an interpolated prose passage describes the efforts of a pal, W. S., to do what H. W. could not. One can go over the whole matter in a 1913 book by Arthur Anderson called *Mistress Davenant*. Needless to say, identifications are deftly made. W. S. is just who you think he is, and Avisa turns out to be Mrs. Davenant. Mrs. Davenant, it seems, had Bird as her maiden name, consequently she is called "Avis" or "Avisa." No deterrant to advocates of this theory are the facts that no evidence concerning Mrs. Davenant's maiden name exists (we don't even know she was a brunette), that the Avisa of the poem is maddeningly chaste, and that the initials W. S. are scarcely unique.

The most persistent candidate, however, is Mary Fitton, whose claims to being the dark lady were brought forth in books by Thomas Tyler and Frank Harris and caused Marchette Chute to comment that "persons who know almost nothing of Shakespeare know he was in love with Mary Fitton." Whether Shakespeare knew her or not, at least she was around London when he was writing sonnets and her claims have an immediacy that neither a "clerical error" nor a "bird-woman" can muster.

Mary Fitton was the daughter of a Cheshire squire who became a Maid of Honour at the Court of Queen Elizabeth in 1595 when she was seventeen. That was at the height of what is sometimes called Shakespeare's "lyric period" when many of the sonnets were no doubt written. An incurable flirt with a desire to marry well, and armed with an easy nature, she soon became a scandalous figure in London. Her first conquest was of Sir William Knollys, Comptroller of Elizabeth's Household and Superintendent of the Royal Accounts. Knollys, who was 48 or 50 when Mary arrived in London, was an old friend of her father's and a steady correspondent with her sister Anne Newdigate. He was even godfather of Anne's first daughter. Asked to "look after" the young Mary, he looked her over instead and fell desperately in love with her in spite of (or perhaps because of) being already married. His wife was wealthy, sickly, and older than he.

Mary, however, played for higher stakes. Ultimately, she got herself involved with William Herbert, third Earl of Pembroke. This maneuver resulted in her being delivered of a dead son and being cast from the court in disgrace, the Virgin Queen preferring virgin maids. Nor did she ever get Herbert to marry her. He needed a wealthy and influential wife, and what's more the escapade put him "out of Court favor" until Elizabeth died in 1603.

Mary doesn't, however, make a totally illogical candidate for the dark lady. She was certainly sensuous, free with her favors, and had an affair with the man to whom Shakespeare's colleagues dedicated the First Folio of 1623. Either she or Anne had some tie to the Lord Chamberlain's Men (Shakespeare's company), for Will Kempe, the comedian who left the group in 1599, dedicated a book, *Nine Daies Wonder,* to Mistris Anne Fitton, Mayde of Honour to most sacred Mayde, Royal Queen Elizabeth. This was his account of morris-dancing all the way from London to Norwich, and he may have become a bit confused from all that jigging, because Anne never was a Maid of Honour like her sister.

Mary's biggest drawback is her coloring. Two family portraits of Mary and Anne Fitton still exist, and there is little to see in them that would encourage Shakespeare to describe her as a "black beauty." Mary is grey-eyed, and even fairer in complexion than Anne. To be sure, the champions of her candidacy have not been deterred. They have questioned the authenticity of the portraits and have even rallied a contemporary painting of "Queen Elizabeth borne in Procession" to shore up their case. Leslie Hotson, "the Shakespeare detective," has put together "the two clues." One involves figures in the fore-corner of the painting: a Maid of Honour with a flaming heart, the emblem of Affection, on her sleeve, led by a young man with ringlets. The other is an anecdote concerning the June 1600 marriage of Anne Russell, also a Maid of Honour, to Lord Herbert, son of the Earl of Worcester. The anecdote is from a letter by Rowland Whyte to Sir Robert Sidney June 14, 1600.

After supper the maske came in, as I writ in my last; and delicate it was to see 8 ladies soe pretily and richly attired. Mrs. Fitton leade, & after they had donne all their own ceremonies, these 8 ladys maskers choose 8 ladies more to dawnce the measures. Mrs. Fitton went to the Queen & woed her to dawnce; her Majestie asked what she was; "Affection," she said. "Affection!" said the Queen, "Affection is false." Yet her Majestie rose and dawnced; soe did my Lady Marques [of Winchester].

As the picture of "Queen Elizabeth borne in Procession" is often (though not finally) identified with the Russell-Herbert wedding and as Mary Fitton and the Earl of Pembroke were almost certainly at that wedding, it didn't take Hotson long to figure that the girl in the corner of the picture with the emblem of Affection on her sleeve is Mary Fitton and the young escort William Herbert, her lover. And what do you know! The girl has a high, white brow and very dark hair. Q.E.D., Mary Fitton was a "dark lady"—why not of the sonnets?

Wasn't it Shakespeare himself who wrote: "All impediments in fancy's course are motives of more fancy"?

At the end of his novel, *The Great Gatsby,* F. Scott Fitzgerald's romantic hero Jay Gatsby is murdered because of his golden girl's carelessness. "He must have felt," reads one passage, "that he had . . . paid a high price for living too long with a single dream. He must have looked up at an unfamiliar sky through frightening leaves and shivered as he found what a grotesque thing a rose is . . ." Possibly that's the way Shakespeare felt about his dark lady, whoever she was, if she was. Surely Louis must have felt that way about Eleanor, and maybe Robert Burns felt that way about Mary Campbell and all his other conquests. For Shakespeare and Louis and Burns all at one time must have believed in the Rose. And the man who idealizes anything, who seeks *la vie, la fille, en rose* is likely to end up "alone and palely loitering" on some "cold hillside." Fitzgerald wasn't the only one who'd noticed that. John Keats noticed it, and Chaucer did too. There is a world of literature about "what a grotesque thing" the Rose can be.

5

GROTESQUE ROSES

In the astrophel-stella relationship which derives from courtly love, one of the major obligations of the lady is to show mercy. And one of the most poignant situations arises when the lover commits himself, as perhaps Shakespeare did, to a woman who has none. *La belle dame sans merci.* That was the title Keats gave to one of the most beautiful lyrics in the English language. The poem tells of the knight-at-arms who meets a fairy's child, "full beautiful" in the meads. She looks at him "as she did love" and goes with him on his steed, directing him to her "elfin grot" where she weeps and sighs and lulls him to sleep with food and drink. Then she deserts him, leaving him to awake "on the cold hill's side" where he encounters other kings and princes and pale warriors who have suffered the same fate. " 'La Belle Dame sans Merci' hath thee in thrall!" they tell him, and he, filled with longing, wanders about the edge of the withered lakeside "alone and palely loitering."

For Keats the poem may well have expressed the frustrations of his own life: his tubercular condition; the fact that he felt, sick as he was, he should not marry Fanny Brawne, the girl he loved; the lack of recognition he was receiving as a poet. He may also have had in mind the dreams of his Romantic contemporaries who hoped to set up ideal communities on the Susquehanna River, free the Greeks from tyranny, and live without encumbrances such as marriage. It matters not, the poem is the finest expression in the English language of the frustration that is likely to come to any person who is seduced by an ideal—whether it be fame, happiness, world peace, the Rose or a golden girl.

When he wrote his poem, Keats almost surely had been thinking of the tale of Thomas of Erceldoune, a thirteenth-century Scotsman who lived in the town that is now called Earlston. Thomas was a clairvoyant, and he claims in his own writings that he gained his power as a gift from the Queen of the Fairies who took him away to Elfland. His legend was put into ballad form, under the title "Thomas Rhymer." It begins:

> True Thomas lay oer yond grassy bank,
>   And he beheld a ladie gay,
> A ladie that was brisk and bold,
>   Come riding oer the fernie brae.
>
> Her skirt was of the grass-green silk
>   Her mantle of the velvet fine,
> At ilka tett of her horse's mane
>   Hung fifty silver bells and nine.
>
> True Thomas he took off his hat,
>   And bowed him lowdown till his knee:
> "All hail, thou mighty Queen of Heaven!
>   For your peer on earth I never did see. . . ."
>
> "Oh no, O no, True Thomas," she says,
>   "That name does not belong to me;
> I am but the queen of fair Elfland,
>   And I'm come here for to visit thee."

She then takes him upon her "milk-white steed" and they gallop off "swifter than the wind." "For forty days and forty nights," Thomas sees neither sun nor moon and hears only the "roaring of the sea." Eventually they pause. The Queen feasts him and comforts him, then shows him three roads: the thorny, narrow one leading to Heaven, the lily-strewn one leading to Hell, and the middle one that goes to Elfland. Telling him he must be quiet or "You will n'er get back to your ain countrie" she takes him down the middle road.

> He has gotten a coat of the even cloth,
>   And a pair of shoes of velvet green,
> And till seven years were past and gone
>   True Thomas on earth was never seen.

When he gets back he thinks the trip has taken but a few days, even though in some variants it is said to have lasted a thousand years.

He was lucky to get back at all. The Celtic fairy is a dangerous, if charming, creature for a mortal to associate with. Originally, these "little people" were the wood sprites and water nymphs of "olden religions"—quite similar to the nymphs of the Hellenic mythologies. However, when Christianity came to the Celts they were given a somewhat different role. They became tenants of the Devil, paying a tithe to him on a regular schedule every thirteen months or seven years. In fact, in one variant of the "Thomas Rhymer" ballad, the Fairy Queen threatens to make Thomas himself the payment. Of course, this is just another manifestation of the way in which the Church went about conversion. The idea was not to eliminate the pagan gods and rituals, but to adopt them to Christianity, giving them new and appropriate symbolisms. One explanation of the elf-people is spectacular. After the Revolt of Lucifer against Awe, Satan and his followers were cast out of Heaven toward Hell, which in the Ptolemaic version of the Universe lay below Earth. As they fell through the orbit of Earth, some of them caught in the bushes and thickets and lakes where they remain today, fairy-folk, still indentured to their Master who dropped on below.

These half-pagan, half-Christian demi-gods are able to transform themselves at will, and they appear as mermaids, mermen, washers at the ford, "wee men," or in a series of changeling shapes. In British ballad tradition, where some of the most haunting stories about them are preserved, they tend to appear in "hollow lands and hilly lands," like the Scottish Catershaugh, where apple trees grow and mists come up over the streams. Dawn or dusk, twilight time, is when one is most likely to meet them, and the results of these encounters are apt to be disastrous, to say the least. Their presence is a convenient way of accounting for all sorts of troublesome matters. A couple produces a child who is "all nose and no forehead"; a girl's true love dives in a lake and never surfaces; a sweet young maid suddenly finds her apron strings won't tie. The fact that the fairies exchanged one of their ugly offspring for the couple's lovely bairn, that the true love was abducted to Elfland by a mermaid, that the maid was seduced by a "wee, wee man" while she strolled abroad make handy, and acceptable, rationalizations.

But it is the lovely fairy women that are the worst of all, for they have the power to create a never-ending longing in the heart of the mortal who succumbs to them. It is a love-sickness that the lady will not satisfy and which will absorb the man forever, leading him on and on toward nothing. William Butler Yeats caught the feeling in his "The Song of the Wandering Aengus." The speaker in the poem has been entranced by a changeling. He catches her, in fish form, but as he starts to "blow the fire a-flame," she transforms herself into "a glimmering girl with apple-blossoms in her hair." She calls his name, but immediately runs away, fading through "the brightening air." He must follow. "Though I am old with wandering," he says, wandering through lands and places where he is liable to encounter his fairy lover, he is sure that someday he will find her and possess her forever. He hasn't got a chance.

Also complicating any relationship a mortal man might enter into with a Celtic fairy is the fact that elfin women are abnormally jealous lovers. The mortal who involves himself must never prove unfaithful and cannot break the arrangement in order to take an everyday mate. George Collins was one ballad hero who found this out. George Collins (he also goes under the names Giles Collins, Johnny Collins, and Clerk Colvill) is quite a ladies' man. "I neer did see a fair woman, but I would sin with her bodie." He leaves his true love, lusty dame Fair Ellen, to go to the Wells of Slane where he meets his supernatural mistress, a washer at the ford (that is, a changeling woman who is sometimes seen by travelers washing clothes at a lonely river-ford). The washer knows where George has come from and that he has engaged himself to a mortal lady, Ellen. In her fury, she gives George a headache, and when he complains about it provides him with a sark to wrap about his temples. The sark, which can't be removed, will continually tighten until George is dead. He realizes what she has done and tries to stab her with a knife, but she is too quick. Turning into a fish, she swims off, while he goes home to curse "the false mermaid" and die. Fair Ellen, who knows nothing of this, is working on her trousseau when she sees a funeral coming down the road. She learns it is George's, runs down, opens the coffin, and kisses the "cold clay lips." Then she goes home, and requesting her mother to make her bed "both wide and narrow" (she is neither virgin nor married), dies of a broken heart.

"The Devil, your master, cast your heart of stone" goes the lyric of an old popular song. It isn't so much that *ces belles dames sans merci* are purposeful. It's rather that they have no feelings, no commitments that they can make except to themselves. Beautiful, irresistible, selfish, they are cruel, without responsibility for it, to hearts that are true. When made into Roses, they can only prove grotesque. The old tales, like the old masters, are never wrong. No one knew this better than F. Scott Fitzgerald.

F. Scott Fitzgerald was not an "everyday young man." Besides being a pain in the neck to many of his friends, he had an uncanny ability of looking at himself objectively. In particular, he liked to analyze his tendency to romanticize rich, lovely young women. So far did he carry this idiosyncrasy that he even recorded from memory his love-making and "sweet nothing" conversations for later use in his books. Of course, this split personality helped him greatly as a novelist, and the one good novel he was able to produce out of a welter of alcoholism and instability, *The Great Gatsby,* is in a real sense Fitzgerald-as-Nick-Carraway-the-narrator looking at Fitzgerald-as-Jay-Gatsby-the-hero in love with golden girl Daisy.

Daisy was actually a composite, made up mostly from Ginerva King and Zelda Sayre—along with himself, the main loves of the novelist's life. Ginerva was his first real crush. He worshipped her when he was at Princeton and she was a pretty, socially prominent Chicago debutante. He was impressed by her popularity, her "taken-for-granted" wealth, and her electricity. To the *parvenu* grandson of a Minnesota grocer she truly seemed the princess of his own märchen. She strung him along, adding him to the other charms on her bracelet and eventually dismissing him. He never really got over it, or her. Still, his capacity for romanticism was sufficient that he soon met and idealized a southern variant, Zelda Sayre. This time the plot came out correctly, and after a rejection or two "Jack" was able to win his golden girl. Unfortunately, they did not live "happily" in the ever after. The post-marital sequel was entitled *Crack Up* by its author (none other than the hero himself) who found great solace in grubbing through the debris left from their "castle built in air."

Besides becoming enamored of Ginerva King while at college, Fitzgerald also became enamored of the poetry of John Keats. The name of his book *Tender is the Night* comes from the fourth stanza of "Ode to a Nightingale," and one scholar has even produced an article with the schizophrenic title *F. Scott Fitzgerald as John Keats*. That he saw Ginerva King, and even came to see his

Zelda Fitzgerald, the model for Daisy in The Great Gatsby, started the flapper movement.

(UPI)

wife, as *une belle dame sans merci* almost goes without saying, and story after story, each with a strong autobiographical tinge, begins with an aspiring knight meeting a fairy's child and ends with the unhappy lover "alone and palely loitering" beside some sedge-withered lake.   He even pushes the parallel so far in *The Great Gatsby* that he gives Daisy Buchanan the maiden name of Fay.

The more one looks at all this, the more one realizes that, for good reasons, Fitzgerald's favorite theme was what a "grotesque thing" a rose can be, or to put it another way: if you think life is a märchen in which heroes win golden girls from ogres you are in for a cold awakening on some deserted hillside.   Actually, *The Great Gatsby* is not much more than a cynical märchen anyhow, set amid the roarings of the Twenties with the "foul dust" of America's culture polluting man's supposedly "incorrupitble dreams."   Daisy Buchanan, a fast, "God, I'm sophisticated" flapper is the princess; her polo-playing, "enormously wealthy" husband Tom is the ogre who holds her in the chains of an unhappy marriage; and self-made bootlegger James Gatz, alias Jay Gatsby, is the hero.

Fitzgerald had explained the development of the hero's hopes in a story called "Absolution" published two years earlier than the novel.   He had originally planned it as an opening chapter, for it was, in the author's own words, "intended to be a picture of Gatsby's early life."   In it, the young Gatsby-to-be misinterprets a priest's remarks during confession and decides there is a "glittering world" in which he can exist free from obligation to "God's moral truths," responsible only to the "promptings of his own imagination."   In the novel, the Dakota farmboy, James Gatz, embraces such an illusion, changes his name, and naïvely enters this "glittering world," giving up the usual roads to success and recreating his life as a "fairy tale" where attainment of Daisy, "golden girl high in the white palace" is the only plot.

The story ends with the hero floating face down in his own swimming pool, murdered by a jealous husband for infidelities the ogre committed and for a car accident in which the heroine was the hit-and-run driver.   Moreover, the heroine, who could have saved "Jack" by risking her own neck, does nothing except flee with the ogre—to where people are "rich together," skipping her hero's funeral at which his hopes are summed up by the epithet "the poor son-of-a-bitch." The "kiddies" who want to read this kind of bedtime story go off to sleep with each other. And there's no doubt that *The Great Gatsby,* inverted märchen, has proved a steady selling item on the Charles Scribner's Sons list. Its popularity in the post-World War II world, especially with college students, certainly tells us something about our Age as well as our youth. But it is only one exposition of a theme that men have rued for years. The classic tale of what a grotesque thing a rose can be, Geoffrey Chaucer's *Troilus and Criseyde,* dates from the fourteenth century.

As Chaucer tells it, Calchas was a Trojan seer who foresaw that the Greeks would sack Troy and so deserted to the enemy. He left his daughter Criseyde widowed and alone to face what barbs and scorn her father's conduct visited upon her. She was armed with no weapons other than great beauty, modesty, and grace of manner. "In my judgment," says Chaucer, "there was none so fair in all Troy city." One of Priam's sons, Troilus, has, it seems, taste similar to Chaucer's. Second only to his brother Hector as a hero, Troilus has had no time for girls. In fact, he mocks his friends for their preoccupation with women and concentrates his time exclusively on his one pleasure: battle. Until, "one enchanted evening," he sees Criseyde. He falls madly, head-over-heels in love, spending all of his time from that moment thinking of her.

But he is shy, and inexperienced, and he hasn't any idea how to approach her or what to say. He turns to one of his best friends, Pandarus, an older fellow who just happens to be Criseyde's uncle and who considers himself an authority on courtship although he has seldom been successful himself. Through varied social maneuvers, Pandarus introduces them, gives them chances to meet, and finally creates the opportunity for them to go to bed together. At first Criseyde is reluctant to get re-involved, to "enthrall her liberty" as a widow. But she is flattered, aware of Troilus' prestige, and she just tacitly lets things drift toward what conclusion they will. As Troilus finally seizes her in bed and tells her she must yield as there's no escape, she wryly comments, "If I hadn't yielded before this, I wouldn't be here now." For Chaucer makes his Criseyde a drifter, that type of woman who amorally follows the line of least resistance. In this story she succumbs to Pandarus' energy in engineering the match and then, happy enough with the result, reasons it is no fault of hers if her beauty attracts Troilus.

Things go well for a bit. Then Calchas, who has been anxious to get his daughter out of the ill-starred city, arranges an exchange: Criseyde for a captured Trojan, Antenor. There is much sadness, sweet sorrows of parting, and promises to be true and to return "though it be ten thousand mile." Criseyde leaves, ominously escorted by an insinuating Greek named Diomede, who at once senses the situation and the nature of the lady involved. While Troilus wanders through the old retreats lovesick to the strains of "our song," Diomede begins to capitalize on Criseyde's loneliness. For the very reasons she gave in to the energy of Pandarus, she allows Diomede to seduce her. She sends Troilus no "Dear John" letter. She just drifts away, and the matter climaxes when Troilus sees the brooch he had given Criseyde on parting pinned to a tunic that Deiphebus, his brother, had torn from Diomede during the day's battling. "His heart goes cold" and he realizes "it's all over." He plunges recklessly into battle, day after day, hoping to encounter and get even with Diomede. But he is frustrated there too. Finally, Achilles kills him and his spirit rises to the "hollow of the eighth sphere" where he looks back on "this little spot of earth," now aware of its vanity and wretchedness and the aimlessness of his own love. And so the story ends.

Chaucer was, to be sure, neither the first nor the last to write about Criseyde. Her story seems to have sprung from the mind of a twelfth-century trouvère, Benoît de Sainte-Maure who worked for Eleanor of Aquitaine's husband, Henry II of England. Benoit devoted about 1,500 lines to it in his 30,000-line *Roman de Troie*. What excuse he had for adding this love story to his "historical novel" rested on a few lines in Homer's *Iliad* and on the works of two frauds, Dares Phrygius and Dictys Cretensis, gentlemen who lived no earlier than the second century but who pretended to have been eyewitnesses at the Trojan-Greek affair. Homer barely mentions Chaucer's three main characters. The hero, Troilus, is dismissed by a single line in the *Iliad*. His friend Pandarus is noticed twice, being described as a great archer and as a victim of the Greek Diomede. The heroine, Breseis (Criseyde's name in Benoît), gets more attention, but she has nothing to do with either Pandarus or Troilus. She and her sister Chryseis get involved in a lover's pentangle with Apollo, Agamemnon, and Achilles—and, according to classicists, are really named Hippodamia and Astynome anyhow. Dares and Dictys follow Homer. But they do raise Troilus' stature so that he becomes the second best warrior (next to Hector) among the Trojans—a creative move that gave him prestige enough for Benoît's purposes.

Benoît let his imagination go to work on all this. Quite aware of the vogue of *fin amor* in the Anglo-French courts of his day, he simply had Troilus fall in love with Briseis, whom he calls Briseide, and used the affair to add interest to those sections in his *Roman de Troie* that deal with the endless "alarums and flights" of a ten-year war. But Benoît failed to capitalize fully on the passions which accompany courtship and consummation. His 1,500 lines, which are scattered through an 8,500-line section, deal only with the prisoner exchange and the grief the lovers feel when they are finally parted.

Probably matters would have stopped here had not a Sicilian lawyer, Guido delle Colonne, decided to rewrite Benoît's *Roman* in 1287. The result, in Latin, was called *The History of the Destruction of Troy,* and it not only superseded Benoît's work as the authoritative account of the important ancient struggle, but did a great deal to make the Trojan legend widely known in the Renaissance. Such was the literary situation in the mid-fourteenth century when a poetic young Italian named Giovanni Boccaccio was sent by his father to Naples to make his way in the business world. There he fell in love with Maria d'Aquino, an unhappily married woman. Though he was unsuccessful in his pursuit of her and though she left him in Naples, she commissioned him to write various stories for her. In fact, even after she left him, she inspired most of his love romances, like the *Filostrato* which was composed in hopes of persuading her to return. To show Maria d'Aquino how he felt, Boccaccio included the Benoît-Guido account of Troilus' ardent suit, devotion after parting, and final unhappiness, retouching it to fit his own situation. In it he renames the girl Criseida, perhaps confusing Briseis with her sister Chryseis, and gives her a personality, making her a widow. She yields to Troilo with token, but proper, resistance. He also develops Pandaro, the archer of Homer's *Iliad,* into a friend of Troilo and a cousin of Criseida, allowing him to rationalize his eagerness to compromise a girl in his own family by arguing that widows are by nature "merry." His opinion seems to be supported by the ease with which this widow gives herself over to Diomede after the exchange. Not that Boccaccio's heroine is a wanton. She is clearly a gentlewoman, but straightforwardly passionate and with a clear idea of "what men are for."

Chaucer took the story right from Boccaccio, probably reading it about 1378 when he went to Italy on a diplomatic mission for the government. He evidently felt no obligation to change the plot when he rewrote it, following the adage of his day that "a story belongs not to the one who tells it first but to the one who tells it best." His great contribution was, of course, the depiction of the heroine, now Criseyde, which is one of the most memorable characterizations in all literature. Amoral, unfaithful, ultimately *sans merci,* Chaucer's Criseyde is also modest, self-effacing, and genuinely sweet. And if she is confident of her power over men, she has a pleasant uncertainty about it, never quite sure that it will really work. She has a quiet, bright sense of humor, and I've never seen a reader yet who didn't like her. For Chaucer makes Criseyde a complicated woman, of great sensitivity, delicacy, and subtlety. He also adds a generation to Pandarus' age and sees him, slightly ridiculous, as a sort of frustrated old chap who participates in Troilus' passion for his niece somewhat in the fashion of an old athlete watching from the sidelines. By doing all this, and by making Troilus the "campus jock" who suddenly finds himself "pale and wan" before a pretty girl, and by making Diomede the wordly-wise wencher who crassly capitalizes on Criseyde's nature, he was able to produce one of the classics of world literature.

For awhile, scholars found some of the behavior in the poem confusing and inconsistent. However, once it was realized that the characters are conducting themselves under the influence of courtly love (after all, their progenitor Benoît did work for Eleanor of Aquitaine's husband), things fell into place. Troilus' inability to act (Pandarus even has to hoist him into bed with Criseyde that night of the assignation), Criseyde's aloofness and sudden capitulation, Pandarus' paradoxical role as both confidant of the lover and supposed family protector of the woman begin to focus. Even so, scholarly rationalizations such as this tend to get overrated. Troilus, Pandarus, and especially Criseyde make good sense in terms of the shy-bold, diffident-compliant crosscurrented behavior of everyday human beings. Chaucer, like all great writers, knew "full well" that behavior is not black hat and white, that real people can feel more than one emotion at a time and can act two ways at once.

However, although the tale of Troilus and Criseyde climaxes with Chaucer's version, its history is far from over. Eventually, the name Cressida becomes a word for whore and Pandarus for "go-between." That switch was the work of a Scotsman, a dour Scotsman indeed.

The fifteenth century is one of the least exciting in the whole history of English literature. The reason given by some scholars is that "Chaucer emasculated it." The remark does show the tremendous influence this poet exercised on those who wrote just after his death. Whether his ghost actually wielded such a scalpel or not, for many decades it was popular to imitate Chaucer, to re-tell tales he had told, or to complete those works that he had left unfinished. John Lydgate, for example, translated Guido's *Troilus,* including in it a long tribute to Chaucer. The anonymous author of *The Tale of Beryn* tries to complete *The Canterbury Tales,* taking the pilgrims into the town and assigning them stories that Chaucer never got around to writing. And one group of Scotsmen went down in literary history under the collective name: the Scotch Chaucerians, King James I even being of their number.

Robert Henryson (also spelled Hendryson and Henderson) belonged to this group, although he did a good bit more with his pen than just copy The Master. Very little is known about him, except that he was a schoolmaster probably connected with the Benedictine Abbey at Dunfermline. Even his dates are printed *c.* 1425-*c.* 1506. One cold stormy night, he claims to have mend-

ed the fire, taken a drink to arm him from the chill, and begun
to read a tale "written by worthy Chaucer glorious." This was
the story of Troilus and his faithless leman. When finished with
the five books of rime royale, instead of going to bed (and it must
have been late indeed), Henryson says "to breke my slepe another queare I toke." The statement clearly implies that he opened
another volume of Chaucer and read on. Of course there is no
other volume of Chaucer, and this seems to have been Henryson's way of lending stature to his additions by pretending they
were part of the original. The extra "queare" that Henryson
"toke" that night continues the story of Criseyde to her tragic
ending after her defection to the Greeks and her infidelities with
Diomede. Called *The Testament of Cresseid,* it simply ignores
Troilus' death at the sword of Achilles, keeping him alive and
reasonably well in spite of his heartbreak.

Now Henryson was a literary man of no mean genius. He
recognized, as Chaucer had done, that the really interesting
person in the whole affair was Criseyde, and that the real tragedy of the story lay not so much in Troilus' learning too late
how roses can be grotesque but in what could happen to Criseyde once Diomede had deserted her. Henryson also knew that
a man such as Chaucer's Diomede was not likely to remain true
for long. His affair with Criseyde had been sensual, and he had
taken her for no better reason than that's what women are for.
Moreover, Henryson knew nothing of the courtly love conven-
tions under which Criseyde's relationship to Troilus had been
functioning. Consequently, he tended to consider her a "merry
widow" (perhaps like Boccaccio's Criseida), a woman whose
business it was to be kept by some convenient, presentable man.
He nonetheless sympathized with her deeply, realizing that she
had not gone through her separation from Troilus or her infidelity with Diomede without considerable pain. He has her bit-
terly reproach Venus and Cupid for the cards they have dealt
her and dream that her case is being tried by the gods. Venus
argues vehemently against her, and the gods vote to punish her
offense with leprosy. Saturn and Cynthia descend to tell her the
verdict, informing her that her lovely face will be covered with
"spottes blake, and lumpes," that where she "comest, eche men

shal flye the place," and that she shall beg from house to house "lyke a lazarous."

When Cresseid awakens her dream has come true, and she ends up on the streets sick and penniless. One day, Troilus rides by her. Looking down from his mount, he sees something in the eyes of the wretched beggar woman that reminds him of his lost love. Impetuously, he pours jewels and money in her "cuppe" without recognizing her. After he leaves, Cresseid is swept with grief. Feeling death coming on, she asks another leper to carry her ruby ring to Troilus and to tell him her unhappy fate. Troilus, seeing the ring, is also frantic with regret, but he has no idea what to do. She was untrue to him—and it's all too late now. Desperate, he erects a monument over her leper's grave.

Henryson's poem was printed in William Thynne's 1532 edition of Chaucer. It comes directly after the "fyfth and laste booke of Troylus" with the statement "here foloweth the pyteful and dolorous testament of fayre Creseyde." For two hundred years it appeared in every edition of Chaucer's work and was even included in a complete works of Chaucer as late as 1810. During these years, only a few scholars knew that the *Testament* was not actually by Chaucer. As far as the general public was concerned the tale of Criseyde was a tale that ended morally in unhappiness and leprosy, designed as Henryson said to warn "worthy women" against "false deception."

And the tale was known to the public. In the 16th and 17th centuries it seems to have been retold constantly by the popular press. Spurred by the common man's inability to understand the subtleties of Chaucer's characterizations and by the convenient moral twist Henryson had conceived, balladeers and playwrights developed Pandarus into a low-comedy clown and Criseyde into "a mark." For awhile, her beauty prevailed. Early in the century poets were happy to compare their mistresses' good looks to those of Criseyde, but the purpose is never very idealistic.

> To grant me grace and so to do
> As Creside then did Troylus to.

And it was only a matter of routine that Pandarus would become little different from other low-comedy pimps and bawds that hustle "in between" on the Tudor-Elizabethan stage and that Criseyde would first light fires with her beauty and then quench them with her compliance.   Characteristic is George Whetstone's 1576 "forewarning" to "all the young Gentlemen of England" against "the companie of inticing dames." In the "Argument" to a poem called "Cressids Complaint" he preaches,

> The inconstancie of Cressid is so readie in every mans mouth, as it is a needelesse labour to blase at full her abuse towards yong Troilus, her frowning on Syr Diomede, her wanton lures and love: nevertheless, her companie scorned, of thousandes sometimes sought, her beggerie after braverie, her lothsome leprosie after lively beautie, her wretched age after wanton youth, and her perpetuall infamie after violent death, are worthy notes (for others heede) to be remembered. And for as much as Cressids heires in every corner live, yea, more cunning than Cressid her selfe in wanton exercises, toyes and inticements, to forewarne all men of such filthes, to persuade the infected to fall from their follies, and to rayse a feare in dames untainted to offend, I have reported the subtile sleites, and the leaud life, and evill fortunes of a courtisane, in Cressid[s] name; whom you may suppose, in tattered weedes, halfe hungerstarved, miserably arrayde, with scabs, leprosie, and mayngie, to complaine as followeth.

And in the complaint itself, Cressid frankly admits that she was always a girl of careless ways, that she enticed Troilus, and was sleeping around with other Trojans while he was madly in love with her. Following Henryson's lead, Whetstone describes her fate as "glad . . . a browne breade crust to gnawe." "Loe!," he concludes, "here the fruits of lust and lawlesse love. . . ." The subtle story of naïve Troilus, paradoxical Criseyde, and meddling Pandarus had become a simple tale of a lusty swain pursuing a pretty kite and obtaining her through a broker-lackey.

Such was the story Shakespeare knew. "Let," he writes, "all constant men be Troiluses, all false women Cressids, and all brokers-between Pandars." His heroine is depicted as a wanton with a "language in her eyes, her cheek, her lips"—even "her foot speaks." The play is a bitter play, cynical and coarse. Not only does he treat the love affair as a sensual one, but he finds the whole purpose of the Greek-Trojan war suspect. Helen is constantly referred to as "an old aunt" and "a whore": Diomede remarks that "For every false drop in her bawdy veins a Grecian's life hath sunk." Achilles is despicable. Although in love with Polyxena, he kills her brother Hector from ambush with the help of a host of Myrmidons to revenge unheroically the death of his "masculine whore" Patroklos. Shakespeare of course sided with the Trojans because his legendary history told him that the British were descended from them via Felix Brutus, Aeneas' grandson, who had settled Britain.

But in truly twentieth-century fashion, neither Greeks nor Trojans know why they are fighting anyhow. They are uncertain of the values they are dying for and are trapped in a lime of false honor and false pride. Chaucer's lovers are made part of the confusion. Like Achilles and Polyxena or Helen and Paris, Troilus and Cressida are trapped, pawns of uncontrollable forces. When Troilus argues vehemently at a council of war that the Trojans must never give up the fight no matter what the cost, the cost quickly proves to be his own Cressida, who he has wooed for two years and loses the day after he gets her. Her father Calchas thinks he's doing her a favor exchanging her out of Troy and has no idea that she is consorting with Troilus or that he is forcing her to leave her lover. Perhaps the most cynical touch of all lies in the fact that Shakespeare doesn't punish Cressida for her infidelities. She is left half-excusing her acts as a normal feminine frailty.

> Ah, poor our sex! this fault in us I find,
> The error of our eye directs our mind;
> What error leads must err; O, then conclude
> Minds sway'd by eyes are full of turpitude.

Since Shakespeare's time, the popularity of the story of Troilus and Cressida has waned considerably. True, John Dryden did a "revision" of Shakespeare's play subtitled *The Truth Found Too Late*. In it, Cressida remains faithful and commits suicide when accused of infidelity. There have been others, but the love-tale that was on "everyone's pen for half-a-thousand years" has the smell of mothballs about it today. And if a story belongs to "the one who tells it best," Chaucer owns Troilus and Criseyde. He owns it because of his sympathetic depiction of the heroine, the classic *belle dame sans merci,* perhaps of all literature. And maybe Robert Henryson deserves just a piece too, for he was the one who realized that Criseyde, like all *les belles dames,* ultimately might prove a tragic figure, if not for her own failings, then for the fact that even the gods would insist on asking more of her than flesh is apt to cope with.

Like Mary Hamilton, standing on the gallows, about to be hung for allowing herself to be seduced by the Queen's consort, any *belle dame* might observe:

> Oh, happy, happy is the girl
> That's born of beauty free,
> For my rosy lip and dimpled chin
> Have proved the ruin o' me.

6

"A WARNING TO MEN
AND MAIDENS ALL"

Ruin may come in many forms, and often the keeper of the roses may prove as grotesque as the flower herself. "Murdered girl ballads" are trite song-stories in which a young man fancies a young girl. She, inconveniently, becomes pregnant and begins to talk of marriage. Unwilling to cooperate to this extent, he *(sans merci)* simply disposes of her. The plot outline, with appropriate accompaniment, comes across clear in this broadside from the Harvard University stacks.

THE LEXINGTON MILLER

Come all you men and maidens dear, to you I will relate,
Pray lend an ear and you shall hear concerning my sad fate,
My parents brought me up with care, provided for me well,
And in the town of Lexington employ'd me in a mill.

'Twas there I spied a comely lass, she cast a winning eye,
I promis'd I would marry her if she would but comply:
I courted her about six months, which caused us pain and woe;
'Twas folly brought us into a snare, and it prov'd our overthrow.

Her mother came to me one day as you shall understand,
Begging that I would appoint a day, and marry her at hand;

It was about one month from Christmas, O, cursed be that day,
The devil put it in my heart to take her life away.

I was perplex'd on every side, no comfort could I find
Then for to take her life away, my wicked heart inclin'd;
I went unto her sister's house at eight o'clock that night,
And she, poor soul, little thought or knew I ow'd her any spite.

I said, come go along with me, out door a little way,
That you and I may both agree upon our wedding day,
Then hand in hand I led her on, down to some silent place;
I took a stake out of the fence, and struck her on the face.

Now she upon her knees did fall, and most heartily did cry,
Saying, kind sir, don't murder me for I am not fit to die;
I would not hearken unto her cries, but laid it on the more,
Till I had taken her life away, which I could not restore.

All in the blood of innocence, my trembling hand have dy'd,
All in the blood of her who should have been my lawful bride;
She gave a sigh and bitter groan, and cast a wistful look,
I took her by the hair of the head and flung her in the brook.

Now straight unto the Mill I went, like one that's in a maze,
And first I met was my servant boy, who deeply on me gaz'd;
How came that blood upon your hands, likewise on your clothes?
I instantly made reply, 'twas bleeding of the nose.

I called for a candle, the same was brought to me.
And when the candle I had light, an awful sight I see;
Now straightway unto bed I went, thinking relief to find,
It seemed as if the plagues of hell, were lodged within my mind.

Next day her body was search'd for, but it could not be found,
Then I was in my chamber seized, and in my chains were bound.
In two or three days after, this fair maid she was found,
Came floating by her mother's house, that was near Wentontown.

Her sister swore against me, she said she had no doubt,
'Twas I that took her life away, as 'twas I that led her out.
It's now my end comes hastening on, and death approaches nigh,
And by my own confession I am condemned to die.

Now fare you well to Lexington, where first my breath I drew,
I warn all men and maidens, to all their vows be true.

The final two lines, which seem to have been left out of this
broadside, should say something similar to:

And take a warning from my fall, all filthy lusts defy
By giving way to wickedness; today, alas, I die.

The "formula" above has certain characteristics that are
worth recording. For one thing the girl, in spite of the fact she
has been sleeping with her lover and is pregnant, is always depicted as "sweet and twenty, and scarcely been kissed." The
lover is hard, a villain—upon second thought not the sort of chap
the girl described as heroine would be likely to associate with,
much less marry. She is, we must conclude, terribly, terribly
naive. The parents are hard-working, loving, confused when the
facts come out. The crime, as described in the ballad, is particularly violent, the motivation unstressed, the girl euphemiz-
ing her pregnancy with a plaintive: "I'm not fit to die." To
the credit of the murderer, he does show remorse once captured, confessing his crime (whether the courts convict him or
not) and warning "men and maidens all" against falling into a
similar fate. Often his main motivation seems to be to avoid
going to Hell. Of course, all murdered girl ballads aren't perfect
"laboratory specimens," but it is astounding how steadily the
actual crimes curve toward the pattern above as they are written up and circulated through folk and popular tradition.
  Where it all began is hard to say. The formula was well
known in Britain as early as 1744 when a broadside entitled
"The Berkshire Tragedy, or the Wittam Miller: With an Account
of his Murdering of his Sweetheart" was successfully hawked.
Though the theme may go back a bit before that, there is little
doubt it is a formula for sentimental, middle class minds and it
established itself as a staple among the city printers in the
late eighteenth and nineteenth centuries when entrepreneurs
like Catnach, Such, and Pitts eyed each other like *Time* and
Newsweek. Such printing and reprinting of a good thing en-

abled "The Berkshire Tragedy" to spawn "The Lexington Miller" and a host of other variants and adaptations that have turned up in oral tradition, in chapbooks and songsters, in the popular music marts, and ultimately on the records of Britain and, particularly, of America.

When you realize that there are literally hundreds of descendants of the old "Berkshire Tragedy" circulating this nation under names such as "The Oxford Girl" or "The Wexford Girl" or "The Butcher Boy," and when you realize that the similar American ballads, like "The Jealous Lover" or "The Banks of the Ohio" have hundreds of variants of their own, you get some idea of the force this simple pattern has had on all "disposable sweetheart" stories. G. Malcolm Laws, Jr., who has indexed and discussed the "murdered girl" ballads in his books *American Balladry from British Broadsides* and *Native American Balladry,* was able to list ten separate songs which reflect the formula. Six of them record actual, well-documented crimes that occurred long after 1744.

Arthur Field, then a young scholar, attempted in a 1950 article in *Midwest Folklore,* to psychoanalyze the Anglo-American desire for the "murdered girl" formula. His conclusion, based largely on the fact that singers almost always sing these ballads in the first person, was that the songs allow people to let out aggression through fantasy, a finding so obvious that it scarcely warrants space in a scholarly journal. Certainly the fact that people just love to be shocked has to be added. Exclamations like: "Are there really such monsters in the world?"; "What sort of upbringing do you suppose he had?"; "She was scarcely more than a child" have their role in such reviews of murder, mayhem, and scandal.

Obviously one can psychoanalyze the singers of "murdered girl" legends best if the crime is a well-documented one and "the doctor" has the opportunity to scan contemporary accounts to see how the known facts have been altered. But the formula is often so strong that fact simply melts under its power and vanishes among the clichés. For instance, neither "The Jealous Lover," in which the man lures his sweetheart "deep, deep into yonder valley where the violets always bloom" and stabs her to death, nor "The Banks of the Ohio," in which he asks his love "to take a walk" and throws her in the river, have been identified with any specific crime, although there is some chance the former originated in a crude nineteenth-century broadside detailing the demise of one Betsy Smith. Like the old "Berkshire Tragedy" they seem to be handy packagings of plot that can be made use of by all men in all seasons—what Arthur Field might have called "ur-crimes." The ballad collector H. M. Belden has listed twenty-one names for the victim of "The Jealous Lover" and seven for the murderer.

On the other hand, we know more than we need to know about crimes like the beheading of Pearl Bryan near Cincinnati and the drowning of Naomi Wise in North Carolina. The murder of Pearl Bryan was even the subject of an M. A. thesis-turned-book: *Poor Pearl, Poor Girl,* by Anne B. Cohen. Briefly the facts of the case go as follows. On February 1, 1896 a boy found the headless corpse of a woman in a farmer's field near Fort Thomas, Kentucky. The coroner's report revealed that the woman was five months pregnant, and it was assumed the crime had been committed by the father of the child and the woman was some tramp from Cincinnati. However, when the body turned out to be "respectable" (belonging to Pearl Bryan, the twenty-three-year-old daughter of a prosperous Greencastle, Indiana farmer), the case gained in significance. Pearl's beau, Scott Jackson, studying to be a dentist in Cincinnati, was arrested and charged with murder, as later was his roommate Alonzo Walling. The prosecution developed the case that Jackson and Walling had attempted to abort Pearl's baby, claiming they killed her and decapitated her when their efforts failed. On March 20, 1897, the two were hanged, although they protested their innocence to the end, and in spite of the fact that a Greencastle lad, Will Wood, was locally known as Pearl's lover and had to flee town after nearly being lynched. Pearl's head, missing throughout the scandal, still hasn't been located.

So notorious was the case that it dominated the front pages of the Ohio River newspapers for thirteen months, inspiring balladeers, songwriters, and newspaper versifiers to produce a flock of Pearl Bryan songs and poems. One of these compositions, hard-plugged by the popular hill singer Vernon Dalhart, has survived as a widely known American ballad. It opens with the cliché,

> Now, ladies, if you'll listen
> A story I'll relate,
> What happened near Fort Thomas
> In old Kentucky state.

Two others have also entered oral tradition. One, widely known, is simply a grafting of the Pearl Bryan story onto "The Jealous Lover." It begins,

> Way down in yonders valley
> Where the violets fade and bloom,
> Our own Pearl Bryan slumbers
> In her cold and silent tomb.

The other, somewhat more quizzical, moves in one of its variants to a conclusion advising,

> So you girls who fall in love,
> You still may be misled.
> Don't take any hasty steps.
> Oh, girls, don't lose your head.

Much of Anne Cohen's study is devoted to showing how the murdered girl formula affected not only the ballad versions of this murder, but the newspaper accounts as well. With the earnest style reserved for theses, she explains the power of cliché:

The result of this formulaic filter, through which information passes, is that stories tend to be altered progressively toward greater and greater similarity to the model. Through time, distinguishing features that one might expect to be remembered because of their striking character are blurred and lost if they conflict with the model. Similarly, features that originally had no part in a story will be drawn to it if they belong to the formula influencing the story.

Anne Cohen, going well beyond Arthur Field, believes legends like that of Pearl Bryan, to be part of the socio-psychological make-up of the rural South and Midwest and that the passive attitude toward disaster taken by heroines like Pearl, when their lovers lure them to lonely spots and batter them senseless with shovels and railroad ties, is simply a "behavior pattern" that says "ordinary decent people" are "essentially passive in their response to events, trusting Providence to direct" matters. She also stresses the influence of the stock figures of the eighteenth- and nine-teenth-century melodramas, where the villain is usually vigorous and urbane while the victim is inactive (to be frank, simple). She feels it inconceivable for someone like Ohio's Pearl Bryan to turn the tables on her would-be murderer the way someone like Britain's Lady Isabel does in the ballad of "Lady Isabel and the Elf-Knight." This self-sufficient beauty is lured, much in the fashion of "the murdered girls," to a riverbank by an evil knight who plans to finish her off just as he has finished off her six sisters. Resourcefully, she explains to him that her gown is too precious to be ruined by going in the water with her and asks for permission to take it off. He agrees. She then tells him to turn his back while she strips. When he does, she kicks him into the stream and holds him under with a branch until he drowns. In a French-Canadian variant, she Gallically asks him to remove her silk stockings and kicks him into the stream as he kneels before her with her lovely leg on his lap. Anne Cohen no doubt has a point, but she doesn't explain why "Lady Isabel and the Elf-Knight" is popular all over the American South and Midwest.

The parents of "murdered girls" are invariably "tender"— weary, tearful, "doing their best" folk. The book *Poor Pearl, Poor Girl* devotes a lot of space to tracing the transformation of Pearl's parents into the formula. In the case of the Bryans, the metamorphosis was extensive. Not only was Pearl's "real" family able to sit through every session of the Jackson-Walling trial without breaking down, but they actively participated in the prosecution of the two youths, at one point threatening them in their cells. Some of them joined a lynch party to speed up Jackson's punishment. But strangest of all, they possessed an obsession to visit the spot where Pearl's body was found, even rewarding the man who first identified the shoes by giving him a pair identical to those found on the body. Not that the "formula" wasn't up to the job. Anne Cohen prints one extract from a news story of the time that might have embarrassed even Louisa May Alcott.

"And did they find the head?" asked the old man through his tears. He was told that at that time the head had not been found. "Oh, I hope they will [find it]. We don't want to have it said above her grave: Here lies the body of a headless woman. That would only serve to perpetuate our bitter recollections. But," and the old man straightened up in his chair, and, raising his hand toward heaven, said in a voice that was chilling in its tones, "Terrible as her fate was, and much as we deplore it, we would rather endure the torture of a daughter lured to ruin by a villain than the infamy of a son who stands charged with such a crime."
As he spoke the words a hush fell upon the room. The mother bowed her head and sobbed, and men and women in the room cried like children. It was a scene that would touch the hardest heart.

After adjustments such as this, there is no way any socio-historian can hope to reconstruct the truth concerning the Bryan murder. "La vie sans rose" implies strongly that Pearl had bestowed her favors on many a country lad before either Will Wood or Jackson came along, that she went to Cincinnati voluntarily to get the abortion, that Jackson and Walling killed her unintentionally and then panicked when they found they had a corpse on their hands, that the trial was conducted "in the press" and wasn't the least fair. But that's not the way anyone is going to hear it any longer.

Nonetheless, the distortions in the Pearl Bryan legend are most marked in the area of characterization, and the plot is far closer to what must have happened than in the ballads about Jonathan Lewis and Naomi Wise. In 1808, Naomi Wise was an orphan girl living with farmer William Adams and his wife close to Asheboro, North Carolina, where the Deep River flows. She was nineteen years old, and naturally reported to have been of "unusual beauty and gentle manner." Jonathan Lewis was much attracted to her and they became sweethearts. She, at least, expected that they would marry. However, Lewis had designs on a more profitable union with Hattie Elliott, the coquettish sister of the man he worked for, and he found his old relationship with Naomi becoming *de trop*. When Naomi began to demand marriage on the grounds she was fully compromised (i.e., pregnant), Lewis evidently made some plans.

One summer evening Naomi tied a few belongings in a package and hid them outside Adams' farmhouse. That night she took the bucket as if to get water from the spring and went out. She was not seen again alive. After she disappeared, footprints assumed to be hers were discovered leading directly to a stump by the spring where they mingled with those of a horse. It was surmised that Lewis had told her they were to run off to be married, that she had met him and mounted behind him voluntarily. The same night, a family living near the mill pond on Deep River heard screams, but disregarded them. The next day, Naomi's body was found in the shallows of the river. She had drowned because she had been knocked unconscious ("kicked and stomped," in the words of the song) and tossed in the river with her skirts tied above her head.

Lewis was, of course, the prime suspect. Picked up and brought to view the body, he was nearly given "a neck-tie party" by the infuriated farmers of the area who were particularly incensed by what they felt was his "exaggerated sentimentality" upon seeing the poor creature he had killed. "Callously," one said, he smoothed the tangled hair from the "quiet face." But he was not to hang for this or any other crime. Put in jail, he escaped. Seven years later, while living at the Falls of the Ohio, he was apprehended and brought back for trial, but by then the evidence was hazy and the jury had to acquit him. He died in Kentucky shortly after.

The story of "Poor Omie" can be collected from most singers with full repertoires in the Deep South. Carson J. Robison, once a well-known hillbilly performer, wrote his own version of the crime, and Olive Burt tells how she came across a "pink paperbacked pamphlet" in Salt Lake City in 1947. It is titled *Naomi Wise, or the Wrongs of a Beautiful Girl:* the author is Charley Vernon who turns out to be Braxton Craven, one-time President of Trinity College in Randolph County. Many a local poet has also given the legend the benefit of his muse. One opens with this Lochinvar-like description of Lewis:

> He was so good-looking, so handsome and brave,
> And to many women his promise he gave.
> His horse was the finest, his clothes, they were new,
> His bearing was knightly, his words were not true.

There is also a spring that has been named after the unhappy girl. It is in New Salem, not far from where she died, and no one in his right mind drinks the water. The spring is "haunted," as is the section of Deep River called Naomi Ford where, at dusk, one can hear "angel voices" singing "in accents sweet."

> Beneath the crystal waters,
> A maiden once did lie
> The fairest of earth's daughters,
> A gem to deck the sky.
>
> In caves of pearled enamels,
> We weave an amber shroud
> For all the foolish damsels.
> That dare to stray abroad.
>
> We live in rolling billows,
> We float upon the mist,
> We sing on foamy pillows,
> "Poor N'omi of the past."

"There is," wrote a local historian in the Greensboro *Daily News* of November 15, 1925, "not a person in miles of Randleman and New Salem that does not know at least one story about her death." He adds that "most of the people list her among the saints and let her stand for all that was pure and holy in womanhood sacrificed to the beast in man."

The characters of Naomi, Jonathan, and the Adamses fit the "murdered girl" formula quite nicely. She was, if not "pure and holy," certainly innocent and in all likelihood "passing fair." Lewis, if not "a beast," was certainly a calculating chap. And the Adamses did nothing that would remind one of the Bryans. It's the plot that gets badly distorted. The ballad has Lewis choke or batter Naomi and "throw her in the river to drown" in quite conventional fashion without using the old rapist's trick of tying her skirts above her head. Such things as the desire of the local citizens to lynch him, his escape from jail, the seven-year lapse between his original apprehension and his trial, and his acquittal are seldom even hinted at—in Anne Cohen's words "blurred and lost" because "they conflict with the model." The ending is particularly conventionalized, the final stanza usually being Lewis' confession to the murder when "a prisoner condemned to die."

Actually, the prisoner's repentance when "condemned to die" is a commonplace extending far beyond the "murdered girl" formula. One of the oldest clichés about condemned criminals is that they compose an "apologia" in their cells before going to the gallows at dawn. Called a "last goodnight," the confession is always "de profundis" and there actually are a number of real ones extant. The labor rouser Joe Hill wrote his twelve-line poem "My Last Will" in his cell just before he was electrocuted in Salt Lake City in November 1915 and it has appeared in print many times. Jereboam O. Beauchamp, the murderer in the notorious killing of Colonel Solomon Sharp at Frankfort, Kentucky in 1824, produced a whole series of prose tracts that have been printed in Loren J. Kallsen's *The Kentucky Tragedy*. But it is the "goodnight ballads" that are particularly remarkable because they are invariably "composed" with music by illiterates who can't play an instrument, much less pick out a tune. Of course, what really happens is some print shop hack sees a chance to turn a profit and pumps out a musical confession which he then has hawked (along with the beer and hot dogs) to the Madame Lafarges clustered about the gallows.

The ballad of Tom Dula (or Dooley as he is sometimes called) offers a fine example of the fusion of the "last goodnight" with the "murdered girl." On page 706, Volume II of the *Frank C. Brown Collection of North Carolina Folklore* is printed the following portion of a letter written by Mrs. Orene Burrell of Lenoir, N. C. to her brother John Foster West, then a student at

Chapel Hill. It summarizes the local traditions about the murder of Laura Foster by Tom Dula, and probably Ann Melton, 80 years before.

I'll tell you all Verlee and I can remember about Tom Dula. . . . Laura Foster was a cousin of Grandpa Harve Foster. She and Dula were engaged. Tom got to running around after this other woman, we can't remember her name. She and Tom planned to lure Laura off and kill her. Laura and Tom were horseback riding in the woods somewhere near Happy Valley, and the other woman stepped out and stabbed her in the side. They stuffed handkerchiefs in her side to stop the blood. People hunted for her for some time, and one day a man found her because the horse he was riding smelled her and was snorting, etc. She was in a shallow grave, her head between her knees. The other woman, on trial, packed it on Tom and he never did tell she did it. She would say on trial, "A rope will never go around this pearly white neck." Tom was hanged, and later, on her death-bed, she confessed. The legend or story goes, and I've heard Grandma tell it a hundred times, that you could hear meat frying and see black cats running up and down the wall of the room she was in when she was dying.

Whatever the truth about the case, Dula was hung for the crime and Ann Melton was acquitted. Not always mentioned in such local accounts is the fact that Tom seems to have contracted a venereal disease (I've never seen mentioned which one) from Laura Foster and passed it on to Ann. Evidentally, he was furious about this (though his logic is somewhat hard to follow), and the State established the infection as a main motive for the crime. A summary of the case against Dula is also printed in the *Brown Collection:*

The prisoner [Thomas Dula] was indicted as principal, and one Anne Melton as accessory before the fact, in the murder of one Laura Foster, in Wilkes county in May, 1866. The bill was found at Fall Term, 1866, of Wilkes Superior Court, and upon affidavit, removed to Iredell. The prisoner and Ann Melton were arraigned together, but, upon motion of the counsel [Zebulon B. Vance] for the former, there was a severance, and he put upon his trial alone. The case, as made out by his Honor, contained a statement of all the evidence and was quite voluminous. There were several exceptions by the prisoner on account of the admission of improper testimony. . . . His Honor overruled the exceptions, and the testimony was admitted. Verdict of guilty: rule for a new trial; rule discharged; motion in arrest of judgment; motion overruled; judgment of death and appeal.

Supposedly Ann Melton confessed her role in the crime on her deathbed. Local raconteurs recall how one lady saw blue flames crackling about her body as she lay dying, that she screamed in agony as her flesh began to burn just before her death, and that she kept asking her friends to save her from the big black man waiting in the corner with a pitchfork in his hand. Another tale has her admit that she and Dula collaborated on the crime and when they found the body too heavy to carry, cut it in half, each picking up part. Generally, one gets the feeling that local belief did not acquit Ann as readily as did the State.

Nonetheless, Dula signed a statement the night before he died swearing that he was the "only person that had a hand in the murder of Laura Foster," and he actually did harangue the throng that gathered to see him hung, instructing them on his preparation to enter "another world." This statement and the speech were enough to make people think he wrote a "last goodnight." Alan Lomax goes along with this idea in his *Folk Songs of North America* where one of the three "Tom Dula" ballads appears. "Even," writes Lomax, "in the ballad he composed during his last days in jail, he did not mention her (Ann's) name." That such a sophisticated scholar as Lomax would print a "last goodnight" as having been composed by a man who probably never wrote a line of verse in his life testifies to the power of this convention.

What is supposed to be Dula's "goodnight" was "immortalized" as a "pop" song in the late 1950's by the Kingston Trio. It begins with lines that most Americans now recognize: "Hang down your head, Tom Dooley, hang down your head and cry." The tune is a dance tune, indecently bright, cheerful, and high-stepping, and the arrangement was based on the variant sung by Frank Proffitt of Pick Britches Valley. It is quite different in tone from "Dula's own song" as collected by Maude Minish Sutton of Lenoir.

> I pick my banjo now,
> I pick it on my knee.
> This time tomorrow night
> It'll be no more use to me.
>
> The banjo's been my friend
> In days both dark and ill.
> A-laying' here in jail
> It's helped me time to kill.
>
> Poor Laura loved its tunes
> When sitting 'neath a tree;
> I'd play and sing to her,
> My head upon her knee.
>
> Poor Laura loved me well,
> She was both fond and true;
> How deep her love for me
> I never really knew.
>
> Her black curl on my heart,
> I'll meet my fatal doom,
> As swift as she met hers
> That dreadful evening's gloom.
>
> I've lived my life of sin,
> I've had a bit of fun.
> Come, Ann, kiss me goodby,
> My race is nearly run.

Surely if Dula wrote a "gay" goodnight of the sort the Kingston Trio sang, the local newspaper description of him during his final hours is accurate. "The hardened assasin [has] a fierce glare of the eyes, a great deal of malignity, and a callousness that is revolting."

They are an unfeeling lot, these "elf-knights." In 1810, Polly Williams, seduced by a wealthy young man who doesn't want to marry her, goes for an afternoon stroll with him along the cliffs near Uniontown, Pennsylvania. Her body is found at the bottom of a ravine and her lover, suspected of the crime, is able to claim Polly committed suicide and go free. In 1847, in Brookfield, New Hampshire, Joseph Buzzell, irritated by Susan Hanson's breach of promise suit, hires half-wit Charles Cook to kill her. Although he changes his mind at the last minute, he can't stop the killing and Susan is shot. Buzzell is hanged and Cook imprisoned for life. In 1868 in St. John, New Brunswick, John Monroe, already married and father of two children, makes love to Sarah Vail who has a child by him. He takes Sarah and her new baby on a trip and murders both. Monroe is captured and hung in February 1870. In 1892, Ellen Smith is shot by Peter deGraph in Mt. Airy, North Carolina. In 1917, in Elkhorn City, Kentucky, John Coyers asks the pregnant· Lula Viers to elope. Nearly six months later her body is found in the Big Sandy River near Ironton, Ohio. Rose Connally is poisoned with wine and stabbed with a "skeever." Catherine Berringer is given "a fatal cup" by a lover who tells her the potion will cure her cold. Nelly Cropsey is murdered by a man named Jim. And Maria Bewell is killed by her stepfather when he can't seduce her. The results, sweetly played in tune, are "The Murder of Polly Williams," "The Brookfield Murder," "The Murder of Sarah Vail," "Ellen Smith," "Lula Viers," "Rose Connally," "An Eulogy on the Death of Miss Catherine Berringer," "Nell Cropsey," and "Maria Bewell." Given time enough, Polly and Nelly, Susan and Sarah, Poor Ellen will be one, a single dear heart confronted by a single scoundrel—heroines of a thousand faces acting out a retold tale which truly makes hungry as it satisfies.

It was inevitable that one of these "retold tales" would attract a writer of real talent. The case of Chester Gillette and Grace Brown did just that. Gillette was executed on March 20, 1908 for tipping his pregnant sweetheart out of a canoe and into New York's Big Moose Lake 20 months before. His motivation was her pregnancy and his desire to marry another. Before the crime was committed, Gillette and Grace Brown traveled a sordid odyssey from cheap hotel to cheap hotel in the Adirondack area while he procrastinated on her demands for marriage. The affair has been described desperate moment by moment in Charles Samuels' *Death Was the Bridegroom,* but it was Theodore Dreiser who brought it to national attention and made an artistic attempt to explain human behavior through it.

Dreiser was a rough, polemic, frank depicter of lower middle class America, and he dominated our fiction for the first quarter of the twentieth century. Believing that the world is without reason or meaning to the human mind, a place where "nothing is proved, all is permitted," Dreiser liked to study individuals as they struggle for power, pleasure, or simple survival in the ruthless environment of American society. Some of his characters succeed, either through sheer strength of purpose or through an inner poise that enables them, catlike, to come down on their feet no matter how Fate drops them. But the sensitive, the indecisive, the ones without that inner poise are crushed. Like a squid in the tank with a lobster, they can't maintain the struggle, they tire, and are destroyed either by one of society's predators or by chance itself.

Dreiser saw this sort of weakness in Chester Gillette, and he built a book from the legend. He calls Gillette "Clyde Griffiths," and models his early life on the one he himself had known. Griffiths comes from mediocre stock, his mediocre mind filled by dreams of American success and American money. His parents, who are impoverished evangelists in Kansas City, are barely able to feed and shelter him and give him a meager education. All of them dream of an escape. His sister Hester tries by running off with an actor and is deserted. Clyde quits school and by working as a soda-jerk and bellhop makes the first money he has ever really had. It goes to his head: he gets mixed up with liquor and brothels, and eventually kills a little girl while driving a stolen car. He leaves Kansas City and flees to Chicago where a wealthy uncle gets him started working at a mill. There he moves up to manager of a small department, in charge of twenty-five girls. He has an affaire with one, Roberta Alden, a pretty, religious, farmer's daughter, who lets him seduce her because that is the only way she feels she can hold him. Roberta ends up pregnant. Meanwhile, however, he has met and fallen in love with a lovely, spoiled rich girl named Sondra Finchley. Although he knows her family will not approve of him, he hopes to marry her and cement his fortune. When he can't find a doctor to abort Roberta who is demanding a hasty marriage, he becomes desperate. Seeing a news account of a couple who went rowing and failed to return, he decides to drown her. From this point on Dreiser's lovers act out the "murdered girl" formula.

> Two mothers are weeping and praying;
> One praying that justice be done,
> The other one asking for mercy,
> Asking God to save her dear son.
>
> The dreams of the happy are finished,
> The scores are brought in at last;
> A jury has brought in its verdict,
> The sentence on Gillette is passed.
>
> He is now in bleak Auburn's dark prison
> Where he soon will give up his young life,
> Which might have been filled with sweet sunshine
> Had he taken Grace Brown for his wife.
>
> But Cupid was too strong for Gillette,
> It was playing too strong with his heart,
> For the one that had loved him so dearly,
> Yet from her he wanted to part.
>
> 'Twas on a hot, sultry day in the summer
> When the flowers were all aglow,
> They started out on their vacation
> For the lakes and the mountains to roam.
>
> Did she think when he gathered those flowers
> That grew on the shores of the lake
> That the hands that plucked those sweet lilies
> Her own sweet life they would take?
>
> They were seen on the clear, crystal waters
> Of the beautiful Big Moose Lake,

And nobody though he'd be guilty
Of the life of that poor girl to take.

It happened along in the evening,
Just at the close of the day,
With the one that had loved him so dearly
They drifted along on South Bay.

They were out of the view of the people
Where no one could hear her last call,
And nobody knows how it happened,
But Gillette and God knows it all.

Two mothers were weeping and praying;
One prayed that justice be done,
The other one asked for mercy,
Asked God to save her dear son.

Dreiser spends forty-five pages on the scene covered in the last six stanzas above, dwelling on things the folk, in their stress upon formula and stock characterization, have little time for. "The flowers all aglow" and "the sweet lilies" are described in great detail, and he philosophizes on the sentimental irony of Roberta's happiness at being with the man she thinks she's about to marry and her enthusiasm over the beauty of what will prove her final day. But most of all he stresses Griffiths' inability to handle the crime coolly and efficiently. No murderer, Griffiths is a Shakespearian hero trying to play a role he is not cut out for, driven toward what Alfred Kazin described as "tawdry prizes he is trying to win." For pages he questions, hesitates, goes forward, steps back, like some lower-middle-class Hamlet attempting to stab Claudius. And he never does accomplish the crime. Roberta, in her simplicity, "suddenly noticing the strangeness" of Clyde's behavior as he looks at her from the bow of the canoe, moves toward him, "since he looked as though he was about to fall forward into the boat—or to one side and out into the water." The canoe rocks. Panicky, he flings out at her, anxious only to "free himself of her—her touch—her pleading—consoling, sympathy—her presence forever," hitting her with a camera he has been holding, capsizing the boat, and knocking them both into the water. She, of course, drowns—conveniently, half by accident. And he is taken, tried, and electrocuted for a crime he intended to commit, but wasn't strong enough to carry out.

Dreiser even has Griffiths compose a "last goodnight" in his cell two days prior to his death. It starts, "In the shadow of the Valley of Death it is my desire to do everything that would remove any doubt as to my having found Jesus Christ . . ." And after telling young men to know only "the joy and pleasure of a Christian life," it ends on the statement: "My task is done, the victory won." Meanwhile, his mother, who has tried repeatedly to get the governor to pardon her son, fails. After the execution, she returns to street evangelism and the novel closes with Griffiths' sister Hester's little bastard by the actor starting out on the very life-road Griffiths had taken a generation before.

Whether *An American Tragedy* is a first class novel is a moot point. As long ago as 1948, when the book was but twenty-three years published, H. L. Mencken had his doubts. Characteristically, he wrote that its success (and it was very successful) was due to its "sheer bulk" and because readers on "the lower and more numerous levels . . like something that will last all winter." But it may be that the success of the novel rests on that same something that has made the "murdered girl" ballads successful, the something that kept Pearl Bryan's case on the front pages for over a year, that enables the *National Enquirer* to publish. For when Dreiser saw the "injustice, imbalance, and deceit of life" in the story of Chester Gillette and his murdered girl, perhaps he also saw something about "ordinary decent people" the less tutored have long wanted to record—as a warning to "men and maidens all."

7

BLACK MAGIC

La dame sans merci who is truly evil is a witch. In fact, any person, male or female, who practices sorcery or has supernatural powers (for better or for worse) is a witch. But, in popular usage, the word has tended to become associated with the ladies and to focus on black or evil magic rather than white or benign magic. And with all due respect to modern "witch associations," made up of men and women who have no harmful aims in the world, it is fair to say that the word carries strong connotations of feminine trouble-stirring.

There are as many kinds of evil women as there are religions. From the Hebrew Lilith, that spirit of desolation who was created with Adam to be his mate before Eve; to the ogres with toothed vaginas who people the western American Indian myths; to Circe who turned Odysseus' men into swine; to the colonial granny women who rode phallic symbols, slipped through keyholes, and could only be killed by a silver bullet—witches cackle, slurp, and haunt their many ways through world folklore. Most Western European witches (the black-weeded symbol of All Hallows' E'en) are folk-religious rationalizations stemming from the fact that rural people did not give up those old orgiastic agricultural rites just because they had been converted to Christianity. True, as we note concerning the elf-people, the

Church Fathers recognized the tenacity of ritual and did what they could to infuse pagan rites with Christian meanings, but they weren't one hundred percent successful in their accomplishments. In many spots, the old rites associated with fertility, firewater, and fire were continued. Where this happened, the Church simply labeled the whole package as the workings of the Devil, calling them Black Masses or Sabats, and suggesting they were being held in purposeful defiance of God. In fact, the image of the Devil as a creature with horns, cloven feet, and a furry body comes from just such an identification of His Evilship with the Dionysian goat that so often was worshipped in Mediterranean areas.

The common Western European witch has particular powers among which are listed the ability to divine the future; the power of transforming herself, others, or objects into whatever her heart of stone desires; invulnerability to harm from such usually fatal mechanisms as bullets, poison, concussion; a knowledge of alchemy, drugs, potions, poisons and spells; as well as the ability to fly, to travel at supersonic speeds, and to lift loads that would make Atlas himself stagger. Traditionally, she has a magic wand made of hazel ("witch hazel") or one of the fruitwoods (pears, apples, and the like are suggestive of the male scrotum and so have magic, fertility potential). The Devil, her Master, usually provides her with an imp or familiar in the form of an owl, toad, or black cat. But her talents have their limits, especially in the face of Christian symbols such as the cross, the name of our Lord, or holy water. Thus, she cannot, without aid, cross a threshold that has been blessed, she is powerless at the crossroads, and one is safe from her in the sanctuary of the local church. Moreover, she can be killed by silver objects (silver seems to have magic powers in most folk communities), and if she loses a paw or is slashed while in animal shape the wound will remain even after her transformation back to normal form. There are other drawbacks too. Most likely, she has a birthmark hidden by the hair of her body, under an armpit, on her head, or (if she be particularly devious) near her genitals. She has abnormally long eyelashes, and her complexion is commonly brunette in keeping with her Master's favorite color. Nor is her life simple. She is compelled to count straws in brooms she happens to pass, holes in sieves, grains of wheat in bowls, sheets in packs of paper. Such idiosyncrasies are not easy to cover up from sharp-eyed observers, though her speed in reckoning may be like that of a computer.

In Christian thought, witches represent the old belief in Providence: that is the direct intervention of God and Satan into world affairs. In a culture that accepts this idea fully, not only can Michael, Gabriel, Jesus or perhaps God himself appear to lead troops to victory or rescue a child drowning in a river, but he can drop into your house for dinner. And Satan may do the same, debating Daniel Webster, tempting Dr. Faustus, or assigning one of his agents the task of taking some innocent Christian's shape and pinching teen-age girls. Consequently, the damage that has been ascribed to witches throughout the Middle Ages and down to more enlightened times has been extensive. Witches have visited innocent people with all sorts of infirmities, cancers, and scrofulas; they have acted as midwives to engineer the birth of malformed and idiotic children; they have ravaged crops, cattle, homes, and even armies with pestilence and plague; they have prevented goodwives from proving fertile; and they have caused innocent men to howl like wolves and run on all fours through the fields. In fact, as far as toil and trouble goes, accomplishments ascribed to them are nearly equal to all the *Apocalypse's* Four Horsemen have been able to do.

Today, it is hard to believe that the settler and missionary alike travelled to Africa, to the Americas, and to oceanic regions convinced they were entering demesnes ruled by the Devil, filled with dark souls who had been kept there from the white purity of the Lord, whose medicine men, customs, and ignorances could only be described as witchcraft. Isolated in such lands, where even the elements themselves seemed under Satanic control, the pilgrim had to remain on sharp lookout for evil. The New England Puritans are famous for the "crow's nest" they kept. To their seventeenth-century minds, it was quite clear that the Devil had his agents hard at work in a continual effort to undo God's colonization program. "That the Devil is come down to us with great wrath," wrote Cotton Mather, "we find, we feel, we now deplore. In many ways, for many years hath the Devil been assaying to extirpate the kingdom of our Lord Jesus here."

Toward the end of the century, as reports of His Satanic Majesty's activities began to pile up, the colony of Massachusetts, particularly its intellectual segment, was in an uproar. An hysterical fear that the Devil was about to take over "Greater Boston" developed, and it was pretty clear that all was lost if God-fearing people didn't move fast. The confession of Ann Foster at her trial in July, 1692 gives some idea of what was occurring. She tells how the Devil Himself came to her in the form of a bird that changed from white to black, sat upon her table, and, promising "prosperity," began to interest her in evil. However, it was one of His agents, Goody Carrier, that made her into a witch. Goody Carrier . . . came to her in person:

. . . . six years ago and told her if she would not be a witch the Devil should tear her in pieces and carry her away, at which time she promised to serve the Devil. Since then she had bewitched a hog of John Loujoy's to death, and had hurt some persons in Salem Village. Goody Carrier came to her and would have her bewitch two children of Andrew Allin's, so she had then two poppets made and stuck pins in them to bewitch the said children, by which one of them died, and the other very sick. She was at the meeting of the witches at Salem Village, because Goody Carrier came and told her of the meeting and would have her go, so they got upon sticks and went said journey. Being there, she did see Mr. Burroughs the minister, who spake to them all. This was about two months ago. There were then twenty-five persons met together. She also said that she tied a knot in a rag and threw it into the fire to hurt Tim Swan, and that she did hurt the rest that complained of her by squeezing poppets like them and so almost choked them.

She even admitted that the witches of the area had definite plans to set up the Devil's kingdom in that very area.

The problem was—how did one know who was an agent of the Devil and who was not? How did one tell a real witch from an innocent falsely accused, especially when the Devil and his army could take any form they wished? The only answer seemed to be trials, and quickly a series of court sessions were held, the most notorious being at Salem. Still, the trials had their baffling

sides too. Only a few of the accused confessed outright the way
Ann Foster had. Some, with the aid of dialectics suggested by
the Black Master Himself, denied all, often in utter defiance of
accusers who swooned in their presence or began to feel pinches
and to itch just from being in the same room with them. Susanna
Martin, "one of the most impudent, scurrilous, wicked crea-
tures in the world," whose trial clearly discovered her to be
such, when asked what she had to say for herself, stated brazenly, in the very presence of the respected Cotton Mather, "that
she had led a most virtuous and holy life."

Today, when one looks at the testimony, he is amazed by the
fact that the accused are just as panicky and just as ignorant
as their prosecutors. Nowhere lies the defense "This is all nonsense!" "What's wrong with you people?" "Calling me a witch
is stupid!"—the immediate reaction of the twentieth-century
mind. No, the defenses are based on the very beliefs that caused
the accusations, and one realizes that persecutor and per-
secuted could easily switch roles. George Jacobs, examined
at Salem on May 10, 1692 along with his single daughter Mar-
garet concerning "high suspicion of sundry acts of withcraft,"
defends himself characteristically. "The Devil," he says, "can
go in any shape. . . . The Devil may present my likeness. . . .
Well! Burn me, or hang me, I will stand in the truth of Christ.
I know nothing of it."

The belief in the witch drifts into the intellectual "out-back"
with the changing fashions in religion and the growth of scientific explanation. When the world is a mechanical phenomenon
that God put in motion and turned his back upon, or when it is
an electrical-chemical accident occurring in chaos, there is little
room for the old recruiting battle between God and Satan for
Everyman's soul. Still, moral distinctions go with civilization,
death and taxes being but two of the inevitabilities, and "whatever Utopia of human virtue and happiness" man may project,
as Hawthorne remarked, he must early recognize the need for a
prison as well as a cemetery. So "unmotivated malignancy"
gives way to explanations concerning chromosome disturbances,
genetic misalignments, trap-like environs, and cold Pablum
served night after night in the nursery, while we ever attempt to

explain why some members of our groups have a compulsion to contaminate the doings of "dear hearts" and gentle folk.

The Satanism of the modern world may be better explained than that of olden times, but it is scarcely less real or less sinister. Souls available at barter, traitors who violate a nation's intimacy, outlaws who thrive "in cold blood," trouble goodmen today as surely as any Mephistophelian sorority of yesteryear. Spying is a particular source of moral consternation. Unmoved by Nathan Hale's rationalization that it is work that must be done and therefore is noble, we would like the "breed of black cat" which gets involved in it to stay out in the cold. For in wars where honor is said to be at stake and where soldiers are asked to fight for God and their country, it is not difficult to classify someone who is willing to sell "Right" for a price with Judas, Iago, and Goody Carrier.

For instance, in the First World War, that attempt to make the world safe for democracy (the form of government clearly preferred, if not practiced, by the Lord), how does one account for Mata Hari who sold the Cause for luxury, who used immorality "straight up" to do it, and who fertilized the poppy fields of France with the corpses of thousands of boys who were trying to "do something for her"? Surely there can be no more tears shed when she cowers before the firing squad than there were for John Huss when he "drank the flames" at the stake or when Ann Foster brazenly heard the word "guilty."

Although the Devil must have engineered her conception, Margaretha Geertruida Zelle was not a bastard child, but the daughter of a part-Jewish father and a bourgeois Dutch mother. Her life began on August 7, 1876 in the little town of Leeuwarden, and her upbringing was normal. Until 14, she went to typical Dutch schools, getting a typical Dutch education; then she entered a Catholic convent. At 18, taking her vacation at The Hague, she met Captain Rudolf MacLeod, a dashing, if fast-fading, ladies' man. There was a mutual attraction, best explained by phrases like "he swept her off her feet" and "she saw an in-some-ways-golden chance to escape from the constrictions of her family and school." The result was marriage. The tale, if one believes a book by her mother entitled the "History of my daughter's

life and my charges against her former husband . . .", reads like
an Edwardian best-seller in which Satan Himself abducts a simple girl, ruining her life and claiming her soul. MacLeod proves
far less rich than he pretended to be; he takes to drinking, gambling, and wenching; a child, Norman, is born to the hand-
wringing young wife. To frustrate the wolf, Margaretha Geertruida is forced to take on a wealthy lover, certainly with her
husband's approval, probably at his suggestion. The birth of
another child, Jeanna Louise, and a military assignment in Java
intervenes. Matters are temporarily eased. Soon though, the rup-
tures in the relationship prove so deep that they will never be
healed and physical violence becomes commonplace. On top of it
all, Norman dies. Then MacLeod, in love with "another woman,"
asks for a divorce, backing his arguments with the statement he
will resort to murder if separation isn't facilitated. The serial
winds on through its tedium of clichés: a transfer back to Amsterdam, a separation-reconciliation period during which Mac-
Leod attempts to abduct Jeanna Louise, debts, drinking, and loss
of respectability, all to the result that Margaretha leaves home,
enters the streets child-by-the-hand with no visible means of support and "barely the threads on their backs to keep them warm."

When Paris beckoned, it became pretty obvious that the Devil
had established claim to another bourgeois soul. Aided by her
father, who seemed to have been anxious to get her out of the
area, about twenty-seven and already a bit worse for wear, the
unhappy girl set forth. She planned a career as a dancer, but she
had no training, so like the little Arkansas girl at the Corner of
Sunset and Vine, she used what she did have and became "an
artist's model." The story of her first job is revealing. Asked to
pose in the nude, she hesitated, not on moral grounds, but because in spite of her fine figure, hypnotic eyes, amber skin, and
Lorelei voice, she had ugly, pendulous breasts, so unappealing
that one of her harsher critics has referred to them as "simply
small dugs." Even when she turned to nude dancing, she never
bared them, making this display of discretion her trademark and
using a jewelled brassiere to hide their repulsiveness. She
claimed she had been mutilated by her cad of a husband during
one of their marital tiffs. However, reports are she wasn't pretty

Mata Hari, the most famous female spy, was executed by the French during World War I.

(UPI)

enough to be a good model anyhow, one acquaintance claiming her features "lacked refinement." In short, she quit modeling and turned to dancing as quickly as she could.

Her debut at dancing aroused her husband, MacLeod, who felt his honored name (and it was a good Scottish name) was being compromised. Quite unsatanically, he treatened to have her incarcerated in a convent if she persisted. And for a while she did "retire," hiding out in Nimegue. But she had seen "Paree," and by 1905 she was back beside the River Seine, this time however with experience, "an act" that she knew she could sell, and a purpose. Margaretha Zelle had become Mata Hari, and a star was born.

"The Red Dancer," she billed herself, "from the south of India on the coast of Malabar, in the holy city of Jaffnapatan, member of a family within the sacred caste of the Brahmins." Her father was so pure of heart that he was called "The Blessing of God"; her mother was a *bayadère* in the temple of Kanda Swany, and died when fourteen years old, on the very day she gave birth to her only child. The priests, having cremated the young mother, adopted the baby whom they named "Eye of the Dawn" or "Mata Hari," shielding her from the world and training her to be a dancer too. By thirteen, she was a *bayadère* performing nude in religious ceremonies. One day a handsome English officer attending the rites saw the nude girl dance, and, fascinated by her lovely eyes, fell madly in love with her. Against all custom and all rule, he spoke to her, so charmingly that she found herself falling too. With daring, courage, and resourcefulness, he abducted her from the priests and married her. Shortly after, a son Norman was born, only to be poisoned in childhood by a treacherous Oriental servant. Distressed into superhuman strength, "Eye of the Dawn" wrung the villain's neck herself.

Mata Hari's act, then, was to perform for Siva, the whimsical, sensual God, the sacred (and, to be sure, nude) dances mastered in her youth—a brave, hurt, mysterious spirit, struggling to keep the things in her life together. She started on the vaudeville stage, where the excitement of her approach soon gained her all sorts of notoriety. This she converted into a string of lovers and a stockpile of material goods. Rapidly, she shifted from public dancing to what became her Parisian specialty: the "private engagement" presented in the apartments of some wealthy dilettante who had selected a group to enjoy an evening of Oriental art. The authenticity of her performances, based on what she had been able to glean from books and what she had observed between skirmishes with MacLeod in Java seems to have passed such "muster" as her clients required. Besides the fact that her nudity covered as much as it revealed, her greatest asset seems to have been that she had utterly convinced herself that her promotions were genuine. Like the youngster who really thinks Keds will make you run faster or the cowboy star from Ohio who begins to walk bowlegged and talk Texan all the time, Mata Hari became a ministrant to Siva. And she even "passed muster" with her act before some "distinguished" Orientalists at the Guimet Museum. Her success was immense. "Engagement" followed "engagement," assignation followed rendezvous, while the coins and jewels rolled in—and out, for like the little girl from Arkansas she lived as if there were no tomorrow.

But, as with most acts based on novelty and/or shock, tomorrow came quickly. By 1907, her Eastern Star was sinking, her performances were being imitated, the press was getting bored, and even her "soirées" were becoming *passée*. She realized she had to find fresh enthusiasms, so she left for Berlin. There she deftly attracted the attention of the aristocratic "stag line," accompanying even such figures as the Crown Prince to the army maneuvers in Silesia. And somehow, for some reason that has never been clear, she became a German spy, ministrant to a God of another fire. It couldn't have been for money. Even a struggling courtesan lives better than a spy. It couldn't have been for political chauvinism, for Mata Hari supported only herself. The idea that she was anxious to "revenge herself on the French" for getting tired of her act is preposterous. Most likely, the answer is "simply for kicks," because she loved excitement, because it gave a purpose to her "dalliances," and because once she was "in" there was no way out.

The Germans wanted Mata Hari because she was the only woman available who had the experience, morals and looks to cultivate intimacy and confidence among highly placed military and political figures in Western Europe. Her technique was always the same, exactly what it had been when Paris embraced her. She moved in the best circles, charming, available, a dancer-courtesan ready to rendezvous. Her price was high, her fidelity of no account. The secrets she gained, she gained from confidences, keeping her eyes open, and by putting *deux et en deux* together.

Her legend has her operating in a house of secret panels, revolving mirrors, and tapped telephones, with no intrigue too absurd to be attached to her name, no treachery too foul to be made the more sinister by her part in it. Actually, she operated quite blatantly, even amateurishly. The British, the Italians, and the French knew her to be exactly what she was, but her legal umbrella was quite waterproof. A courtesan, she could always excuse her contacts on "business" grounds; a courtesan, she always had something she could use to "twist arms" in high places in the various governments. She was allowed to operate largely because it was no easy matter legally or politically to "pin anything on her." When unassailable evidence did appear, she was apprehended.

Like most *belles de nuit,* Mata Hari had consummate scorn for the men who pursued her. She described one with "his hyena's snout and his swindler's mien." Another she calls "as puritanical outside as he is licentious within"; another she says would "sell his God if he could find a buyer." "Bah," she remarks, "their jewels and their flowers weary me. . . . Men are vile! They who adore me would devour each other for my smiles." Nonetheless, she demanded lovers who would maintain a fine temper. One aspiring "boulevardier" who took her on because of her reputation as the most extravagant, as well as the most notorious, woman in Paris, "lost all" with a simple remark at an expensive dinner he gave in the Bois. In spite of the vast sums spent on the affair, when the *maitre d'hotel* offered him a box of cigars, he brushed them aside disdainfully, remarking, "I already have some excellent ones, and what's more they don't cost so much." Hearing him, Mata Hari is supposed to have said to her other dinner partner, "The stingy old Devil! A woman such as I could never make love to a creature such as that." She closed her door to him at once.

The break in her case came in the form of an intercepted and decoded telegram from the naval attaché at the German Embassy in Madrid, a gentleman called Lt. von Kroon by biographer Thomas Coulson, but listed as de Krohn in the *Almanach de Gotha,* who was handling German espionage in Spain at that time. The message was to Headquarters in Amsterdam asking for money to enable H 21, Mata Hari's spy name, to travel to Paris. She even had the check in her possession when on February 13, 1917 she was "captured" upon her arrival. Noting her favors came high, she claimed the money to be "love pay" from de Krohn in spite of the fact it was in the form of a government check, for throughout she seems to have thought her cover as a dancer-courtesan would explain all her relationships with political and military figures to all suspicious minds. Moreover, she seems to have been taken completely off guard when the French Second Bureau confronted her with the case against her they had long been assembling.

The French had a good case by the time they took her in, and it may well be that the Germans supplied them with the concrete evidence needed to "get rid of" H 21. For some time before her arrest, the information which she had been sending had been clearly inaccurate. The reports, conveyed in the form of seemingly innocent letters to her daughter through official pouches carried by Dutch diplomats from Paris to Amsterdam, may have aroused suspicion that the French and British were on to her and were purposely providing her with false information. And engineering an arrest has long been standard operating procedure for dismissing spies who no longer are useful.

To us, today, Mata Hari's treacheries seem long ago: advance information on troop movements for battles we never read about, spots where surprise attacks might be launched, routes of fliers who would drop spies behind the lines, nose-counts of soldiers gathering in some forgotten staging-area. The results are equally dulled: ambushes, surprise resistance, flaming plane-crashes, elation, victory, heartbreak, defeat. But once it was all lethal and vital, and many of us have an ancestor or two among the 50,000 dead men that the French authorities have attributed to her activities. Major Thomas Coulson once wrote that there is "a great gulf that separates the foyers of the elegant Champs-Elysées from the bivouac fires. . . . Yet over this yawning gulf between selfish lust and heroic self-sacrifice went the fluttering feet of the Red Dancer and her partner, Death. . . ." The statement is only melodramatic because the past always seems to have been some preposterous movie.

Nothing in Mata Hari's career as a spy was as preposterous as her trial, however. Although the French Second Bureau had a truly impregnable case against her by the time she was taken into custody and although she had done immense damage to the national cause, "40 million" princes, statesmen, savants, and artistes rose to her support, Frenchmen romantically standing by a woman, in some cases their once-woman, in her moment of need. Her legal defense was undertaken by a former lover, Maître Edouard Clunet, by then a distinguished and internationally known legal figure. Though 72, he was most urbane, charming, with snow-white hair and dignity—as impressive a bastion as she could have wished for. Personally acquainted with President Raymond Poincaré, he seems never to have doubted that he could free his former mistress, counting heavily on fear of scandalous revelations to cause direct intervention from high state officials. He failed simply because the whole matter was "shut and closed," and his final emotional appeal citing her unhappy married life, the persecutions of her wretched husband, and her need to combat poverty, arguments which she had always used effectively in the bedroom, failed both in court and in the "smoke-filled" back chambers. When she was finally judged guilty and condemned to death, the old advocate burst into tears. Margaretha Geertruida merely smiled and bit her lip. And one soldier of the guard exclaimed in admiration: "That one, my God, she knows how to die."

Placed in Cell #12 at Saint-Lazare, she lived out her last weeks in the company of three Sisters of Mercy who formed an intimate guard for her. Her hope was not utterly erased by the verdict. Maître Clunet continued to marshal an array of powerful figures in his efforts to gain clemency. He even went so far as to ask President Poincaré to intervene in the name of their friendship. But nothing availed. Still, most Frenchmen, convinced as they were that Mata Hari was guilty of everything charged to her, felt that someone, somehow would get her off—if not through influence, then by rescuing her from the prison. Some, naïvely, felt the Germans would engineer a release or an escape. And one persistent rumor centered on a degenerate nobleman, supposedly named Pierre de Mortissac, who had dissipated a fortune and had once tried to win Mata Hari from a German lover. It was said that even though this de Mortissac had known all sorts of women as he ran through his millions, he had never really been in love until he met the Red Dancer. His passion for her became a life-long obsession, surviving the efforts of his German rival to discourage him, surviving rejections from Mata Hari herself, and surviving long periods of separation from her. His "plan" to free her, and so claim her, was designed to win the heart of any lady who has been to too many movies or to a few Italian operas. The officer of the firing squad was said to have been bribed to have his soldiers fire blank cartridges during the execution. Mata Hari's arms were to be loosely bound, so that she could sink to the ground as the blanks went off. Thus, she would be able to crumple up and feign death as the troops marched by her after she was supposedly killed. Her body was then to be placed in a coffin specially built so that she could breathe underground, and she was to be buried in a grave that was dug abnormally shallow. A select group of de Mortissac's agents could then dig her up and spirit her away to the arms of the certain-to-be-rewarded lover.

Many people have accounted for Mata Hari's poise during her last weeks as proof that she was "well aware" that de Mortissac's rescue would be effected. Though imperious and demanding during her early days on "death row," she did become remarkably tractable and resigned before the end. Without doubt she believed that one or another of her influential friends would prevail. At any rate, it is a fact that she danced for the Sisters the day before her death, that she slept well the night before the execution which was scheduled for 5:47 in the morning, and that she held the hand of one of the Sisters to reassure her just before the final moments. This one, in fact, did know how to die.

Clunet was not to be outdone by de Mortissac, however. Frustrated in all his attempts to gain clemency through influence, the urbane lawyer is reported to have pulled a final ploy just before the execution took place. Knowing that under the French penal code a woman who is carrying a child cannot be executed, he announced Mata Hari to be pregnant. When he was countered with the fact that no possible lover had visited the accused in her cell, he gallantly admitted that in spite of his seventy-two years he was the father. Mata Hari was actually greeted the morning of her execution by a group of French officials bearing both the unhappy news that Clunet's pleas had failed and the hope that if she were indeed pregnant with her seventy-two-year-old lawyer's child she could not be executed for a while. To her credit, if not to her kindness, she burst into laughter at Clunet's suggestion and dismissed her final hope, one of her comments being that on any other day she would not forgive the gentlemen from awakening her at such an hour.

Margaretha Geertruida Zelle was executed at Vincennes on October 15, 1917. Before she faced her death, she was baptized by an Anabaptist minister, and she faced the firing squad without covering her eyes. She offered no excuse for her life or her treasons, and she gave the world no Nathan Hale-ism to remember her by.   Her last words, addressed to the young officer in command, seem to have been: "Merci, monsieur"—a simple phrase, but one that does carry a certain meaning considering the life she had led.

As so often happens when a notorious figure dies, word immediately spread that Mata Hari had not really been killed. The idea that she had escaped her fate and been carried off by the lovesick de Mortissac (to some foreign land where they are dancing out a life of luxury and lasciviousness) re-kindled at once. In truth, some of the details of the de Mortissac "plan" did come to pass.   The gendarmes never did bother to knot the rope with which they tied Mata Hari. Her body did slump. And her grave was soon empty.   However, she did die, just as surely as Hitler and Gandhi and King Arthur died. A doctor examined the body after the shots struck home and declared her dead. However, as there was no one to claim the corpse, a medical school disinterred it and spirited her off to their dissecting rooms. For those who accepted this a-romantic medical end to the greatest spy of them all, legend still offers succor.   Another rumor reported that de Mortissac, knowing his plans had failed and that his beloved Mata Hari was dead, had retired to a Spanish monastery where he is measuring out his old age, an Abélard frustrated in both similar and different ways.

There is no doubt something awe-ful in the utter self-centeredness of Margaretha Zelle. To be able to sacrifice 50,000 youths in a businesslike exchange for luxury, approbation, and excitement and never give their tragedies a thought is a proposition almost impossible for "a properly brought up young person" to conceive. Still, the very scope of her immorality demands a certain respect, and we have a niche of heroism in our cultural heritage where she and others with her sort of intensity can fit and be honored. One mustn't forget that much of our literature has "advocated" the Devil, whose agents have proven more interesting, on the whole, than Virtue's soldiers. The "best role" in the morality play is always Vice. The hero of *Paradise Lost* is Lucifer, not the Winner. Actors squabble to play Iago, while Robin Hood, Jesse James, Bonnie, Clyde, Billy the Kid *et al* have had movies and TV shows to glamorize their deviations.

Nowhere has this quirk in our moral nature been more obvious than in the American glorification of the outlaw. Citizens of a land cradled in rebellion, students of a history which has sanctified the chronic troublemaking of our Hancocks, Ethan Allens, and Tom Paines, we have always been happy to embrace rebels, particularly those who can rationalize their maladjustments by citing environmental hardship or cultural imbalance. So we pay our warm nickel to see Frank James, Shakespeare-quoting killer, as the main attraction in the Buffalo Bill Wild West Show, so we cluster about the marshmallow sticks to chorus the praises of a demented Pretty Boy Floyd, and so we reach out to the frozen soul of Eldridge Cleaver, as cozily and myopically removed from their villainies as we are from Iago, fretting within "the wooden O," or Lucifer flaming down the Ptolemaic sky.

What we have come to believe about Belle Starr is most characteristic. Called "completely bad all the way through" by Sylvester Violante, who knows more about the American West than anyone, Belle Starr has become a heroine for a life pattern which must have evoked "lewd delight" in whatever committee Satan assigned to review it. In fact, if the definition of a witch is a woman who has had sexual intercourse with the Devil, the odds alone may well have given her a literal initiation.

Myra Belle Shirley was probably born, like Abe Lincoln and a thousand others, in a log cabin—February 5, 1848, on the Missouri frontier. Her father was named John and her mother Elizabeth. No one knows much about Elizabeth, but John was a loner and a wanderer who bought 800 acres of land near Carthage and eventually became a tavern-keeper in the town. Belle spent her youth in Carthage and was educated there—actually quite thoroughly for the time and place. However, affairs such as "Bleeding Kansas" intervened. Raids like those of Quantrill and inevitable retaliations like those of Jim Lane and his Red Legs churned up the local youths, launching the careers of the James Boys and their cousins the Youngers, and ending the life of Belle's brother Edward, who died in the bushwhacking and shooting. Belle is given credit for participating too, at one point supposedly reconnoitering a Federal (that is, "enemy") camp and warning her brother's group of a planned attack. However, the source of this information is Frank James' "autobiography" *(Written by Him-self),* a volume considered by most scholars about as reliable as its author. One thing is sure: all this excitement was bad for the tavern trade. So Shirley sold out in 1863 and was soon "gone to Texas" to move in with one of his sons, Prescott, near Dallas. There the family seems to have established a reputation for hostility, crudity, and isolation that has echoed down to the present.

Meanwhile, back in Missouri, the Civil War came and went. Missouri ceased to be a healthy place for Confederate guerrillas, many of whom refused to let things simmer down and went right on with their pillaging after the war was over. Northern sympathizers tended to burn farms, lynch those who hung around, and forego any efforts aimed at "reconstructing" stubborn neighbors. Many of the most determined Southerners, like the Jameses and the Youngers, used Northern persecution as an excuse to continue "the fight," robbing banks, mugging Federal guards, and shooting up towns as though the war were still on. Though they were protected and aided by sympathetic friends in the area, things were uneasy for them. They were labeled "outlaws" (which indeed they Federally were), and prices were put on their heads. On February 14, 1866, Frank and Jesse James and the Youngers engineered the first "western style" bank robbery, shooting up Liberty, Missouri and killing a fourteen-year-old boy in the process. Public outrage was intense, and the sometime guerrillas fled to Texas to hide out until their smoke settled down. Most of the anecdotes that attempt to connect Belle Starr with Jesse James date from this period, and it may be that the Jameses, as well as their cousins, made use of the Shirleys' sympathy toward ex-Confederates, hiding out with them in their moments of need. At least Cole Younger did, one side effect being that Cole "saw and conquered" Myra Belle, who was pregnant by the time he rode off.

Much has been made of how handsome and what a ladies' man Cole Younger was. Tales are told of how he always stood up when a woman entered the room and how, even with eleven bullets in his body at Northfield, Minnesota, he struggled to his feet in the wagon that lugged him off to prison and waved at the ladies gathered round. It is little wonder that "every girl he met" fell madly in love with him. However, his pictures do not show him to have been particularly handsome. Evidently he had a good line, was theatrical, and most of all paid attention to women in a world where they were often handled like cattle. Whatever his appeal, it was strong enough for Belle, and daughter Pearl resulted.

Cole Younger had, however, no intention of marrying Myra Belle. Conveniently, she never pressed the issue, finding whatever solace she required in a string of eight "marriages" (not counting less permanent yokings) with a string of "bad guys" and "Indians." The names are hardly important now: Jim Reed, whose "wedding" to her was officiated by another outlaw, Jim Fischer, and who was killed by a member of his own gang; Blue Duck, a Cherokee who met her while negotiating over a herd of stolen cattle; Sam Starr, who actually did go through a sanctified service and was shot in a drunken brawl; Jim French, Jack Spaniard, Jim Middleton, Jim July (all of whom met violent deaths). They loved her, says folklorist Ben Botkin, "in a kind of sloppy, over-lapping fashion." Reed, who fathered her son Edward while they were hiding from the law in California, and Starr, who gave his name to what one wit called "her posterity," are the most important. But it was Cole Younger for whom she seems to have really "carried the torch" and when she built her famous home on the Canadian River in Oklahoma Indian Territory, it was Younger's Bend that she named it.

From 1875 to her death in 1889, Belle operated a kind of sanctuary for selected outlaws in the Indian lands. From Younger's Bend she supervised rustling, fenced stolen horses, and built a reputation as "someone you could trust while the heat was on." Although she helped many criminals flee the area, records do not show her to have been involved directly in such things as train robberies, bank jobs, murders, or "necktie parties."

Belle called her outlaw buddies "jolly good fellows," stressing that she wanted nothing to do with those "common thieves" who can be found in any locality and who would betray a friend or a comrade for their own gain. Sometimes, today, it is hard to realize that there were good and bad badmen in the old West. But there really were, and the ex-Confederate outlaw is closer to

today's revolutionary guerrilla than to anything else. The men
Belle Starr harbored were ex-farm boys, brought up no worse
than any farm boy of that era. Many of them had simply become
involved in the Kansas-Missouri skirmishes when very young—
the Jameses and Youngers were teen-agers when they began raid-
ing. When the war ended they were young adults who knew nothing else. They had no desire to go back to the drudgery of the farm,
they were scared to settle down where Northern revenge might
reach them, and in some cases they were grotesquely unrecon-
structable. When they robbed a train or a bank, they weren't
doing anything that differed markedly from what they had done
for years, and a good many of the local folk applauded their efforts. In spite of an "accident" now and then, they respected
"non-combatants," trying hard not to harm women, children, or
preachers. Brought up in family environments, they respected
home and mother and knew well the value of women in a world
that had few about. They also had learned a bit of "readin' and
writin' " (Frank James could quote Shakespeare), knew the Bible
and had attended church when little (the Youngers are supposed to have sung in a Dallas choir in between "jobs," while Bill
Doolin threw Red Buck Weightman out of the Dalton gang for
shooting a minister). They expected, and got from their comrades,
"decent Christian burials," and though it is hard to see what such
"jolly good fellows" planned to tell St. Peter, they were not the
genetic and environmental derelicts that make up the "common
thieves . . . in any locality" either.

Belle Starr was the first woman tried for a major crime before
"Hanging Judge" Parker in the Federal Court of the Eastern Dis-
trict of Arkansas at Fort Smith. In 1883, along with husband Sam,
she was charged with being "the leader of a band of horse
thieves." The trial caused a sensation and the press did much during it to color her career and insure her fame. She was judged
guilty and given a six months sentence. Sam got a year. They
both served their time in Detroit. Before leaving, Belle is said to
have written a letter to Pearl in which she apologizes to her child
for her sins. The language of the "extant text" is somewhat confusing, as Pearl was "full-grown," had already "been on the
stage," and had developed a solid reputation as a madam by the
time of her mother's sentence.

I shall be away from you a few months, baby, and have only this con-
solation to offer you, that never again will I be placed in such humiliat-
ing circumstances, and in the future your little tender heart shall never
more ache, or a blush be called to your cheek on your mother's account.

The note goes on to philosophize that the prison "is said to be
one of the finest institutions of its kind in the United States, surrounded by beautiful grounds and fountains and everything that
is nice" and that there "I" can have "my education renewed"
and that Sam can "attend school . . . the best thing that ever happened for him."

Actually Sam spent his months in prison on the rockpile and
came out as ignorant as he went in. Belle also had little to do
with books. She made chair bottoms out of split cane. However,
both were docile and were released with time off for good behavior. Yet by 1887, Sam Starr was dead, killed in a drunken
argument with an Indian deputy, and Belle was "remarried" to
another Indian, Jim July, who had his name changed to Starr to
"make things more pleasant" for his new mate. That same year,
she was again arrested for horse-stealing, though the case was
dismissed, while son Ed, less fortunate, took his summer vacation behind bars in the Federal Penitentiary at Columbus, Ohio.
Pearl "baby," not to be outdone, had selected the spring to present her mother with a bouncing, illegitimate grandchild.

Belle died a death not unlike those of most of her lovers, shot
by a bushwhacker near her home on February 3, 1889. She would
have been forty-one two days later. No one knows who committed the crime, or what was the motive, if there was one beyond
robbery. Many rumors centered on a neighbor named Watson,
but such interesting candidates as Jim Middleton, brother of lover John Middleton; Jim July-Starr, her husband; and son Ed
have been considered. Pearl hired a stonecutter to put an inscription on the monument that now rests over her mother's
weed-covered grave, near the site of her famous home. It reads:

Belle Starr

Born in Carthage, Missouri, February 5, 1848

Died February 3, 1889

Shed not for her, the bitter tear,
Nor give the heart to vain regret,

> 'Tis but the casket that lies here,
> The gem that fills it sparkles yet.

On the top of the stone was carved the likeness of Belle's favorite horse, Venus. In a way it is too bad Pearl didn't include Belle's description of herself: "A woman who has seen much of life." Compared to most ladies of her day, she had indeed.

Woody Guthrie, the composer-singer whose naïveté and inspiration usually flew well in advance of his training, once endeavored to compose a poem about Belle in the fashion of François Villon's "Ballade of Dead Ladies." The result begins:

> Belle Starr, Belle Starr, tell me where you have gone
> Since old Oklahoma's sandhills you did roam?
> Is it Heaven's wide streets that you're tying your reins
> Or single-footing somewhere below?

To Guthrie, this Oklahoma "bad girl" is a sort of poor man's "snow of yesteryear"—truly belle, a dazzling Maid Marian who led a happy-go-lucky group of Lincoln Greens through the "glorious days of the Old West."

> Eight lovers they say combed your waving black hair,
> Eight men knew the feel of your dark velvet waist,
> Eight men heard the sounds of your tan leather skirt,
> Eight men heard the bark of the guns that you wore.

Persons who are content with Guthrie's physical description of Belle are also happy to accept other "facts" about her: for instance, that she was educated, a talented musician, and a complete "lady" at all times. Legend tells us that she wrote continuously, kept a piano in her living room, and demanded courtly conduct from the heterogeneous group of outlaws, bushwhackers, and half-breeds that made up her court. "And if she was a bit rough, foul of mouth, and extra-legal in her activities, she had a 'heart of gold', could out-ride, out-shoot, and out-swagger any man she ever met."

The truth differs. Unlike Mata Hari, or many other daughters Satan has unleashed upon decency, Belle Starr was not beautiful,

Belle Starr, shown at left with her paramour "Blue Duck," got a most touching tombstone (center). But what admirer could have foreseen her reincarnation as Gene Tierney (right) in the 1941 movie?

not even "attractive." Nor was she goodnatured or "a lot of fun." John Horan once described her as "a hatchet-faced woman with the disposition of a rattlesnake." Still, she had certain assets. First, she was about the only thing available. Second, she had "easy ways" and her willingness to hop into bed undoubtedly served to improve her "complexion" (as the Elizabethans would have called it). Third, the men she consorted with were no matinee idols themselves and didn't expect any more bouquet in their women than they did in their liquor.

Nor was Belle a woman of any learning. Her formal education had consisted of a few years at the Carthage Female Academy, a private establishment that taught its "young ladies" such arts as readin' and 'ritin', plus 'rithmetic, and exposed them to deportment, music, and the classics. She was literate all right. She could speed through the federal "Wanted" posters that were of interest to her and write letters, and probably knew that Homer and Virgil weren't off-oxen, but educated, say the way her contemporaries Susan Anthony, Lydia Pinkham, or Queen Victoria were—hardly. Undoubtedly she could play the piano. But her ladylike behavior was as "relative" as her larnin'. Belle almost always dressed in a long dark velvet gown, carried six-shooters at her side, and rode side-saddle with a high collar, chiffon waists, and black leather boots, often crowning the effect with a cream-colored Stetson with an ostrich plume. The gown and the style of riding gave her a feminine (not a ladylike) appearance and encouraged anecdotes such as the one about the time her hat blew off while she was riding with Blue Duck near Fort Smith. Her consort, untutored Cherokee that he was, made no move to retrieve it. Belle decided a lesson in decorum was called for, so she whipped out her pistols and told the "ignorant bastard" to "get the hell down and give a lady her hat again" or she'd blow his ever-lovin' brains out.

The big thing, of course, was that Myra Belle Shirley did things that people who go to Sunday School and then get married think they would like to be doing. And she did those things with a flair, attracting "considerable attention wherever she goes" as the Dallas *News* once commented—"a dashing horse-woman and exceedingly graceful in the saddle." With her mount named "Venus" and her concern for those "jolly good fellows," she was able to establish a reputation for hospitality, humor, and honor among thieves. The dime novelists took her up, largely because her sex gave her a uniqueness in the western outlaw history available to their "research." Richard Fox was particularly drawn to her activities, filling his *Police Gazette* with columns about her, labeling her "The Petticoat Terror" and "The Female Jesse James." It was in those pink pages that her legendary character developed, the plots centering on her humor, her musical talents, and her honor—which always remained bright within her own frame of morality. The *Police Gazette* had her, like Huckleberry Finn, cast aside town life because of her natural independence, lawlessness, and nomadic soul, having her rob trains, hold up stagecoaches, and shoot it out with lawmen—things the real Belle never cared to do. They even mixed her up with Belle Boyd, the notorious Confederate spy, and gave her a role in the Civil War. Because the *Gazette* was so widely read in the Old West, the real

Belle Starr and the fictitious one quickly became confused, blending in the rumor mills, the news accounts, and ultimately in the legends that developed about her.

But Belle Starr was not the girl a man "who had a mother" brought home. Her activities are only colorful and appealing when they exist in history or fiction or imagination where some God (Time or The Author or Unreality) can protect us from the havoc she would wreak upon our necessary ways. When Lucifer is able to introduce her into our everyday lives, she becomes every bit as real a threat to our "armies of unalterable law" as another of his agents was to the cause of God and our Allied Country.

8

INTO THE EARS OF BABES

Each age, whether hunting and gathering or industrial, finds it
necessary to have its Mother Goose, or several of them, with
rhymes and tales which instruct the goslings how golden eggs
are laid and how the huffing wolf is kept from the door. Traditionally the role has fallen to women, to the Cleopatras, the Sweet
Helens, even the Cressidas and Belle Starrs, transposed to mom-
mies and grannies. But in societies where women have flown this
particular nest, the group has seen fit to re-assign the task, if
only to the daily attentiveness of the comic strip or the warm
breast of the TV tube. For it appears that whatever wonders
are to issue out of the mouths of babes must be poured into their
ears first.

Mother Goose is a force, then, as real a force as sex or evil,
and mankind has seen fit to glorify the narrators of what the
Britishers William and Cecil Baring-Gould once referred to as
"Nobody-Really-Knows" lore. The Baring-Goulds' name is a
good one, not only for the texts which range from counting-out
jingles, tongue-twisters, and simple stories to weather verse and
prayers, but also for the goose-mother herself. Actually the
rhymes and stories are but a folklore of children, learned by little
boys and particularly little girls in the kindergartens of history,
used for a year or two as caches for wisdom or as accompani-

ments to simple games, then passed along to the "next generation" of kids, ending up in some warm corner of the memory.
Because they are folk, editors and compilers who publish them
forth in chapbooks, "garlands," and "melody miscellanies" often
print the resultant volume under the aegis of an author with a
never-never name like Peter Puzzlewit, Gammer Gurton, Tom
Thumb, Mother Hubbard or Mother Goose. Most such "pseud-
onyms" have long since been forgotten or gone to serve other
masters: Gammer Gurton her Tudor "W. S.," Tom Thumb his
Henry Fielding and P. T. Barnum, Mother Hubbard her Sarah
Martin, so that the field of children's rhyme has been left to
Mother Goose. And rightly left to her. She was perhaps the first
such anonymous author—and has always been the most popular.

In spite of wild speculation that has identified Mother Goose
with figures as fanciful as the Queen of Sheba, the chances are
extremely good that the name comes from France where the
peasants long retained the belief that there is a bird-mother who
tells tales to children. This bird-mother is now impossible to identify. Because the motif is widely known among the Celts, perhaps she was once a feminine creator in the hierarchy of gods
worshipped by a Breton group long since overwhelmed by the
mix of Gauls, Franks, and Romans that has given us France.
For *Genesis* to the contrary, the mythologies of many peoples
have been quite willing to postulate that a "hen" (as well as the
"egg") preceded the rooster. Stith Thompson's *Motif-Index of
Folk Literature,* where such matters are filed, offers a good many
examples of female-creator motifs running from "Creative
mother as source of everything" and "Old Woman as creator" to
a story that explains how man began from some salty stone acti-
vated by the licking tongue of a great Cow.

Bird-mother Goose may well have explained to some savage
brain the origin of children or how children are to be reared.
Animal nurses, at least, are known world wide in folklore. There
is, of course, the famous wolf who suckled Romulus and Remus,
as well as bison-, serpent-, bear-, tiger-, and even crab-mothers.
One African Zulu story tells about a bird that provided a family
with milk. Hidden by the woman who owned it, the bird each day
filled as many jugs as the family needed. The children, however,

discovered the bird, and, taking it out to play, lost it in the woods. Searching for it, they were caught in a terrible storm. The bird, grown enormous, appeared and protected them with its wings. When the storm was over, it carried them off and brought them up properly and carefully, eventually returning them safe, healthy, and well-trained to their family. From that time forth the villagers have worshipped the bird and they are supposed to be visited by it regularly. So there is much reason to suspect that some pre-French group left fragments of its own bird-mother, child-educator myth with those who came after them.

Naturally, if such a bird-mother is still remembered, she won't be remembered as a legitimate religious figure in a country that has become Christian. If people continue to believe in her, she will be treated as an historical or legendary figure and identified with recognizable settings. If people no longer believe in her, she will not necessarily be ignored, but may, like Br'er Rabbit, Anansi, and Juan Oso, survive as a never-never figure in märchen, to be grouped loosely with the other inhabitants of fairytale-land.

The bird-mother of France seems to have been remembered both ways. By the seventeenth-century the phrase "*comme un conte de la Mère Oye*" was a proverbial phrase and the goose-mother was an established matron of all sorts of children's rhymes, games, and philosophical bric-a-brac. Charles Perrault's famous 1697 collection of fairy tales (märchen) has a frontispiece that depicts an old woman spinning and telling stories to a cat and some children, and the subtitle for that book is *Contes de ma mère loye.*

On the other hand, there were already well-established efforts to identify her with Berte, who was both wife of Pepin and mother of Charlemagne. Berte lived until July 12, 783 and was considered to be a patroness of children. She evidently had one foot that was noticeably larger than the other, for she was called Berte *au gran pied* (not Berte *aux grands pieds* as some footnotes have it). As *La Reine Pedanque* her name has been translated by eager scholars as Queen Grosfoot or, better still, Queen Goosefoot. Whether the original Mother Goose or not, her name has attained genuine legendary status in France, where she is cited as one of the "dead ladies" by François Villon and where her early life follows the old folktale pattern already "lived" by the Trojan

Paris. Daughter of the King of Hungary, she is betrothed to Pepin. Blessed with a servant who looks almost exactly like her, she goes to meet her new husband. Because she feels ill, she asks the servant to spend the wedding night with Pepin. The faithless girl decides to continue as queen, and, between the sheets, persuades Pepin that the real Berte should be put to death. Berte is imprisoned, then taken out by an executioner to be killed in the woods. She is so sweet he cannot bring himself to do it, so he simply abandons her, figuring a bear or something will finish her off. Simon, *Le voyer,* comes by, finds her, and gives her a home. By chance, Pepin meets her, recognizes her, is told what happened, takes her to Paris, and has the false "queen" executed.

The whole matter is fogged by the fact that tradition frequently confuses Pepin's Berte with Berte, the wife of Robert II of France, who lived at the end of the tenth and the beginning of the eleventh centuries. The latter Berte is also associated with barnyard fowl and children. She was the daughter of Conrad, *Le Pacifique,* King of Bourgogne, and the first wife of Eude, the Comte de Chartres. She and Eude had five children. After his death, she found it expedient to marry Robert II in one of those medieval moves by which political interests were protected. Robert was, however, the godfather of one of her five children by Eude and so ineligible to marry her. There were other "spiritual" complications, and the confusion was sufficient that the church excommunicated him for the alliance. Rumor had it that the Lord revenged Himself on Berte and Robert by having her bear a child who was half goose. Rumor doesn't jibe with the fact Robert, under pressure, "excused" Berte about the year 1000 on the grounds she was sterile. Though he quickly married another, he seems to have been fond of Berte, for ten years later he tried to get the Pope to renegotiate his excommunication and the annulment-remarriage so that he and Berte could join again. The Pope refused.

That one or the other of the Bertes was the original Mother Goose is possible, but it is more sensible to speculate that their patronage of juvenile matters combining with the rumors of one's goose-footed build and the other's gosling-babe identified both with a once mythic bird-nurse already in tradition.

Legend's most persistent claimant to the crown of Mother

Goose is, however, a simple Boston woman who was named Elizabeth Foster. Practically nothing is known of her early, middle, or late years. She was born in Charlestown on April 5, 1665. Twenty-seven years later, she married a middle-aged widower with ten children and promptly bore him six more. His name was Isaac Vergoose, Goose, or Verboose (spellings were casual then), and they lived in a house on Washington Street, opposite Temple Place. Six years after her marriage, she joined Old South Church. In spite of having so many children, she seems to have known what to do, gaining a reputation for reciting rhymes to amuse her own brood and their friends. She was ninety-two when she died in 1757, and is allegedly buried in her son-in-law's family tomb in the Old Granary Burying Ground near a monument to another favorite of Americanists, Paul Revere.

Her oldest daughter, also named Elizabeth, was married by Cotton Mather to a hack printer, Thomas Fleet, in 1715 and these two kept house above his shop, "The Crown and Heart," on Pudding Lane, now Devonshire Street. Fleet is supposed to have published his mother-in-law's rhymes. Exactly how this came about is not known. Romantic speculation has it that he liked to listen to "grandma" cooing the verses to his baby son and decided to make the materials available to others. This idea is supported by the fact that a major portion of his business was devoted to children's books, broadsides, and playlets. The more cynical feel that "driven distracted" by her desire to be an "author" he printed the rhymes to keep the old girl off his back. For it has been reported that Mrs. Vergoose had nursed "publishing ambitions," as well as children, for some time.

No matter. About 1720 a volume of verse, claimed to be from the repertoire of Elizabeth Foster Vergoose, is reported to have sold for two coppers under the title *Songs for the Nursery or, Tales from Mother Goose.* Fleet's original edition of these rhymes has not been seen by a modern scholar. However, the second edition, subsequent revisions, and the offspring of Fleet's volume are still about. Over the years, the verses have been spiffed up, the illiteracies of Mrs. Vergoose eliminated, and her rhyming tuned a bit. If she actually is the author of some of the introductions attributed to her, Mrs. Vergoose had a rather inflated idea of her own literary merit. One reads:

My dear little blossoms, there are now in this world, and always will be, a great many grannies like myself, both in petticoats and pantaloons, some a deal younger, to be sure; but all monstrous wise and of my own family name.

These old women, who never had chick nor child of their own, but who always know how to bring up other people's children, will tell you with very long faces that my enchanting, quieting, soothing volume, my all-sufficient anodyne for cross, peevish, won't-be-comforted little bairns, ought to be laid aside for more learned books, such as THEY could select and publish.

Fudge! I tell you that all their batterings can't deface my beauties, not all their wise pratings equal my wiser prattlings; and all imitators of my refreshing songs might as well write a new Billy Shakespeare as another Mother Goose.

We two great poets were born together, and we shall go out of the world together.

> No, no, my melodies will
>   never die
> While nurses sing, or babies
>   cry.

However, the real question about Mrs. Vergoose is not how good she was vis-à-vis Billy Shakespeare, but whether she actually composed Mother Goose rhymes at all. Like most informants, she seems to have laid claim to all sorts of material that she took from tradition. Folksingers and tale-spinners do this all the time, pointing out the very mountain where Fair Charlotte lived before she froze to death on her way to the ball or taking you to the exact spot on the highway where the ghostly hitchhiker waited for a ride. To many informants the fact that they are the ones in the community who sing or tell the legends makes them the "authors" of those legends, and it may well be that Elizabeth Vergoose claimed authorship of Mother Goose material in this fashion. At any rate, while Mrs. Vergoose may have made up a ditty or two and known a flock more, she certainly didn't write "classics" like "Cock Robin," "Old King Cole," "Little Miss Muffet," "Tommy Tucker," "Jack Horner," "Jack and Jill," or "The Dish Who Ran Away with the Spoon," "The Man in the Moon," or

"Eeny Meeny Miny Mo"—all of which volumes like the 1833 *History of the Goose Family* have given her credit for.

In fact, the background of such old rhymes has absorbed scholars almost as thoroughly as has the identity of the bird-mother. In the Baring-Goulds' fascinating book, *The Annotated Mother Goose,* many theories of origin and explanation are set down. Most of them, whether correct or not, negate Elizabeth Foster Vergoose's claims to authorship. For example, even if the Cock Robin of

> Who did kill Cock Robin?
> I, said the Sparrow,
> With my bow and arrow

is not "a metrical rendering of . . . the Norse tale of the death of Balder, the god of summer sunlight," he most definitely was used to mock Sir Robert Walpole, the most powerful man in the English government during the "reign of good King Geo. I." Walpole, who functioned on the basis of the slogan: "Every man has his price," ran a ministry that was popularly called Robinocracy. Either way, Elizabeth Vergoose in Boston loses out. She surely knew nothing of Balder and even were she urbane enough to be satirizing London's Robert Walpole (a most unlikely chance), she did not create the verse she used. The "Cock Robin rhyme" seems to date from the Middle Ages, if only because the word "shovel," which was once pronounced as though spelled "shouell," is rhymed with "owl" in one variant.

Similarly, she surely knew nothing of Old King Cole, one of the legendary kings of ancient England; or of little Patience Muffet, whose entomologist father died among his collection of spiders in 1604. Nor did she make up the name Tommy Tucker, a very old label for someone who is grabby or selfish. The same sort of mind that is willing to accept Elizabeth Vergoose's authorship of the rhymes will be attracted to Katherine Elwes Thomas' 1930 book, *The Real Personages in Mother Goose,* in spite of the paradox that Mrs. Thomas identifies many Mother Goose characters with political figures Elizabeth Vergoose had never heard of. Mrs. Thomas sees Jack Horner as Thomas Horner, the fellow who sup-

posedly stole a plump deed to Mells Manor from a Christmas pie
in which he was delivering a dozen such documents to London.
This was in the days of the Dissolution under Henry VIII. She
sees Jack and Jill as Cardinal Thomas Wolsey and his coadjutor
the Bishop of Tarbes on their way to France to arrange the marriage of Mary Tudor. Miss Muffet, no entomologist's daughter,
is Mary, Queen of Scots, and the spider, John Knox, who de-
nounced her frivolity from his pulpit in St. Giles until he betook
himself to Holyrood, where he sat down beside her and, in his
own cobby way, demanded her recantation. The Dish and the
Spoon (the Court Taster of Food) who ran away together are none
other than Edward, Earl of Hereford, and Lady Katherine Grey,
sister of Lady Jane Grey. They annoyed Elizabeth R. with their
secret marriage and were confined to the Tower for seven years
where they passed some of the time by producing two children.

The fact that such politically oriented speculations have little
more chance of being accurate than the idea that Elizabeth Vergoose wrote them has bothered few editors. Many have gulped
down a bait even more tasty—namely, the attempts by early folklorists to identify nursery rhymes as residue of ancient myths.
The theory that Cock Robin is Balder is typical. Jack and Jill are
really Eddaic characters, Hjuki and Bil, the masculine name Bil
changed to Jill. "The Man in the Moon" is a folk memory of a
godly visitation to Earth. And "Eeny Meeny Miny Mo" is based
on an old Druid sacrificial chant.

This last theory was postulated by the late Charles Francis
Potter in no stranger reservoir of scholarly theory than *Harper's
Bazaar.* Using the older variant,

> Eena, meena, mona, mite,
> Basca, lora, hora, bite.
> Hugga, bucca, bau;
> Eggs, butter, cheese, bread
> Stick, stock, stone dead—O-U-T!

Potter showed that "meena" and "mona" referred to the Island
of Mona (now Anglesey) and the Menai Strait which separates
it from North Wales; that "hora" and "lora" are the Latin for the

fatal hour and the binding straps which held the victim; that
"bucca" was the Cornish word for hobgoblin. To Potter, the
references are clearly to the ancient Druidic sacrifices in which
victims, chosen by lot, were bound, placed in wicker baskets or
cages, and taken to the sacred island where they were sacrificed
to the gods. Eggs, butter, cheese, and bread are sacred foods,
used here as part of the incantation in order to confound evil
spirits. Even the word "eeny" is explained. "Eeny," it seems, is
the first word of an old Anglo-Cymric shepherd's score, later
used by fishermen to count fish: "Eeny, teeny, ether, fether, fip."
It combines with the final line "Stick, stock, stone dead—O-U-T!"
to indicate that the rhyme was part of the lottery selecting the
scapegoat.

For the exact reasons the whole Bird-mother Goose business
serves so well to illustrate the interworkings of folktale, it proves
too complex to be explained in terms of one person or one theory.
La Mère Oye appears to have served her time in myth, in legend,
and in märchen, to say nothing of the romantic doodlings of
"scholars." Today, her name covers all sorts of rhyming, singing,
playing, and yarn-spinning in all sorts of times and all sorts of
places. Hundreds of composers, bright children, and clever grannies have contributed their genius to this vastness, not only the
Bertes and Elizabeth Foster Vergoose, but the professionals like
the eighteenth century's Harry Carey (who wrote "Sally in My
Alley") and that child who decided "Eachy Peachy Don Ameche"
sounded appropriate for picking up jacks.

It would be inappropriate to leave Mother Goose and her
friends without indicating that all is not well with her world. In
1952 a British watcher of the morals, Geoffrey Handley-Taylor of
Manchester, observed that while "the average collection of 200
traditional nursery rhymes contains approximately 100 rhymes
which personify all that is glorious and ideal for the child" it is
unfortunate that "the remaining 100 rhymes harbour unsavory
elements." In one collection, for example, he finds two cases of
death by choking; one case each of death by cutting a human
being in two, decapitating, squeezing, shrivelling, starving, de-
vouring, boiling, hanging, and drowning, plus eight unclassified
murders; along with four cases of killing domestic animals, one

case of body snatching, seven cases of mutilation, two cases of masochism, and one of cannibalism.

In the twentieth century the "telly" and the comics have come under similar attacks. Perhaps this is because these modern "animal nurses" are elbowing Mother Goose aside and assuming her household duties. At least usurpers such as Little Orphan Annie have been able to shock the Handley-Taylors quite as well as a bird with a bonnet on. "Violence," wrote *Time Magazine,* "is the little carrot-top's constant companion: in one three-month period, 75 acts of murder or mayhem were committed within her ken. But Little Orphan Annie is insulated against all misfortune by one priceless possession: eternal youth."

For that matter, Annie's origin as well as her career is as spectacular as that of any bird-mother. Not only did she step fully-developed from the forehead of her creator, but she changed sex immediately after birth. Since then, bathed in a shower of gold, she has lived the plot of a sort of "mod märchen," set in history, but as fanciful as any tale of glass forests and giant beanstalks.

In 1924, Harold Lincoln Gray, a professional cartoonist working on the Chicago *Tribune's* "The Gumps" strip came up with an idea for his own cartoon. It centered around a little orphan named Otto, then Andy, whose sex was switched because the publisher Joseph M. Patterson remarked upon seeing Gray's pilot: "The kid looks like a pansy," and suggested they draw a skirt on him. "Make it for grown-up people, not for kids," he added. "Kids don't buy papers. Their parents do." The name Annie was borrowed from James Whitcomb Riley's widely read Hoosier poem,

Little Orphant Annie's come to our house to stay,
An' wash the cups an' saucers up, an' brush the crumbs away,
An' shoo the chickens off the porch, an' dust the hearth, an' sweep,
An' make the fire, an' bake the bread, an' earn her board-an'-keep;
An' all us other children, when the supper-things is done,
We set around the kitchen fire an' has the mostest fun
A-list'nin' to the witch-tales 'at Annie tells about,
An' the Gobble-uns 'at gits you
      Ef you
      Don't

Watch
Out!

and a character who was to become as familiar as Mother Goose herself entered American tradition.

Little Orphan Annie flourished until Gray's death in 1968; in fact, was kept going for almost six years after by five successors. Gray, who grew up on a farm near Chebanse, Illinois and who was in the Class of '17 at Purdue, had many of the political and social biases normally associated with the rural Midwest. These he enthusiastically incorporated "for the grown-up people." Annie, who solves her problems with the "I, the jury" technique later made famous by such activists as Mike Hammer and James Bond, dislikes many of the things the Chicago *Tribune* has been famous for disliking over the years—in particular Madison Avenue, the welfare state, Lord Keynes, and whatever else is left of center. Accompanied by the expletive "leapin' lizards" and her "arf-ing" dog, Sandy (he looks like a cross between a polar bear and a German shepherd), and in conjunction with her billionaire foster father, Daddy Warbucks, or his two devoted enforcers, Punjab and Asp, she enters town after town to right wrongs and solve crimes with a dispatch even the Lone Ranger has never matched. In the process she outboxes bullies twice her weight and strength, outwits gangsters and petty politicians who have spent a lifetime perfecting their trades, and reforms misers more devoted to their crabbiness than Scrooge ever was. All this in spite of the fact she is about twelve years old; in spite of the fact she is, as *Time* called her (9-4-'64), "physically deformed, an achondroplastic with legs like sewer mains and untenanted circles for eyes"; and in spite of the fact that Warbucks "dependably defaults whenever she needs him most" and has never "given her an extra dime."

Still, robber baron Warbucks, who appointed himself Annie's guardian in 1924, clearly fashioned his ward's standards before he let her and the dog go it alone. A munitions tycoon who made fortune after fortune in war-profiteering, Warbucks believes in the old adage that there are just two kinds of people: winners and losers. And when the chips are down you turn to the "winners" for guidance, power, and final decision. His philosophy is frequently given dramatic illustration in the strip. "I suppose," he remarks during one climax, "plenty of fine, kindly folks would be aghast at our drowning these fifty cutthroats before they could kill us."

Annie was one of the winners. In the nearly forty-five years Gray drew the strip, she never let "Daddy" down. Living on her "grecian urn", she and Sandy have remained without humor, uncompromisingly reactionary, their singleness of purpose and threshold of pain to be marveled at. During their crusade, this righteous twosome amassed a host of enemies who, because they were beyond the confines of the strip, were also beyond the intervention of Gray. These have been ministers, teachers, lawyers, and advertisers who took umbrage at her influence on vast audiences (at one time the readership of 350 newspapers) to whom she drummed the iron fist-velvet glove lesson that crime is best solved by wiping out the criminals and that the person who is basically honest ("with a heart of gold," Gray said) and can take care of himself is the only person worth his chemicals. "Sweetness and light—who the hell wants it?" Gray remarked to a *Time* reporter. "Murder, rape, arson. That's what stories are made of."

*The indestructible
Little Orphan Annie.*

And along with Jack London, Joseph Conrad, Theodore Dreiser, and Ernest Hemingway, he saw the strong as having the best chance of weathering life's plots.

But Annie made friends too. Even today, almost a decade since Gray died, an older group will reminisce at a cocktail party by breaking into snatches of the song that introduced her radio program in the 1930s.

> Who's the little chatterbox?
> The one with curly auburn locks,
> Who can she be?
> It's Little Orphan Annie.
>
> She and Sandy make a pair.
> Never seems to have a care,
> Cute little she,
> This Little Orphan Annie.
>
> Bright eyes, always on the go,
> There's a store of healthiness—and
> If you want to know,
> "Arf", says Sandy. . . .

For there are still people who can find an Ovaltine mug in the attic and who have long felt a security knowing "she was there" in the daily paper (maybe in life, too)—even if they never read a strip for months on end. And Little Orphan Annie did "come to our houses to stay," developing for many Americans the same reality that Tom Sawyer's fence and Elizabeth Vergoose's talents have developed—a reality which almost makes her märchen-like adventures a part of our legendary past.

There is, however, an urge in man that won't let even the maternity of Mrs. Goose or the independence of Orphan Annie gravitate free from sex. For in these post-Freudian and post-Jungian days, it is fashionable to see everything, whether its present form is legend, märchen, comic strip, or novel, as related to myth and those rituals myth symbolizes. The fashion reflects a belief in what Jung called the "collective unconscious" and a feeling that all men in all times use similar symbols to express their similar urges, and has enabled its true believers to uncover all sorts of memories of past crises, mass psychological conflicts, and group-shared dreams in story matter (in nursery rhymes and Ovaltine promotion) that once seemed most direct and easy.

Erich Fromm's extreme interpretation of the story of another little girl, Red Riding-Hood, reflects most the dangers inherent in what one cynic described as "the dreamy approach to literature." It appears in his suggestively titled book, *The Forgotten Language* (i.e.: the language of myths, dreams, and the unconscious).

Fromm uses a text which he calls "Little Red-Cap" and for which he cites no source, locale, or date. #333, "The Glutton" (Red Riding-Hood) is described as follows in Stith Thompson's *The Types of the Folktale,* the professional's handbook for such matters:

The Glutton. (Red Riding Hood). The wolf or other monster devours human beings until all of them are rescued alive from his belly. Cf. Types 123, 2027, 2028.

I. *Wolf's Feast.* (a) By masking as mother or grandmother the wolf deceives and devours (b) a little girl (Red Riding Hood) whom he meets on his way to her grandmother's.

II. *Rescue.* (a) The wolf is cut open and his victims rescued alive; (b) his belly is sewed full of stones and he drowns; (c) he jumps to his death. Motifs:

I. K2011. Wolf poses as "grandmother" and kills child. Z18.1. What makes your ears so big? F911.3. Animal swallows man (not fatally).

II. F913. Victims rescued from swallower's belly. Q426. Wolf cut open and filled with stones as punishment.

Thompson lists many European printings of the tale, the sources ranging from Scandinavia to Turkey, from Russia to France, even including Puerto Rico and the West Indies. Generally, the plot is pretty well standardized. Most of the variants available today stem from a 1697 book, Charles Perrault's *Petit Chaperon Rouge,* though the *Kinder- und Hausmärchen der Brüder Grimm (Grimm's Fairy Tales)* is a source of the more complex texts. *The Standard Dictionary of Folklore, Mythology, and Legend* actually goes as far as to state "the story . . . seems literary to the extent it derives from Perrault and the Grimms." As just about all the texts derive from these two compilers, this is tantamount to saying that were the story ever traditional its tradition has died out and its popularity is due to the printed texts. In Perrault's version, the adventure ends when the little girl is eaten. However, in Grimm, a hunter appears and, killing the wolf, slits him open. Little Red Riding-Hood and her grandmother both emerge undigested from the wolf's stomach. As the tale has traveled, it has varied a bit. In one Italian text, often called "Caterinella," the little girl goes to the wolf's house to borrow a pan in which to make fritters. On the way back she eats the fritters herself and then, rather boldly for a little thing, substitutes horse-buns in their place. The wolf is understandably irritated, and though she hides from him he sniffs her out and eats her. In a Russian variant called "The Cannibal Godfather" that guardian of her soul is the one who devours her. In Africa, the tale sometimes mingles with "The Three Little Pigs." The wolf eats little goats or pigs left unguarded at home by their mother, only to have a hunter cut open his stomach, rescue the "kids," and put rocks in their place so that the wolf sinks and drowns when he jumps in the water. The heroine is called Tsélané in Botswana, and she stays home when her parents go forth to find fresh pastures for their cattle. A cannibal, who has swallowed hot stones to make his voice sound like that of her mother, deceives Tsélané into opening the door. He puts her in a bag and lugs her away. But he gets thirsty and, leaving the bag with a group of little girls, goes to find water. The girls run and tell Tsélané's mother, and the mother puts scorpions, vipers, and a dog in the sack in place of her daughter. When the cannibal returns from his drink and opens the bag for a feast, the scorpions, vipers, and dog bite him. In the Western Sudan the tale is told with a hyena replacing the wolf, and on the Guinea Coast "Little Red Riding-Hood" is a boy.

Erich Fromm quite arbitrarily selected but one variant of this complex group for analysis, treating it as though it were the only way human beings tell the tale and interpreting the events without regard for the whole picture. His unidentified text is, he writes, "a good illustration of Freud's views while at the same time offering a variation of the theme of the male-female conflict. . . ." For folklorists, his commentary has become "a good illustration" of how and why psychologists and psychiatrists ought to be careful to learn something about folktales before they fool around with them.

Fromm bases his remarks on three ideas. 1) Folktales like "Little Red Riding-Hood" are culture dreams, standing in relation to the culture as a whole the way every-night dreams do in relation to individual lives. They can, like every-night dreams, be interpreted by trained psychologists. 2) There was a time when women ruled a matriarchal world. Eventually, female rule gave way to male rule, creating a conflict which is still echoed in our folktales. 3) The story of "Little Red-Cap" (as he suggestively entitles the variant he analyzes), properly interpreted, not only preserves this battle of the sexes in symbolic form but reveals how ever-present the conflict is in today's unconscious. His "once and only" interpretation is given below:

Most of the symbolism in this fairy tale can be understood without difficulty. The "little cap of red velvet" is a symbol of menstruation. The little girl of whose adventures we hear has become a mature woman and is now confronted with the problem of sex.

The warning "not to run off the path" so as not "to fall and break the bottle" is clearly a warning against the danger of sex and of losing her virginity.

The wolf's sexual appetite is aroused by the sight of the girl and he tries to seduce her by suggesting that she "look around and hear how sweetly the birds are singing." Little Red-Cap "raises her eyes" and following the wolf's suggestion she gets "deeper and deeper into the wood." She does so with a characteristic piece of rationalization: in order to convince herself that there is nothing wrong she reasons that grandmother would be happy with the flowers she might bring her.

But this deviation from the straight path of virtue is punished severely. The wolf, masquerading as the grandmother, swallows innocent Little Red-Cap. When he has appeased his appetite, he falls asleep. . . .

The male is portrayed as a ruthless and cunning animal, and the sexual act is described as a cannibalistic act in which the male devours the female. This view is not held by women who like men and enjoy sex. It is an expression of a deep antagonism against men and sex. But the hate and prejudice against men are even more clearly exhibited at the end of the story. Again . . . we must remember that the woman's superiority consists in her ability to bear children. How, then, is the wolf made ridiculous? By showing that he attempted to play the role of a pregnant woman, having living beings in his belly. Little Red-Cap puts stones, a symbol of sterility, into his belly, and the wolf collapses and dies. His deed, according to the primitive law of retaliation, is punished according to his crime: he is killed by the stones, the symbol of sterility, which mock his usurpation of the pregnant woman's role.

This fairy tale, in which the main figures are three generations of women (the huntsman at the end is the conventional father figure without real weight), speaks of the male-female conflict; it is a story of triumph by man-hating women, ending with their victory.

Fromm's three basic assumptions are at best "highly hypothetical," certainly not to be accepted without detailed documentation. Most likely they are "just plain wrong." One wonders how, exactly, Fromm *knows* the symbolic values he assigns to the incidents in his variant and why a relatively recent, most literary tale such as this one of necessity carries messages about a man-woman struggle that supposedly occurred generations before its composition. Of course, I have already stated that the matriarchal theory of civilization "lies wheels up in the junkyard of ideas" and that, while it sputters forth now and then, it is something against which respectable anthropologists brace themselves much in the way Elizabethan scholars brace themselves against the idea that "Shakespeare didn't write his plays." But probably the worst weakness in Fromm's discussion lies in the fact that he considers but one variant of the many Red Riding-Hood tales. Anthropologist Melville Herskovits, who reviewed *The Forgotten Language* in the *Journal of American Folklore* of 1953, was particularly troubled by this. He notes Fromm's selection of the title "Little Red-Cap":

Why Fromm prefers this translation of the title of the German version of "Little Red Riding Hood" one cannot say. Perhaps his predilection may arouse a suspicion that some unconscious mechanism was at work in his mind, for folklorists will find his rendition—its source not cited—has many incidents that are not present in the tale as commonly read by and recounted to American children. Certainly it will be of interest to folklorists to learn, for example, that the " 'little cap of red velvet' is a symbol of menstruation," to name but one of the hidden meanings of sexual significance revealed to us. It is a pity, however, since Fromm concludes that the "sexual act is described as a cannibalistic act in which the male devours the female," that he did not have recourse to the version in a book of fairy stories which I borrowed from a young neighbor. For in this version, when the little girl reached her grandmother's house and was told to "come and lie down" with the disguised wolf, she "undressed herself and got into bed" with him.

What, one ponders, would he have done had he consulted the African texts in which the male girl-eater places "Little Red Cap" in his bag or in which the heroine turns out to be a boy! Surely *Ma Mère L'Oye* and perhaps even the indomitable Orphan Annie would find their minds boggling before such Freudian perspectives.

9

LUCKY STARS

Bordered by primroses though it may be, few paths have led young women more directly to reward than the theater. Whether the aim is "a good marriage," fame and fortune, or simply a place in the sun, for about 300 years acting has been the way. Furthermore, nowhere since the doll house was built has woman attained the old "hunting and gathering parity" more completely than on the boards. There, salaries, publicity, recognition, and success or failure have been, if not "regardless of sex," "regardless of which sex."

It wasn't always that way. In England, for instance, not until the Restoration did women replace apple-cheeked boys in the feminine roles. This was when Charles II returned from the Continent (where such things had been going on for awhile) to re-establish public performances after a Puritan-imposed lapse of nearly twenty years. From the very first, the actresses' effect on men was a great asset. Not only did it broaden avenues for writers and producers, but it gave ambitious *belles* like Elizabeth Barry and Nell Gwyn a means of attracting attention which they were able to parlay into profitable attachments, often re-casting themselves at the very top of society's playbill. Perhaps it was their self-interest and open reliance on sex appeal that gave birth to the idea which by 1800 had been elaborated into the "star system"—the belief that the man or woman playing the role is more important than the drama in which it occurs or the author who wrote it.

A star at the apogee needs no particular vehicle, simply one that will show him or her off. The best, like Sarah Bernhardt, can make almost any role memorable as long as it is reasonably appropriate to her. Others, like Mae West, make all roles into the same role anyhow. And once in a while along comes a part which makes a star out of almost anyone who plays it. Polly Peachum in John Gay's *The Beggar's Opera* is, or at least was, such a role. Surely no other part in the history of the theater has taken such a variety of women so far.

The year 1728 was a bonus year for literature. Oliver Goldsmith was born, Alexander Pope published *The Dunciad,* and Gay's classic was produced. "First musical comedy," "democratic opera," "play with song," whatever you wish to call it, the theater had seen nothing quite like *The Beggar's Opera* before. Neither Gay nor his friends Jonathan Swift and Pope (who had given him the kernel of the idea and helped him through the writing of it), not even the producer, John Rich, had any idea whether it would succeed, much less become "the talk of the town." That it would run for sixty-two consecutive nights the first season (an incredible run for those days), that it would be produced every year until 1800, that it would continue to be played steadily throughout the nineteenth and twentieth centuries, or that it would be re-written, revised, and reviewed about the world for 250 years was nowhere among their "fondest hopes." But it did all these things, making as the saying went: "Rich gay, and Gay rich."

The plot is simple enough. Peachum, an opportunistic fence, betrays highwayman MacHeath. As MacHeath is married to Peachum's daughter Polly, he figures to gain control of a good bit of loot through this ploy. However, Polly loves MacHeath and doesn't want to see him hanged. MacHeath, on the other hand, has a number of girl friends. One, Lucy Lockit, helps him escape. But he is recaptured, tried, and condemned to death. Reprieved, he promises to remain constant to Polly, in spite of his song "How happy could I be with either."

Joseph Spence, in his *Anecdotes, Observations, and Characters* (London, 1828), records Pope as describing the first night this way:

We were all at the first night of it, in great uncertainty of the event; till we were very much encouraged by overhearing the Duke of Argyle, who sat in the box next to us, say, "it will do,—it must do!—I see it in the eyes of them."—This was a good while before the first act was over, and so gave us ease soon; for the duke, (besides his own good taste) has a more particular knack than any one now living, in discovering the taste of the public. He was quite right in this, as usual; the good nature of the audience appeared stronger and stronger with every act, and ended in a clamour of applause.

And James Boswell, in his *Life of Johnson,* cites one Mr. Cambridge as commenting:

that there was good reason enough to doubt concerning its success. He was told by Quin, that during the first night of its appearance it was long in a very dubious state; that there was a disposition to damn it, and that it was saved by the song,
            "Oh ponder well! be not severe!"
the audience being much affected by the innocent looks of Polly, when she came to those two lines, which exhibit at once a painful and ridiculous image,
            "For on the rope that hangs my Dear,
            Depends poor Polly's life."

However, *The Beggar's Opera* was written to succeed. Supposedly penned by a vagabond from St. Giles, it offered the bored public a fresh dramatic form, ballad-opera. Combining fashionable lyrics with widely popular English street tunes, its strong plot made fun of almost everything the audience wanted to see made fun of: the government, Italianate fashions in music, local London personalities. Written by a Tory, it struck out at the greed and graft of the Whig leader, Sir Robert Walpole; at his relationships with his mistress, Maria Skerrit; and at the freedom allowed petty criminals like Jack Sheppard and Jonathan

Wild. The characters were, or seemed to be, recognizable figures of the day.

MacHeath, a highway robber, is the lead, and Thomas Walker, playing him, was able to take the town by storm. Eventually he drank and roistered himself into oblivion. Legend has it that after performing MacHeath dozens of times, he forgot his lines. When chided by Rich, he replied, "I have a strong memory, but you can't expect it to last forever." The heroine, Polly Peachum, served the ladies every bit as durably. Lavinia Fenton, the first Polly, had formed a "permanent attachment" with a member of the nobility by the end of the opening season. Her successor, Miss Ann Warren, married a gentleman of some fortune. And four of their successors were "ennobled" by lords who were enamored of them in the role. The result was what has become known as the "Polly Peerage": besides Miss Fenton and Miss Warren, Miss Hannah Norsa (Lady Orford); Miss Mary Catherine Bolton (Lady Thurlow); Miss Catherine Stephens (Lady Essex); and Miss Mary Anne Paton (Lady Lennox). All of these women went into the part lowborn and, with the exception of Miss Warren, came out members of the ruling class.

Lavinia Fenton's rise was representative. According to her *Life (The Life of "Lavinia Beswick," alias "Fenton," alias "Polly Peachum"*—as sold in May, 1728 for one shilling), she was "nobody's daughter." Nobody seems to have meant an army lieutenant and the mistress of a coffeehouse. She attended boarding school for awhile, then "made her own way" by selling oranges in the theatre, singing ballads in her mother's establishment, and engaging in sundry "amours." In 1725, when she was seventeen years old, she decided to go onto the stage, getting a job at "the Hay." There she was "but little known," although she gained a certain distinction by having a duel fought over her. In July 1726, John Rich, the beleaguered owner of Lincoln Inn Fields, hired her to do a Davenant play. She was learning her trade—all facets of it.

At twenty, she was considered one of the promising theatrical singers of her day. Well-trained by her mother in music, well-versed by her experiences in coquetry, with physical grace, genuinely "flashing eyes," and a winsome way, she was armed to captivate the gentlemen of any audience. The role of Polly seemed made for her. William E. Schultz, who did a thorough study of *The Beggar's Opera,* describes her as follows:

The thief-taker's daughter, though a product of low life, is pictured as an innocent, earnest lass who looks at the world through big, round, credulous eyes; and who, never seeing through the falseness of her lover, adores him before and after his *execution.* Gay seems to want us to believe that the Captain really cares for Polly, though often deceiving her when his other amours are close to exposure; that his affair with her is different, being real romance. Polly, for all of the fact that we smile at her artlessness, remains a charming representative of her sex, a rose among thorns.

Although Lavinia Fenton played the role for but one season, January 29 to June 19, she started a vogue in all matters Polly. Pope wrote that "her pictures were engraved and sold in great numbers, her life written; books of letters and verses to her pub-lish'd; and pamphlets made even of her *sayings* and *jests.*" The ravings over her resulted in prints, Polly Peachum fans, and street ballads. Even Hogarth joined the throng, doing one of his earliest oil works of her—a likeness which now hangs in the National Gal-lery, London. The various journals and gazettes of the day printed a host of verses on her telling how *"Courtiers* and *Peers* contend in praising Thee."

> Ev'n thy *own Sex* thy shining Charms extol,
> And, young or old, acknowledge *pretty Poll;*
> While Envy *is itself in Wonder lost,*
> *And* Factions *strive who shall applaud Thee most.*

Particular emphasis was placed on her amours and the gentle-men who contested for her favors. One enterprising publisher even threatened to print a list of admirers "just as he had been provided it by the actress herself." He pointed out that the gen-tlemen whose names were to appear on this list could pay him according to their rank and have private matters kept secret, "if they so wished." The excitement to be caused later by Johann

Strauss, Benny Goodman, "Frankie Boy," or the Beatles was not to be greater.

Miss Fenton's biggest success was with "Oh Ponder Well," the very song that Mr. Cambridge claims "saved the opening night." Listed as Air XII, it comes during Scene X of the First Act when Peachum is planning to obtain "the comfortable estate of widowhood" for Polly by having MacHeath "peach'd the next Sessions" and hung. Polly, who loves her robber-husband, is aghast at the idea and sings to her parents:

> Oh, ponder well! be not severe;
> So save a wretched wife!
> For on the rope that hangs my dear
> Depends poor *Polly's* life.

The song carries little weight, however. Her mother upbraids her "for being particular." "Why, wench, thou art a shame to thy very Sex." "What would many a wife give for such an opportunity!" "Those cursed Play-books she reads have been her ruin." "Hang your husband, and be dutiful."

The melody is old. *The Stationers' Register* of 1595 licenses a song about two children abandoned to die in the woods. That title reads: *"The Norfolk Gentleman His Will and Testament—and how he commytted the keepinge of his children to his owne brother who delte moste wickedly with them and how God plagued him for it."*

> Now ponder well, you parents dear,
> These words which I shall write;
> An awful story you shall hear
> In time brought forth to light.

Also known as "Chevy Chase," it was a frequent "accompaniment" of broadside, chapbook, and songster lyrics, as well as being used in nineteen ballad-operas other than Gay's.

Whether Gay's variant saved the opening night or not, the song sung by Miss Fenton enraptured Charles Powlett, the Duke of Bolton, who was then forty-three years old. Night after night he attended Lincoln's Inn Fields to hear Lavinia Fenton sing. By the end of the season he was not only madly in love with her, but had taken her out of the role, off the stage forever, and set her up as his mistress. Gay wrote to Swift on July 6 of 1728, less than three weeks after the season had closed: "The Duke of Bolton has run away with Polly Peachum, having settled four hundred per year on her during pleasure, and, upon disagreement, two hundred more." Twenty-three years later, when he was sixty-six and she forty-three, he was to marry her and make her the Duchess of Bolton. There is a touching anecdote about this final arrangement. One day "Polly" and the Duke had a violent quarrel. He "dismissed" her in his rage. This was no small matter to a woman of her age; all seemed over. But as a last resort, Miss Fenton decided to try to recoup her fortunes by dressing as Polly and singing Air XVII, from Act I, Scene XIII:

> O what a pain it is to part!
> Can I leave thee, can I leave thee?

The heart of the Duke melted at once. Repenting his rage, he swept "Polly" into his arms, telling her she was no longer his mistress, but from then on his wife!

C. E. Pearce, who did a 1913 biography of Miss Fenton, seems to have been another who fell in love with Lady Bolton. He states bluntly that "in the hands of anyone but the ingenuous damsel of Lincoln's Inn Fields Theatre" the role of Polly Peachum would not have "achieved celebrity" and that the play itself "would simply have taken its place in the long list of dramatic productions the names of which alone" survive.

Despite Pearce's enthusiasms, the role continued to serve its other "occupants" nearly as well as it served Lavinia Fenton. What *Mist's Weekly Journal* had to say about the Irish performances of 1728 might well apply to every Polly for 100 years after: ". . . the Dublin Polly Peachum is already £150 the richer, and many Degrees handsomer for acting that Part." Miss Warren, who had the role during the second London season, took over much of Lavinia Fenton's success at once. The sister of a famous bone-setter at Epsom, one Mrs. Mapp, Miss Warren was always referred to as Polly by the press; had broadsides, verse, and poetry written about her; and had fans and the equivalent of T-shirts with her name emblazoned upon them. The Misses Sterling and Barbier in Ireland; Miss Norsa, who got the role when Rich moved his company to Covent Garden; even the famous Peg Woffington (who like many actresses often played MacHeath) used the role to further their purposes. Miss Woffington made her stage debut as Polly, when thirteen and working in a Dublin children's group. In 1759, Miss Charlotte Brent, a talented singer, had a great success with the role, the play lasting fifty-three nights that season. It even served one chap named Bannister who played the "innocent, earnest lass" for a farcical 1781 Haymarket production in which all the sexes were "most whimsically and indecently" reversed. The *St. James Chronicle,* commenting on his performance, remarks that it was given "with so much sensibility . . . that at length in Spite of his Figure, it almost grew affecting, and ceased to be ridiculous."

The stature that the role attained can be seen graphically from the feud which theater historians call the Clive-Cibber controversy. Two actresses—Kitty Clive, who had played the role as early as 1732, and Susannah Maria Cibber, *parvenue* though wife to producer-actor Theophilus Cibber, had a cat-fight over who would be Polly in the fall of 1736. The waulings were so vicious that they took up much space in the papers of November and December, absorbing almost all the energies of the theatrical gossips of the time. Miss Clive finally won out, and she, rather than the "upstart pretender" opened in the role.

One of the great charms of *The Beggar's Opera* was that it was considered to be immoral, not only in its own day, but for many years after. Daniel Defoe took a typical swipe at it in his *Augusta Triumphans,* three years before his death.

We take pains to puff 'em [rogues] up in their villainy, and thieves are set out in so amiable a light in "The Beggar's Opera" that it has taught them to value themselves on their profession, rather than be asham'd of it by making a highwayman the hero and dismissing him at last unpunished.

One critic comments on the whole matter after a 1920 revival, remarking that "A fierce brandy, a hundred years old, becomes

mild and agreeable. So Gay's opera, in its day capable of de-
bauching the debauched, will now do no harm and increase the
gayety of the town."

However, even when the brandy was still fierce, all the results
were not debauchery. One tale tells how a professional thief,
Joseph Powis, went to a performance and, seeing MacHeath
brought on stage in fetters, was seized with a fit of trembling in
fear that he too would someday be condemned. The "fever"
forced him to give up robbery for an entire week. The lesson
was not, it seems, enduring. In 1732 he graced a Tyburn tree for
burglary.

It is appropriate that the sequel to *The Beggar's Opera* was
entitled *Polly*. However, *Polly* didn't have the sort of success
"Polly" had enjoyed. Not only was it markedly inferior to its progenitor, but it never got out of rehearsal, being banned from the
stage by the Lord Chamberlain under orders from King George
II, who was undoubtedly counseled by Sir Robert Walpole and
his Whig followers. Gay, as well as his cronies Swift and Pope,
were "of the opposition," and *The Beggar's Opera* was scarcely
a subtle satire. First it included a character named Robin of Bag-
shot, whose unrefined manners, indulgent ways, robbery of the
public, and aliases (Bob Booty, Bluff Bob) all suggested Walpole,
who was widely called "Robin" by the public. Second, it included
an interrelationship between MacHeath, Polly, and Lucy Lockitt
which certainly suggested Walpole's relationship with his wife
and the merchant's daughter, Molly Skerrit, whom he kept and
eventually married. Third, persons involved in the politics of the
time could draw a parallel between the fathers, Peachum and
Lockit, who "go halves in MacHeath" and Walpole and Charles
Townshend who were "going halves" in the illegal rewards re-
sulting from the way they ran England. Although the play isn't
a frontal attack on the notoriously corrupt Walpole, there are
few opportunities through which Robinocracy, as the Whig
power was called, isn't taken to task.

Polly, which is really much milder than *The Beggar's Opera,*
was banned "because" and for no other reason. Gay did, however, reap a good harvest from it, even though it didn't see the
boards until June 1777, forty-five years after his death. Skirting

the ban on performances, he had it printed and offered for subscription. So hot an issue was this ploy that the Duchess of Queensberry, who took Gay's cause to heart, was asked to leave St. James by none other than His Highness. It seems she had been soliciting subscriptions to the printed *Polly* among the innermost circles of royalty—and was even discovered doing this by George himself. He sent a special messenger telling her that her presence at St. James was no longer fitting. Her husband, the Duke, rallied to her cause and in the resultant friction resigned his two posts under the crown. Neither appeared at St. James for many years, though the Duchess must have had some satisfaction when, in her old age, she did attend the first performance of *Polly*, forty-eight years "too late."

The role of Polly Peachum, daughter of a fence, wife of a highwayman, is a remarkable vehicle. No matter who plays it, somehow it remains unchanged, making all actresses one. It may be well that Mae West never tried, for truly that would have been the "irresistible force" meeting the "immovable role." Mae West never changes either. To her, all roles are one.

Mae West was born in Brooklyn, New York on August 17, 1892. Her father was Jack West, a brawler in and out of the ring; her mother was a corset fashion model. Talents that were to shape her career showed themselves early. At seven, dressed in pink and green satin with gold spangles and a white lace picture-hat, she won an Elks Amateur Night contest at the Royal Theatre on Fulton Street. She billed herself as "Baby Mae" and called her song and dance routine, "Movin' Day." This success prompted other routines: "Doin' the Grizzly Bear" and "My Mariooch-a Make-a da Hoochy-ma-cooch." By the time she was eleven, she had graduated to somewhat sterner roles in classics such as *Mrs. Wiggs of the Cabbage Patch, Little Nell,* and *East Lynne.* Soon she had developed another talent to go with the theatrics: a huge bust which protruded from her then 5' 2" frame. This adornment seems to have caught on with the local youths, making her a favorite with that audience. By fourteen she was in vaudeville, working with Frank Wallace, the only man ever to become her husband. They were married in Milwaukee when she was still seventeen, partly because a sager vaudevillian advised her that such a move would "look respectable." She left Wallace after a few months, though she didn't get around to divorcing him until thirty-two years later. She has never had children, letting what motherly urges well up release themselves in caring for pet monkeys.

She developed into a solid, but not totally successful, music hall performer, her "curriculum vitae" distinguished by a role opposite Ed Wynn in Rudolph Friml's *Sometime* and the performances through which she introduced the shimmy to white audiences. This embellishment was included after seeing blacks do it, and she was using it in her routines before Gilda Gray made it a national craze.

Mae West did not hit the big-time, that is Broadway, until 1926, when she and her mother produced Mae's own play about a waterfront prostitute after the Shuberts turned it down. Because her director kept insisting that the scenes "reeked sex" like nothing he had ever seen and that Mae had "a low sex quality," the play was named *Sex*—a daring title for the mid-twenties. It turned out to be a real hit, running for eleven months. Badly written, poorly acted, with a vaudeville-level scenario, it caught the fancy of the "flapper set" and "all the sad young men" because of its blatancy and its breezy approach to what was a generally taboo subject. Of course, the play was raided and the performers charged with indecent exposure, Mae herself being fined $500 and spending eight days in jail. The affair was a good investment, for the resultant publicity (emphasizing tidbits like: "Miss West's tender body, so used to silken underthings, is badly chafed from the prison clothes") made her into "a success."

She tried to follow *Sex* with the even higher voltage *Drag,* a play dealing with homosexuality. But "the Big Apple" wasn't ready for that one in the 1920s and the closest the play came to Broadway was Paterson, New Jersey. *The Wicked Age* and *Diamond Lil* followed. From the four she got her theme: shock and sex. And from *Diamond Lil* she honed the image that most people carry of her: the "she done him wrong" girl of the Bowery music halls. Well-kept, well-endowed, well-jeweled, Lil wed Mae to the song that was to become her trademark, "Frankie and Johnny."

Nobody cares, but the Diamond Lil "Frankie" is a musical-historical anachronism. Sung by a Gay Nineties music hall queen doing a 1920-style shimmy within a circle of refugees from the Charles Atlas body-building course, it came to be backed by a danceable, insinuating band playing ragtime as it was played in the 1930s. The heroine and her setting are a long way from the St. Louis "Tenderloin" and the mulatto prostitute about whom the text of the ballad was originally written. For the Frankie Baker who shot her lover at 212 Targee Street in 1899 was a *belle* of more sordid *nuits* than Diamond Lil.

"Employed" on a circuit that included such towns as Memphis and Omaha as well as St. Louis, Frankie Baker was involved with eighteen-year-old Allen Britt, whose only distinction is the rumor that he never wore a pair of full-length pants in his life. Britt was killed with a pistol that the understandably wary Frankie kept under her pillow, and the motive seems to have been his interest in "another woman." Police accounts stress the fact that he was black and she mulatto, and the "mug shots" extant show her to be of "doubtful beauty."

The ballad, almost certainly composed by a black, may well have been rewritten out of an older song. It was called "Frankie and Albert" (not "Johnny") and told the old black tale of a kept man, not a kept woman. It should be sung "blue," with a dirty guitar or "ragged" piano accompaniment, and through African vocal chords. It probably gained its popularity from the singing of Mammy Lou who worked Babe Conners' "high brown" bawdy house in St. Louis, where whites and blacks both heard it.

> Frankie was a good girl
> As everybody knows;
> She paid a hundred dollar bill
> For Albert a suit of clothes,
> Just because she loved him so.
>
> Frankie took them to him;
> Albert put them on,
> Went stepping off down the broad highway,
> Saying, "By, by, Honey, I'm gone
> For I'm your man who won't treat you right."

Frankie went to the beer shops
And called for a glass of beer,
Saying to the bar-room keeper,
"Have you seen little Albert here?"
"Oh, no, no, Frankie, no."

The keeper turned to Frankie,
Says, "Frankie I told you a lie;
He left here about an hour ago
With a girl he called Alice Fry;
I know he's your man; he won't treat you right."

Frankie went to the bar-room;
She called for a glass of gin,
Saying to the burie-be,
"I'm going to get drunk again;
I'll kill my man, who won't treat me right."

Frankie went down the broadway,
With a razor in her hand:
"Stand back all you loving girls;
I'm hunting my gambling man;
I'll kill my man, who won't treat me right."

She went down to the pool room;
She looked in the pool room door,
And there she spied the man she loved,
A-sitting in the middle of the floor,
Saying, "I'm your man who won't treat you right."

"Come to me, little Albert,
I'm calling through no fun;
If you don't come to the one loves you,
I'll shoot you with my old gun;
For you're my man, who won't treat me right."

Albert went behind the counter;
He fell upon his knees—
Look right up into Frankie's face,
Saying, "Frankie, don't shoot me please,
For I'm your man who won't treat you right."

Frankie got up next morning,
About nine o'clock.
She picked up that forty-four gun,
And fired the fatal shot,
She killed her man, who wouldn't treat her right.

"Turn me over, Frankie,
Turn me over slow;
Turn me over on my left side;
Those bullets hurt me so.
You've killed your man who wouldn't treat you right."

People all said to Frankie:
"Little girl, why don't you run?
Don't you see that chief police
With a forty-four smokeless gun?
You've killed your man who wouldn't treat you right."

Frankie went down to the river;
She marched from bank to bank;
"I've done all I could for a gambling man
And yet I got no thanks
For killing my man who wouldn't treat me right."

Frankie went to the funeral;
She rode in a rubber tired hack;
When they lowered him into the grave,
She screamed, "He'll never come back,
He'll never come back, he'll never come back."

Frankie had two children,
A boy and a girl;
She told them if they ever saw their papa,
They would see him in another world.
She killed her man who wouldn't treat her right.

Frankie sat in the court-room,
Fanning with an electric fan.
Whispering to her sister, she said,
"Never love a gambling man,
For all you do, he won't treat you right."

Judge said to the jury:
"Jury, I cannot see,
Though Frankie has killed the man she loved,
Why she should not go free
For killing her man who wouldn't treat her right."

Frankie walked out on the scaffold,
As brave as a girl could be,
Saying, "Judge, you tried me
Murder in the first degree,
For killing my man, who wouldn't treat me right."

Now little Frankie is buried;
She's sleeping by Albert's side;
Albert was a gambling man,
And Frankie was his bride;
She killed her man, who wouldn't treat her right.

"Frankie and Albert" had become an immensely popular folk song among both races when, in 1911, the Leighton Brothers decided to use it in their act. A vaudeville team which had a good bit to do with the popularity of "Casey Jones," too, they had the song rewritten and it was copyrighted for them and music composer Ren Shields in 1912. Their variant, with Allen-Albert's name changed to Johnny, became one of the "pop hits" of the day and was widely sung by troops during the First World War. As fate often has it in folk matters, these soldiers returning to their hill homes, farms, and ghettos brought the "Johnny" variant back with them. With its lively tune and more sophisticated lyric, it rapidly supplanted or modified the old "Frankie and Albert" ballad until today one finds the two so intermixed that separation is pointless. The hybrid, with a heroine who is called Josie, Maggie, Sadie, Lillie, and Annie, as well as Frankie, is the most widely sung and best known native American ballad. One scholar, Robert Gordon, was able to collect over 100 texts of it.

Frankie Baker, absolved of the crime, eventually ran a shoeshine parlor in Portland, Oregon, where she achieved a distinction few outright prostitutes have attained: she was given an award for good citizenship. However, with a sort of Calvinistic justice, the ballad continued to haunt her. Mae West had practically made it her own, and Paramount built the 1933 movie *She Done Him Wrong* around it. John Huston made a play of it. All sorts of singers and big bands recorded it (Guy Lombardo even re-setting it in a soda fountain for the teen-age set). In 1938 Helen Morgan, best known for sitting on a piano and singing "He's just my Bill," starred in a Republic pictured called "Frankie and Johnny." Frankie Baker decided to sue, and her lawyers focussed on Republic Pictures in a $200,000 claim for defamation of character and invasion of privacy. This was one of a series of famous cases involving folksongs, who wrote them, and who is harmed by them. Ones involving "Home on the Range" and "The Wreck of Old '97" are others. Because folksongs are so hard to date and because so many minds go into the development of their revisions and variants, such suits are legalistic nightmares. Frankie Baker never got a cent, and the case, which lingered in the courts until 1942, was dismissed. She died in Portland ten years later, on Old Christmas Day.

Still, it is only the experts who associate Frankie Baker with "Frankie and Johnny" these days. Mae West took the song from her and made what had been a sordid account of ghetto jealousy into a jaunty statement of one of the truisms of our culture: a woman has a moral right to take stringent measures against "her man" if he plays with her virtue and then "does her wrong." And in Mae West's parable, the girl is no "circuit rider," but a sardonic, ambitious, "diamonds are a girl's best friend" beauty; and the man is no short-pantsed pimp, but a top hat, white-tie-and-tails cad who clearly deserves the fate he gets.

The stock market crash and the Depression proved to be lucky for Mae West. As times became tougher and tougher in the legitimate theatre, she packed up Diamond Lil and Frankie and took them west to Hollywood. There she amassed a fortune, and, as one columnist put it, became "an institution, a living legend, as much a part of American folklore as Paul Bunyan or Tom Sawyer or Babe Ruth"—an interesting statement in that the illiterate folk groups are probably the only people in the nation who have never heard of the four. In the movies, a new ingredient was added to the old "shock and sex" broth—comedy. Realizing that the guar-

*Mae West as she appeared in the
1933 movie, "She Done Him Wrong."*
(CULVER PICTURES)

dians of family morals were not about to let her get away with
"nature in the raw" as Broadway had, she began to mock herself,
outflanking the Johnson blue pencil with caricature. For Diamond Lil, the step was short anyhow—people loved it. And once
she had the formula she stuck with it for the rest of her career:
the illicit or "near-illicit" woman, stage center, exaggerated in
figure, dressed in fancy clothes, bedecked with furs and jewels;
her Brooklynese husky and insinuating, delivered with a bounce
of bustle or bust; the male population destroyed by her passing
like the host of Byron's Sennacherib.

Movies with titles such as *Night after Night, She Done Him
Wrong, I'm No Angel, Belle of the Nineties, Goin' to Town, Klondike Annie, Go West, Young Man, Everyday's a Holiday, My
Little Chickadee,* and *The Heat's On,* featuring songs like "I'm
an Occidental Woman (In an Oriental Mood for Love)," "I Like
a Guy What Takes His Time," "He's a Bad, Bad Man (But He's
Good for Me)," as well as the reliable "Frankie," created a Mae
West vogue. Lines like "Come up and see me sometime," spoken
to a Salvation Army officer; "Beulah, peel me a grape"; "I used
to be Snow White, but I drifted"; "It's not the men in my life, it's
the life in my men that counts" became clichés. Sagacities like

"When women go wrong, men go right after them"; "Between two evils, I always pick the one I never tried before"; "Give a man a free hand, and he'll try to put it all over you"; "all Betsy Ross ever made was a flag" entered "Joe Miller's Jokebook." Scenes from her movies were recalled and rehashed—the most famous from *Night after Night* where she enters a saloon festooned with jewelry. "My goodness," exclaims the hat-check girl, "what beautiful diamonds!" "My goodness," says Mae, "had nothing to do with it." In *Klondike Annie,* she told Victor McLaglen, "You ain't exactly an oil painting, but you're a fascinatin' monster." Told that a famous portrait of a lady is "an old master," she comments "It looks more like an old mistress to me."

She had a knack of saying what was expected of her in her interviews. "Sunday School always gave me a headache"; "Sex was always natural for me, it was never a strain"; "My sex urge resulted from being born with a double thyroid." Asked to be on educational television, she replied, "Why not? Everything I've ever done has been educational." Joseph Wood Krutch stated that "her curves were laid out along epic lines." One priest ventured that "she was a wonderful, spiritual person," while Will Rogers wryly contributed that she was "the most interesting woman in Hollywood." In Paris, socialites staged a Mae West party at the Eiffel Tower. Princeton scientists made a magnet curved along her lines, and British aviators named their bulging, inflatable life-jackets after her.

She was banned from all NBC networks after an "Adam and Eve" skit with Edgar Bergen, Charlie McCarthy, and Don Ameche. CBS cancelled her "Person to Person" interview with Charles Collingwood after hearing the tapes of the show. Asked for her views on current events, she had told Collingwood, "I've always had a weakness for foreign affairs"; asked why she had so many mirrors in her bedroom, she said, "I like to see how I'm doin'." Actually, it was her delivery, rather than the lines themselves, that got her into this kind of trouble, a simple phrase like "hello, tall, dark, and handsome" sounding like a proposition when issuing from her smoky voice box. Of course she became the heroine of dirty jokes and night club routines, sharing that particular limelight with her exact opposite, Eleanor Roosevelt.

"What's the difference between Mae West and a country girl? The country girl is fair and buxom." "And now to introduce Mae West! Here they come!" "No point buying a Mae West doll; it's already busted."

Many of Hollywood's top male stars had their moment in the shadows opposite her. Besides George Raft, Cary Grant, and W. C. Fields (her three most famous leading men) Johnny Mack Brown, Randolph Scott, Lloyd Nolan, Edmund Lowe, William Gargan, and Victor McLaglen took turns playing up to her shenanigans. She actually discovered Grant, seeing him on a movie lot and exclaiming "He's the best-looking thing in Hollywood . . . if he can talk, I'll take him." Used to being stage center, she systematically stole scenes from every one of them. And, in the spirit, they all acquiesced. All except Fields, who was as committed to up-staging as she was. Though *My Little Chickadee* was "a classic," they developed a lifelong dislike for each other early in the filming. Mae was particularly bitter, as she had long since become unreasonable about drunks, and Fields was a convinced alcoholic. When but a girl, she had "sworn off" for life following a drunken brawl with her mother.

Her star faded after World War II, though she broke records back on Broadway and on various tours with shows like *Catherine Was Great, Come on Up,* and a revival of the ürform, *Diamond Lil.* In 1954 (over sixty) she had a night club act at Las Vegas singing "I Like to Do All Day What I Do All Night" while surrounded by eight musclemen in white loincloths. In 1959, ready for Social Security, she stopped an Academy Award night telecast with her rendition of "Baby, It's Cold Outside." The same year she published her autobiography, *Goodness Had Nothing to Do with It.* But time was passing, and in spite of a "camp" revival of her old movies she began to seem as remote as Lillian Russell and Nora Bayes. Soon "wind-up dolls" that immediately got undressed or got pregnant became Marilyn Monroe or Jayne Mansfield or Jane Russell dolls. But she has never given up. In her seventies and even now in her eighties, she lives in quarters whose appointments might well have been selected by Diamond Lil herself. On her off-white piano resides a statue of her in the nude overlooked by an equally nude painting, the latter insured by Lloyds of London for six figures. Old enough to be a great-grandmother, her name is still sufficient "box office" that here and there a producer asks her to do shows—figuring, it seems, that if Paul Bunyan is still on grade school walls, and Tom Sawyer still has a motel in Hannibal, Missouri, and Yankee Stadium is still "The House that Ruth Built," maybe Mae West can fire a few furnaces under America's snow-thatched roofs.

The role of "Polly" may make a "golden girl" of whatever actress is lucky enough to play it, and Mae West is no doubt "a legend in her own time," but neither "Polly" nor Mae have the stamp of a true Juno upon them. Sarah Bernhardt did. Madam Sarah was not only a "living legend" (quite as *fameuse* as any Hollywood star) and not only built a repertoire of "can't miss" roles (particularly Lady of the Camellias), but she was an utterly first-rate actress to boot—something not even the most vigorous press agent could claim for Lavinia Fenton or Ann Warren, the rest of the "Polly Peerage," or Diamond Lil herself.

Cornelia Otis Skinner once asked her father if Sarah Bernhardt was the best actress he ever saw. "I don't know;" he replied, "certainly she was the greatest show woman." On the boards for over sixty years, she is not lightly described as "the greatest personality France has had since Jeanne d'Arc," and it is no exaggeration to say that accounts of her doings, her reviews, and her remarks on the passing parade, if laid end to end, would truly circle the globe; that a pile of her photographs would dwarf the Eiffel Tower itself. If, as F. Scott Fitzgerald suggests, "personality is a series of successful gestures," Sarah Bernhardt may have been the "most" of them all, upstaging Cleopatra and Elizabeth R., in addition to her theatrical competition.

Daughter of a Dutch Jewish milliner who came to Paris and rapidly switched to the more comfortable profession of courtesan, Sarah was never really certain who her father was. Speculation has identified Edouard Bernard, later a notary in Havre, as the most likely candidate. At least she was originally named Henriette Rosine Bernard and it may be that she was born in his Left Bank student quarters. The date is also vague, either October 22 or 23, 1844. Brought up by nurses, an aunt, and her mother (when business didn't interfere), at one point nearly dying of tuberculosis, she was understandably a morose, moody child, given to long periods of silence, daydreams, and violent temper tantrums. Her first school was a pension for young ladies, and it was here that the earliest of many legends about her took root. Cast as the Queen of the Fairies in a one-act play, she was doing splendidly until midway through when her mother, her aunt, and two "friends" appeared to watch her. Seeing them enter, she froze, forgot her lines, and ran sobbing into the wings. As the adult Bernhardt suffered more than most from stagefright, it has been common to trace her abnormality to a deep-seated memory of her unhappy debut.

The pension was followed by a stay in a Catholic convent at Grandchamps near Versailles, a stay which made her devoutly religious. At fifteen her formal education ended, giving way to the informal sort that results from listening, reacting, reading, and absorbing the way only a woman trained to be "attractive to men" ever fully knows. Her confidante, only real friend, and sort of substitute mother during these teen-age years was Mme. Guérard, a youngish widow who lived in an apartment above Sarah's mother. Mme. Guérard was eventually to become her social secretary, constant companion, and lady-in-waiting. Tuberculosis still bothered her, and the general conse⹁sus was she would not live into her twenties. Her fate was discussed openly, and Sarah began to see herself as dying—a pattern that may well have set the stage for her mastery of so many great death scenes later on. The family, objectively, purchased her a rosewood coffin lined with white satin, and she kept that coffin throughout her life, making it one of her most famous trademarks.

Aided by Alexandre Dumas and Charles, Duc de Morny, she was admitted to the National Conservatory of Music and Declamation, passing her audition by reciting La Fontaine's *Fable of Two Pigeons*. So her career began. There is little point in tracing her steps upon the stairway to the stars. It is the oft-told story of theatrical ups and downs, petty jealousies, unhappy love affairs, and marriages. Yet it was a long and glorious career, first with France's two national theatres, then again and again with her own companies touring Europe, England, America, and eventually the world. By the time she was done, she had acted every sort of thing everywhere and anywhere—in the best houses, in private homes, on makeshift, open-air stages, in circus tents. And she *was* a remarkable performer throughout.

Able to do classics like Racine's Phèdre with freshness and a sensuality they had never known before, she was also able to take "soap opera" plots with "soap opera" lines leading to "soap opera" death scenes and make critics as well as audiences think they were art.   Victorien Sardore tailored role after role of this sort for her.   But especially she "made her own" Dumas fils' Marguerite Gauthie in *La Dame aux Camélias,* which she did many more than a thousand times.   George Bernard Shaw described her "style" as "hackneyed and old-fashioned," but there was more to Mme. Sarah than that.   At forty, even when in her sixties, she was able to convince audiences that she was the nineteen-year-old Jeanne d'Arc.   And when she was over seventy, her leg amputated, the butt of such gags as "Here she comes!" as the hammer blows signaled "curtain going up," she was able to tackle roles as varied as Portia, Cleopatra, and an "unknown soldier" of France.

Evaluations of her talents saying that "when she walked down a staircase it seemed as though the staircase turned about her,"

*Sarah Bernhardt in the death scene
from Shakespeare's play,
"Antony and Cleopatra."*

(NEW YORK PUBLIC LIBRARY
PICTURE COLLECTION)

that "she gave the impression of weightlessness as she crossed the stage," that "if she were no great beauty, she could create the illusion of great beauty," that "her sense of timing was perfect," that "she is the Muse of Poetry herself . . . reciting as the nightingale sings," that her voice was *"un voix d'or"* similar to a "symphony of golden flutes," that "she plays with her heart, with her entrails" are not the remarks of press agents, but of critics whom she entranced with her presence. But presence didn't do it all. No one worked harder or trained herself more thoroughly than Bernhardt. A theatrical genius, yes, but a completely dedicated and schooled one as well, and the publicity, affairs, debts, and heartbreaks that went with it never distracted her from her dramatic purpose. For she followed to the letter the advice a fellow actress gave her early in her career:

Be prepared to rise on a pedestal constructed of calumnies, gossip, adulation, flattery, lies and truths. But once you're up on it, stay there and cement it with your work and your excellence.

Looking back, it is impossible to tell how much of the Bernhardt story is true and how much is calumny, gossip, lie, or truth, for the people who knew her and Bernhardt herself were not a whit more scrupulous about her doings than were the "tub-thumpers" for her shows. Even her personality was inconsistent enough to make her nearly impossible to describe. She alternated irresponsibility, self-centeredness, and arbitrary ways with do-good, nose-to-the-grindstone activities, generosity, and sagacity about as whimsically as she alternated cheerfulness and ire. With her, one was no surer where he stood this moment to that than was some supplicant on his knees before Chaucer's Goddess of Fame. Certainly, almost anything that is reported about her temper tantrums is believable. There seems no reason to assign to the legend-makers displays like the one focussed on the man who may have been her father. At a "family" gathering to decide upon young Sarah's future, he scoffed at her announcement she planned to become a nun and marry God, calling her a silly fool and suggesting that she ought to be dispatched to a house of correction. Her reply was to physically attack him—pummeling him, scratching him and tearing out a clump of his hair. Such vigor squares with later stories of her slapping Madame Nathalie, *sociétaire* and a leading actress at the *Comédie Français,* and depositing this lady on her ample rear during a squabble that occurred when Sarah was still a first-year *pensionnaire* with that rank-conscious group; of her smashing plates during dinner because her son and daughter-in-law called Dreyfus a traitor; or of her much-publicized attack on Marie Columbier who had written a scurrilous, anti-Semitic, pornographic biography of one Sarah Barnum. Bernhardt went after that upstart with riding-whip and dagger. All who knew her attest to the violence of her rages— and to how quickly she forgot and forgave. Such exercises even stood her in good stead on the stage. One of her most memorable scenes was as Cléopâtre losing her temper at the slave bringing news of Anthony's marriage. Bernhardt needed no rehearsal to stab the knave, throw goblets about, rip down curtains, and wreck the palace room.

There are almost as many stories about her own palatial quarters as there are about her tantrums, her ideas of decor like her temper seeming to reflect the lack of security in her youth. Her taste ran to profusion and money, to appointments like lavish rugs and ankle-deep furs on the floor, damasked walls, Oriental draperies, with all sorts of chairs, couches, settees, and doodads— some very valuable, some utterly tasteless—completing the scene. Always there were plants and flowers, many a by-product of the stage door and curtain call, mingling their odors with the scents of the various animals she kept. For during most of her adult life she had a veritable "home zoo": boa constrictors, alligators, monkeys, parrots, cheetahs, wildcats, dogs. Stories recalling how her pet alligator ate her Manchester terrier or how her cheetah and wolfhound made a shambles of her tea party, chasing three terriers, the monkey, and the parrot in and out among the guests are typical. They ring generally true, unlike straight publicity releases that report how she "always has two quail-fed lion cubs in her dressing room" or how "she keeps a supply of stray cats which she hurls into the stove when particularly annoyed or frustrated." For Sarah did love animals, and one winter even spent 2,000 francs for rolls to feed the starving sparrows of Paris.

Her rooms kept nearly as many lovers as animals. If one believes her or her biographers, it would appear she had an affair with every actor who ever played opposite her and with just about every man who came within the pull of her centrifugal sex appeal. The list is impressive, from Prince Henri de Ligne (the father of her son Maurice) to silent film star, Lou Tellegen (who was seventeen years younger than the same Maurice). The stories about these love affairs are romantic to say the least. Supposedly she met Prince Henri, who was a member of a distinguished Belgian family, when she started to recite a Victor Hugo poem before the Bonapartist Court—a breach of political taste that prompted the Emperor and Empress to leave before she was barely underway. Upbraided rather violently by the gentleman in charge of her group, she was rescued from the abuse by a handsome stranger (Prince Henri, of course) who not only kissed her hand before he parted, but set the stage for becoming her lover and eventual father of her son. To be sure, after falling under Sarah's spell, Henri did try to persuade his family to sanction his marriage to this half-Jewish actress on whom he had produced a bar-sinister child. Needless to say, the family broke up the match. All kinds of scenes have been recreated about the break-up, most variations of nineteenth-century melodrama. One has Sarah, rejected when pregnant, coming to see her Prince after the baby is born. Child in arms, she asks for a minute of Henri's time. The footman, however, comes back with a note saying: "Yes, I know a woman named Bernhardt, but I do not know her son." And even though she was eventually able to persuade the Prince to come to the door, she had no luck convincing him he was the father of the child. He is said to have closed the discussion by calling her indiscriminate and quoting an aphorism from Augustine Brohan to the effect that it is hard for one who sits on a bundle of thorns to know which prickle has caused the pain.

Sarah's own variant of Henri's rejection appears to be modeled on a scene in her favorite play, *La Dame aux Camélias*. In this text she sacrifices her feelings to protect the young Prince's future and family, eventually forced by his protestations of devotion to lie to him, telling him she could never be happy with the restrictions of marriage, saying that her only "career" is to act. Her reward for this sacrifice is a stream of vile accusations and invectives centering on her lack of morals, fidelity, and respectability, climaxing in a slammed door. Her curtain scene was to swoon and remain in a coma for several days. Actually, she told all kinds of stories about Maurice's parentage, listing at one time or other Victor Hugo, General Georges Boulanger, and others as the "real" father. Once she even selected the Duke of Clarence for the lead, in spite of the fact he was born the very year that he was said to have begotten Maurice.

Prince Henri's name may well have "led all the rest" in her memory. However, there are others whose claims to being her truest love are impressive. One was Jacques Damala, an Athenian rake who was stationed in Paris as an attaché in the Greek diplomatic corps. Eleven years younger than Bernhardt, he was a vain, despicable Adonis, over whom a good many women had lost their heads. Reputed to be the cause of a number of divorces and at least one feminine suicide, he was addicted to morphine and had such a bad reputation that the Parisian authorities requested he be stationed elsewhere. Bernhardt fell in love with him at first sight, and after a whirlwind affair in St. Petersburg, where he had been sent, he was able to persuade her to let him act in her troupe. Acting was a lifelong ambition of Damala's, but a profession for which he had restricted ability, his "talent" largely being good looks, a fine speaking voice (which was hard to follow because of his Greek accent), and confidence. In April of 1882, she married him. A bad, bad man, he did not turn out to be good for her. He treated her abominably, was jealous of her acting ability, drifted under the influence of dope, ran up bills, deserted her—and, worst of all, returned. He died in 1889 at the age of thirty-four in a hovel in Paris, a "wreck [as Shelly might say] of Paradise."

One reputed lover was the future Edward VII of England, who probably entered into some sort of "relationship" with her when as the Prince of Wales he was gallivanting in Paris in the late '70s and early '80s. It is hard to jibe his reputation as a lover of the insatiable Sarah in France with legends of his "bedroom incapabilities" in England, no matter what Gallic wonders she may have worked. But he did know her well, well enough to take part in one of her plays. Appropriately perhaps, he posed as the corpse of her lover in *Fedora.*

Most of her leading men were linked with her in fact or public fancy, as were prominent members of the Parisian *beau monde.* Today the names mean little and the scandals are cold. No one cares that poet-author Jean Richepin became her lover after Damala deserted her or that he beat her husband up for what he had done; no one cares that she lost a diamond and a tiara given her by Near Eastern millionaire Kevin Bey in a fire her enemies say she started to collect the insurance; no one cares that she was linked with Edouard de Max, a notorious homosexual, who used to invite his boy friends over to watch him bathe in rose-strewn water. Today the public is pretty blasé about such matters anyhow, Hollywood having taught us that the "affairs" of leading men and leading ladies are as integral a part of the "build-up" as feuds between boxers.

The press had a particularly happy time with her American tours. As she barnstormed, she was accused of such Heraclian activities as seducing all of the male rulers of Europe, including the Pope; of supporting a family of illegitimate sons, the roster of whose fathers included Louis Napoleon, the Czar of Russia, her hairdresser, and a condemned murderer; of engaging in the sins of Sodom as well as Gomorrah with the assorted animals that lived with her. Nor did the Marie Columbier pamphlet, *The Memoirs of Sarah Barnum,* hurt. This little volume was a "labor of revenge" by an actress in her troupe who became outraged during one American tour when roles promised to her were given to Sarah's half-sister Jeanne. Without taste, it detailed the rise and fall of a foul woman, clearly Bernhardt. Columbier, well known for her own "freedoms" and called *"le plat du jour"* by her opponents, wrote with the pen of experience, and the salacious reader finds his cup runneth over as he walks through this valley of the dolls.

Even slander "too good to be true" was given a certain credence by Bernhardt's thirst for the limelight and desire to shock. Charles, Duc de Morny, watching her throw a tantrum when a child, said "the girl is a born actress"; and she was on stage at all times, even, one suspects, when she was alone. In time, she herself probably didn't know what she had actually done, what her press said she had done, and what she hoped she had done. "She'll say anything for the pleasure of saying it," was one of Mme. Guérard's assessments of her. She autographed photos and programs for perfect strangers with comments such as "To you my dear, to whom I owe it all." She would promise anything to anyone, forgetting what she had said half an hour later. One anecdote has her inviting an army colonel, his wife, and six children to visit her, only to order them sent away when they show up, the whole thing having slipped her mind. She cultivated the motto, *"Quand même,"* a phrase which translates roughly "No matter what" and which in her case might well have a bit of "What the heck" in it as well.

One time she took a relatively dangerous balloon ride during the *Exposition Universelle* of 1878. She had the name of her current role emblazoned on the side of the basket, and let float in her wake the rumor that she and her lover had gone aloft to see what intercourse in the skies was like. She walked on the back of a dying whale that had been tied up to a wharf in Boston's Charles River, "ripping" out a bone that had been carefully placed in the animal's back so that the next day's papers could print a picture captioned "How Sarah Bernhardt gets whalebone for her corsets." She carried her money around in a chamois bag, shunning banks and paying off her cast in gold pieces. She wore a chinchilla coat all year round, even during heat waves. She rode in a "Palace Car" which was filled with the decorations, indulgences, and finery associated with her suites in Paris. Talk-of-the-town anecdotes telling how she sat a divorced couple facing across her dinner table because "you two must have such a lot to say to each other"; how the call-boy would knock on her dressing-room door to remind her, "Madame, it will be eight o'clock when it suits you"; how she would cheat at tennis or quit unless the ball were hit directly to her, stalking off the court if anyone were indiscreet enough to defeat her; how she would smoke cigars and dress in men's clothes; how she ate nothing but mussels for days on end; how she had her dressmakers fit her clothes on a skeleton she kept in her closet—and dozens more were carefully gossiped about.

None was as shocking and titillating as the talk about her famous coffin. Rumor called it "the sepulchre built for two" and said that she and her lovers embraced there. Poet-dandy Robert de Montesquieu also was reported to have conducted mock funerals over her body as she lay there looking lovely and dead. "When Mme. Bernhardt is world-weary," *Theatre Magazine* of December 1903 revealed, "she gets into this coffin . . . and covering herself with faded wreaths and flowers, folds her hands across her breast and, her eyes closed, bids a temporary farewell to life"—reawakening "only when dinner is announced."

There's no doubt that she acquired the morbid object when she was about fifteen, at a time when the doctors predicted she would die of tuberculosis. Her granddaughter has quoted her as saying she pestered her mother to buy a coffin, for like the rest she was certain she was soon to die and didn't want to be laid in an ugly, unfamiliar bier. Her mother finally gave in and purchased the rosewood casket with white satin lining. Bernhardt had herself photographed in this coffin while still a teen-ager and seems to have used it as an "extra bed" when the occasion demanded, particularly when her half-sister Regina was sick with her final fever. But she never took it on her travels as the publicists would have the world believe, although the Bettmann Archive picture of her lying in it, decked with flowers, a taper aglow on her left, her hands crossed on her breast is one of the most famous ever taken of her.

By-products of such publicity were all sorts of cartoons and gags. Until plumpness overtook her in her middle years, Bernhardt's gawky, slim build was a favorite topic. She was caricatured as a cane with a sponge on the end of it, as an animated rope, as a seductive boa constrictor. Remarks like "An empty cab drove up and Sarah Bernhardt got out," "She escaped the press by hiding between two paving stones," "She better watch out or some dog will mistake her for a bone," "She is such a liar she may really be fat" swept Paris, London, and the States. Her incessant tours, brought on by high living and large debts, were ridiculed too. In 1912, the New York *Globe* ran a jingle called "Boo-Hoo" that begins,

Who's done Camille in ev'ry clime
From here to Zanzibar,
And trickled briny tears enough
To float a man-o'-war?

Henry James belittled her by saying she was "too American not to succeed in America." Nor was such sarcasm unjust. She billed five straight American trips as "Farewell Tours."

Famous herself, she was quickly incorporated into stories about other famous people. Mixed among the genuine friendships and adventures she shared with Victor Hugo, the two Dumas, George Sand, Ellen Terry, Edward VII, and Thomas Edison, go "Silver Screen" anecdotes like the following. Mme. Sarah is donating her time as a nurse in the Franco-Prussian War. A young soldier who had seen her perform at the Odéon is brought in wounded. He asks for an autographed photo. When she wants to know to whom she should dedicate the inscription, he says "Foch—Ferdinand Foch." Oscar Wilde, dying, states that there were three women that he admired above all others in his life. "I would," he gasped, "have married any one of them. Sarah Bernhardt, Lily Langtry, and Queen Victoria." Mary Todd Lincoln is about to fall down a companionway on a storm-tossed ocean liner. Bernhardt grabs her, and the President's widow is impressed that while an actor killed her husband, an actress saved her from dire injury.

At least once, a story about her has developed in genuine oral tradition. This is a folktale from the unlikely spot of Rochester, Iowa. In 1966, Ruth Beitz published the following sentimentalized text in the *Annals of Iowa,* calling it "The Rochester Legend":

For many years a fascinating legend has persisted concerning the village of Rochester, Iowa, not far from West Branch, the birthplace of Herbert Hoover. It originated in an incident that happened one night in 1905:

The evening train snorted up to the tiny station at West Branch and stopped with a ferocious grinding of brakes. From one of the cars descended a woman muffled in a thick veil and carrying a long pasteboard box.

She had hardly set foot on the ground, when the driver of a waiting hack from the local livery stable stepped up to offer his services. He'd been hoping for some business that night, and this lady looked like a good prospect. Anybody could see she was out of the ordinary, all swathed up like that; and then, the way she carried herself . . . head way up in the air, like a queen. Perfume, too! He sniffed deeply. Didn't smell like Bay Rum, or any of that stuff you could get at the local drug store.

"Where'd you want to go, Lady?" He waited eagerly to hear her voice. It was low, throaty, and undefinably accented.

"To Rochester—and back". . . .

"You got folks at Rochester, Lady? Just whereabouts was you wanting to go?"

The deep but chill tones of the response startled him. "You will please drive me to the cemetery at Rochester, leave me at the gate, and then return in half an hour."

"All right, Lady, no offense intended. Business is business." He shut the door, climbed up to the box, and roused the somnolent horse to action.

With every turn of the carriage wheels, the driver was putting two and two together—or rather, it was three and three: Veiled lady . . . pasteboard box . . . cemetery. What former resident wouldn't want to be recognized . . . lived a long way off . . . and had somebody buried out there? Suddenly he snapped his fingers in jubilation. He had the answer! Sure, it must be the King girl that had run away nearly half a century earlier. After her mother had up 'n died and was put away six feet under, she'd been a hard one to handle by all accounts. Got stagestruck after seein' some travelin' troupers. Then her relatives wouldn't have anything more to do with her . . . said she'd disgraced them. And after that *she* got high and mighty and wouldn't have a thing to do with them, either.

He whoa'd at the cemetery entrance—the place wasn't shut up at night—and bustled out to hand down the passenger. She never said a word until he was back up on the box. Then: "Please drive on. I wish to be alone. Return in half an hour."

The cabbie was so excited that he hardly knew where he drove during that interval. Did the young lady speak with a French accent? If his guess about her identity was right, that was where she'd told people she'd been born, and had it put in all that printed stuff about her. It'd be worth losing his profits on the trip to drive back from the station and find out just where she'd put those flowers—if they were flowers.

When he returned, right on the dot, to the cemetery, the mysterious passenger was waiting, minus the box. The cabman put the horse to the trot; he could hardly wait to get to the station and turn around. As the lady paid her fare, he tried to draw her out some more; but he might as well have been talking to a wooden post. Anyhow, she didn't dispute his bill!

After she'd gone into the waiting room, he climbed back on the box and urged the horse over the road until once more the white headstones glimmered like shafts of twilight through the gloom. The cabbie threw down the reins, jumped out and rushed to the grave of Mrs. John King. Eureka! There, propped up in the pasteboard box, was a bunch of the most expensive roses you could buy! And what was more, there was quite a dent in the little decorative mound of mussel shells piled up near the marker. The veiled lady had undoubtedly taken a handful of them away with her as a memento.

Next day, all Rochester and all West Branch, too, heard the story; and afterwards it kept ringing through the years, 'til the date was as fixed as the A.D. on the courthouse cornerstone. Folks had looked up the city papers and found that Sarah Bernhardt had played at an Iowa theater a night or so earlier, and that clinched matters.

Back in the late 1840's Mr. and Mrs. John King and their small daughter, Sarah, started from New York to the Mississippi Valley, where they expected to join the John Finefield family. Mrs. King, *nee* Castle, a vivacious French Canadian, looked forward to a reunion with her daughter and the grandchildren at Rochester. The death of her husband en route made the meeting a sad one; but comforted by her married daughter, Mrs. King and young Sarah remained for a lengthening stay.

Sarah King played happily with Scott and Fred Finefield and their sisters until Mrs. King died. What was to become of the young orphan? It was decided that she would accompany the Finefield girls to Muscatine, where they could all learn the millinery trade. The city on the shore of the Mississippi River held many attractions; too many, in fact, for carnivals and showboats would tie up at the wharf to offer the community a glimpse into what many considered to be a sinful life. Sarah simply would go to the shows; there was no keeping her away, and her relatives feared the worst. Nevertheless, it was a distinct shock when they heard that she was actually going to join a carnival. One of the female players had fallen ill, and there was a chance for Sarah to learn the part and get a billing on the posters of *Uncle Tom's Cabin*.

The parting was cold; the stubborn girl may not actually have been told never to darken the family door again, but she was made to feel that she was bringing disgrace upon them all. It was some time before they heard from her again, but she did write John Finefield. He never answered. From devious sources he heard how she had left the carnival to attend a French convent in St. Paul and had later departed from there for France. After that came a long gap. At last out of the void there materialized the renowned Sarah Bernhardt of Paris. The relatives had always been alert to the success of any actress named Sarah. They inspected the pictures of this Divine Sarah, read the lavish press agent notices, and decided collectively that she was their long-lost cousin and aunt.

The Finefields bided their time, for in those days all great troupers visited Iowa if only for a farewell appearance. And sure enough, one night Sarah Bernhardt played at Davenport. The Finefields took care to be there, accompanied by some friends who remembered little Sarah King.

As the audience thrilled and chilled at the joys and anguish of *Camille,* the Finefields commented on a fancied resemblance of the leading lady to Norah Briggs, Sarah King's niece. Scott Finefield sent his name to the stage door, but received no invitation to enter. Persistent, he went to the train station, hoping to encounter the actress as she stepped into her own private car. He learned with dismay that the car had not arrived at the staion, but had been sidetracked some distance beyond the city limits. When sought out, the porter of the car said the proceeding was a mystery to him; he had served Sarah Bernhardt for several years and she had never done a thing like that before—seemed as though she didn't want to be bothered by any admirers. It looked as though the assembled friends and relatives of Sarah King would not have a chance to meet the French actress face to face. And they never did. Then came the astounding episode of the veiled lady, the box of roses, and the country cemetery.

It is small wonder that an old Frenchman, told he was dying, welcomed the news. "I depart this life willingly," he whispered, "for I shall hear no more of Sarah Bernhardt." He had best not count on it. For any actress's press agent ought to be able to get releases by St. Peter or Cerberus, as the case might prove—and if Sarah's can't do it, Mae's can; and if Mae's can't do it, Lavinia's. . . .

10

SIDE BY SIDE

There is a large group, maybe two dozen, British broadside ballads in which a girl, impatient for her lover's return from war or irritated because her parents have pressed her lover to sea, dresses in man's attire and goes in search of him. Her adventures follow a pattern in which she enters the service, poses as a cabin boy or a warrior, even captains ships, fights victorious battles, and wins back her boyfriend or gets herself a higher-ranking bunkmate.

> Come all ye good people and listen to my song,
> While I relate a circumstance that does to love belong,
> Concerning a fair maiden who ventured we are told
> Across the briny ocean as a female sailor bold.

As long as there are roles for men and roles for women, there will be sensation in such activities, or in any activity in which traditional conduct is switched. It is not so much that Polly or Molly or whatever the heroine is called is heroic (often she cries and seeks the aid of the captain): the interesting thing is that she has been unorthodox. And it is important in dealing with legendary females to distinguish those whose "fame" rests largely on the fact they have "unsexed themselves" to do what men usually do from those who are truly outstanding human beings. After all, would the world have noticed the Amazons, John Henry's Polly Ann, or Sweden's Queen Christina had they just been "persons" and not "fair maids"? They are newsworthy to the extent they have denied their femininity, cutting off a breast to facilitate their aim, driving "Oh Lordy" steel like a man, bestriding a mount and exhorting the troops. And for a moment forgetting the sanctity and the sacrifice, is that legend of the Maid of Lorraine so different from that of "The Female Sailor Bold" or "The Female Warrior" whose "waist is too slender, whose fingers are too small, whose face is too delicate, to face the cannon ball?" No, legend has embraced many women only because they are doing things that "silly little heads" and "dolls" aren't meant to be able to do, or at least aren't expected to do when there are he-men about to handle them.

Ever hear about Phoebe Anne Oakley Mozee?

Late in the afternoon on a day in spring of the year 1865 the manager of the Gibson House [in Cincinnati, Ohio] waited impatiently as Jesse Jago tossed the lines, sheathed his rifle and began his impressive descent from the Martin and Chenowith stage. The ritual over, he approached the driver.

"Jesse," he said, "is that A. Oakley still up in Greenville?"

"Yep," Jesse said. "Be sendin' more quail any day now, from what I hear."

"Never mind about the quail, can you get him up here?"

"What for?" Jesse asked.

In answer, the manager produced a four-sheet poster announcing in circus-style letters the appearance of, "FRANK BUTLER, WORLD'S CHAMPION RIFLE SHOT."

"Ever hear of this fellow?" the manager asked, gesturing to the poster.

"Reckon I have," Jesse said.

"You know he has a standing offer of a hundred dollars to anybody who can outshoot him?"

"Has he now?" Jesse said, stroking his chin.

"That's right. And what's more I've already bet him another hundred dollars that I know a fella who can beat him. Word's all over town. Everybody's betting on that Oakley fella. Can you get him to come up?"

"What sort of a match?"

"Rifle. Best out of a hundred."

"I'll fetch A. Oakley, providin' one thing—the match goes on regardless of Oakley's age or size or looks."

"I don't care what he looks like. He can shoot, that's all that we care about."

"Oakley'll be here Saturday."

Never was there such a crowd on hand to greet the Greenville stage as there was that Saturday. Quail shot through the head had been the talk of Cincinnati for months. Word of it had passed up and down the river and now it seemed that everyone was at the Gibson House for the coming out of A. Oakley.

No one waited for Jesse Jago's ceremonious descent. Eager hands pulled open the coach door. There were two passengers, an alert, athletic-looking man and a young woman. Quickly the male passenger was hoisted to several pairs of broad shoulders. Necks were craned and excitement ran high as the crowd closed in. It was some time before the protesting stage passenger could explain that there'd been some mistake. He was Oliver Toth, correspondent for *Leslie's Weekly,* and what was going on anyhow?

The lithe, willowy girl who had also come in on the stage approached the center of excitement. A plaid skirt hung nearly to her ankles. A sunbonnet framed her finely chiseled face. There were tiny crow's feet alongside a pair of extraordinarily bright hazel eyes. The young lady addressed the man who was making the most commotion.

"I beg your pardon," she said, "I reckon I'm the one you're lookin' for. My name's Annie Oakley."

A roar of protest went up from the crowd. The quick-thinkers rushed to cover their bets, the others surged around the manager of the Gibson House demanding that the match be called off.

Jesse Jago came up then, and for once he had forgotten to sheathe his rifle. He handled it casually, almost carelessly. The hubbub died.

Jesse spoke softly, as he always did.

"One of the conditions of this match was that it goes on exactly as scheduled, no matter what A. Oakley looked like."

There was a sharp protest but it died quickly as Jesse made a particularly careless gesture with his rifle.

"Get your gun, Annie," he said.

The rest of the story is still told on winter nights when men are fondly cleaning their favorite rifles. The little girl from backwoods Ohio fired shoulder to shoulder with the world's champion rifle shot, scoring hit for hit. On the last round, the one hundredth, Frank Butler missed. Annie Oakley never missed.

The real Annie Oakley

*. . . and Betty Hutton in
the film, "Annie Get
Your Gun," shown with
Louis Calhern.*

If, as Walt Whitman has been acclaimed for writing, it is "as great to be a woman as it is to be a man," honesty must become impatient with "female warriors." Opinion favors women whose legends depend on the power and the glory of what they did, rather than on the eccentricity. At least this final chapter is about three such women: an activist who cared little whether she were male or female and two active ladies, the first who "rested easy" in her sex, the other who threw herself against it. In the long run, though, all three (for their own reasons) would surely have chosen to be "women again" had Fate somehow decreed them that chance. And mankind, as well as God, was able to love them, with due apologies to Yeats, for something other than their "yellow hair."

For that matter, it is likely Mary Magdalene Garland, better known to the folk-singing world as Aunt Molly Jackson, never contemplated her femininity at all. She simply did "what came naturally," mothering, nursing, mating, while her soul burned with the same sort of a-fleshly passion that drove Wat Tyler, Jeanne d'Arc, Lenin, and Che Guevara. An activist almost from birth, she chewed tobacco as a child, saw things with the clarity of ignorance, and brooked no interference with her concept of right. Born in Kentucky to that stock generally called hill-billies (hill-fellows), she was the child of a mountain farmer and ordained minister who at nineteen had married a fifteen-year-old country girl. When she was fifty-nine, she was quoted as saying, "I've had a turrible sight of trouble in my life"—and that is an understatement. She saw her mother die of tuberculosis when she was six, saw her father blinded by a piece of slate that fell on his head in a coal mine, saw her brother Richard killed by a boulder which fell on him in a coal mine, saw her son killed by a rock and slate slide in a coal mine, saw her sister's child starve to death, saw another brother blinded, and was crippled herself in a bus accident. Even at that, she never considered herself particularly unusual, feeling that all the men and women who were exploited by the coal operators as America swept from an agricultural to an industrial society were pretty much in the same fix.

Had the world remained as it was in earlier times, Mary Garland would undoubtedly have grown up to be one of those old "singin' ladies" who serve as keepers of the culture in a folk community. Able to sing and use a tune almost as soon as she could talk, she had a vast repertoire of Anglo-American ballads, hymns, and lyrics. In her "Memorial Issue" of the *Kentucky Folklore Record* (October-December, 1961), scholar D. K. Wilgus wrote that "She knew the old ballads and had a fundamentally 'right' way of rendering them in the old 'high lonesome' style," and her professor-friend John Greenway added "nothing that ever entered her mind was forgotten; she could reproduce a song she composed as a child or give the precise day, date, and hour of a strike skirmish, and both would be accurate—if she chose to have them so." She herself once said that the songs she sang were nothing but "what folks compose out of their daily lives, out of their sorrows, and out of their happiness and all." Two hundred four of them have been recorded for the Archive of American Folksong in the Library of Congress.

But the world didn't remain the same, and mining rather than farming became the main occupation of many hill-fellows. Aunt Molly's father was typical, leaving his farm and opening a general store where he sold food and supplies on credit to mine workers. "Trusted ever'body hither and yon, and lost ever'thing he had" is his daughter's analysis. Like others who were desperate and broke, he went into the mines where he worked six days a week for the rest of his life, spending his Saturday nights and Sundays preaching. Active in the union movement, he took little Molly along with him. From the time she can remember she was involved with picket lines, carrying messages, and seeing "union people." She soon began to turn her ability with song to the cause: the effort to reform practices of the mine operators and to enable workers to earn a decent, and what was even more, a reasonably safe, livelihood.

Though she is quite unreliable in such matters, she claims to have written her first song when four years old, being inspired by her mother's reading of the Good Book. This was two years before she had learned to read and "write by hand." The song begins,

> My friends and relations, listen if you will,
> The Bible plainly tells us we shall not kill.

In spite of stories about Wolfgang Amadeus Mozart and John Stuart Mill, one has to be skeptical of Molly Garland's self-proclaimed precocity, especially when at another point she cites her first jail sentence (six years later) to be the time she first began to write her own pieces. Jailed for blackening her face and dancing around as though she were "a nigger," she reports that the sheriff, a man named Cundiff, felt sorry for her and failed to lock the door, telling her to sing to the onlookers through the bars, then to walk out when everyone dispersed. She replied that she "hain't goin' to sing nare word unless every man gives me a dime and a plug o' Cup-Greenville tobacker." Having collected 37 dollars in change and ten plugs, she sang a song called "Mr. Cundiff, Won't You Turn Me Loose" which recounted the whys and wherefores of her trial. ". . . and that's how I began makin' up songs," she is quoted. "I reckon I've wrote hundreds since then."

No matter when she started, she did write hundreds more. So many, in fact, that Ben Botkin listed her "among the folk bards and minstrels of the mountains," calling her "a militant symbol, with her songs that set the miner's troubles to traditional tunes and patterns." The subject matter is almost always the same, the ballads telling of organizers shot or maimed or framed by the bosses and law officers, of miners killed because of poor job conditions, of children starving while the owners and their wives ride around in diamonds and silk, of strikes and the "hungry blues":

> Ragged and hungry, no shoes or slippers on our feet,
> We bum around from place to place to get a little bite to eat.

The messages she preached were all learned firsthand, "from tough hard struggles and nowhere else." The best deal with the plight of the children. For nearly fifty years after her mother died when she was six, she had children in her arms, taking care of her half-brothers and sisters, her own, and the nearly 900 babies she delivered as a registered nurse and midwife. Much of her ire with the miners' lot rose from and centered on "starving faces." In her preface to "Hungry Ragged Blues" she used to reminisce,

On the seventh day of May, 19 and 30, during the strike, the miners built a soup kitchen out of slabs over in a meadow. When it was finished I told all of the wives to bring everything we had from our mining shacks and put it all together, and go around and collect vegetables from the farmers to make soup as long as the farmers had anything to give. By the middle of October we was desperate; we did not see how we was going to live. For two or three days we did not have anything to make soup out of. On the 17th morning in October my sister's little girl waked me up early. She had 15 little ragged children and she was taking them around to the soup kitchen to try to get them a bowl of soup. She told me some of them children had not eat anything in two days. It was a cold rainy morning; the little children was all bare-footed, and the blood was running out of the tops of their little feet and dripping down between their little toes onto the ground. You could track them to the soup kitchen by the blood. After they had passed by I just set down by the table and began to wonder what to try to do next. Then I began to sing out my blues to express my feeling. This song comes from the heart and not just from the point of a pen.

And her most moving song, "Dreadful Memories," tells how thirty-seven babies died in her arms during the last months of 1931 when the company doctor boycotted families of miners who had joined the union:

> *Dreadful memories! How they linger;*
> *How they pain my precious soul.*
> *Little children, sick and hungry,*
> *Sick and hungry, weak and cold.*

> *Little children, cold and hungry,*
> *Without any food at all to eat.*
> *They had no clothes to put on their bodies;*
> *They had no shoes to put on their feet.*

> *Dreadful memories! How they linger;*
> *How they fill my heart with pain.*
> *Oh, how hard I've tried to forget them*
> *But I find it all in vain.*

> *I can't forget them, little babies,*
> *With golden hair as soft as silk;*

Slowly dying from starvation,
Their parents could not give them milk.

I can't forget them, coal miners' children,
That starved to death without one drop of milk,
While the coal operators and their wives and children
Were all dressed in jewels and silk.

Dreadful memories! How they haunt me
As the lonely moments fly.
Oh, how them little babies suffered!
I saw them starve to death and die.

She married a miner, Jim Stewart, when she was fourteen years old—a normal age for her culture. Stewart was killed in a rock fall in 1917, and her second husband was Bill Jackson, who she claimed was from "the same tree as Old Hickory" ("All the Jacksons in that part of Tennessee and Kentucky belong to the same generation. . . ."). It was while married to Jackson that she became notorious as a labor organizer, singer, and troublemaker, and he divorced her in 1931, supposedly to free himself from the reprisals directed at her for her activities. That was the year that she was exiled from mine country in Kentucky and went on a tour of thirty-eight states singing the trouble of the miners and begging funds for their relief. This was also the time that Aunt Molly Jackson became nationally known. In 1932, during the tour, a bus she was riding turned over in Ohio, seriously crippling her. She sued, but the bus company escaped payment by going bankrupt. She then eked out her living singing and composing, spreading her message to industry, particularly to those parts of it to which hill-folk were gravitating. Married to Gustavos Stamos, she died on August 31, 1960.

When one looks over her life and efforts objectively, he sees the profile of every reformer: the mixture of singleness of purpose, uncompromising idealism, and energy. Molly Garland, told by her uncle that she would grow up to be a fool if she stayed home with her stepmother all day taking care of her father's fifteen children, went to school, learned to read and write, and unlike most mountain girls studied books while rocking the inevitable babies to sleep. The result was the woman who passed a group of mothers with children dying of starvation and immediately entered the local store, ordered a bag of groceries, and walked out, telling the owner she would pay him the $5.90 bill when she saw that kind of money—for now, hungry babies couldn't wait. When he tried to stop her, she pulled a six-shooter and threatened to aerate him. Then she left, saw the children were fed, and went home to await the sheriff. He came quickly, saying "So you've turned robber, eh?" But she explained so sincerely and so vividly that he ended up promising to pay the bill himself, swearing he'd be "damn glad" if he got into trouble for not arresting her.

Yet the result was also the woman who upbraided a utility company in New York City for refusing to make an installation on Christmas Day with the comment, "Just because Jesus Christ was born nineteen hundred and thirty-six years ago I can't get no electricity today?" And the woman who was irascible to song collectors and scholars when they pointed out that some of her "compositions" were not original with her. Though she never saw the article, she would have been "cursing mad" had she known that her friend John Greenway demonstrated in the *Journal of American Folklore* that her series of beloved Robin Hood ballads were not traditional and in some cases not even hers. Greenway makes it completely clear that she either made the texts up out of her respect for the Lincoln green "reformer" or memorized them verbatim out of the Kittredge-Sargent collection of English and Scottish ballads lent her by another collector, Mary Elizabeth Barnicle, claiming them either as her creations or as songs long known in her family.

I spent a lot of time in the spring of 1939 recording all of the songs that she could then remember, for the Library of Congress. At last even Molly ran dry. When I came around for my next visit, she sprang this Robin Hood thing on me . . . I recorded enough to not embarrass her, and then checked with my friend, Dr. M. E. Barnicle, who was Aunt Molly's friend, support and mentor for at least a decade. Molly had made a visit to her house and had borrowed Child's *English and Scottish Popular Ballads,* and, apparently, had given the Robin Hood cycle the once-over. By the time she sat down in front of my microphone she was able to reel off scores of verses of it purely by memory, and interlarded with rich Kentucky-isms. The text, then, was obviously a direct lift from Child, set to favorite Molly Jackson tunes. Perhaps she made further and confusing revisions over the years—but that is how the whole thing began—a delightful jape, played on a government folklorist.

I never told her that she hadn't fooled me—it wouldn't have been polite.

Typical reformer, Aunt Molly always felt her ends justified her means, and she was quite willing to distort truth when she felt it needed distortion. She saw things but one way: "take from the rich, give to the poor." Partial to violent overthrow, extra-legality, and justice slanted to her variations on the theme "one for all and all for one," she couldn't understand why people thought she was dangerous or called her a Marxist for doing things Marxists had long advocated. "I've been framed up," she said once, "and accused of being a Red when I did not understand what they meant. I never heard tell of a Communist until after I left Kentucky— then I had passed fifty. . . ." But even if she understood more than she let on and even if she had absorbed "industrial revolution" indirectly without realizing it, her heart and voice were in the right places. And it is no fault of hers (just as it was no fault of Robin Hood's) that there appears to be no "way of the world" down which all men can walk hand in hand.

Certainly her ideas weren't new, even the proper Bostonians had felt them. And if people like Lydia Pinkham were too polite for Aunt Molly's brand of activism, long before and far away from the labor movement similar drums had thumped. Lydia Pinkham too might have "marched in thirty-eight states," trumpeted out rallying songs, and spoken her piece from pulpits along with Aunt Molly's "sisters" Lucretia Mott and Susan B. Anthony. But Lydia would not. All her life she stayed "just a housewife." Yet Lydia Estes Pinkham was the first highly successful American business-woman, was the author of the first "sex handbook" for "married women and those about to be," and was the person who did the most to convince the men of the world, as well as the women, that it was possible to be female and still feel good. Moreover, in the 1880s, when Annie Oakley was the top marksman for the Buffalo

Bill Wild West Show, it was Lydia Pinkham's face that was the "most easily recognized" of any contemporary American's. And all the time she maintained her role as "chief cook" and literally "bottle-washer" for an ineffectual husband and four children, was active in local politics, community affairs, and organizations, spun and knit "in the sun" with the rest of the girls, seldom leaving what we now call Greater Boston.

Her fame turns on a "vegetable compound" which sounds as though it had been bubbled together during the dark of the moon by the Weird Sisters themselves. A "sure cure for all female complaints," it was brewed from eight ounces each of true and false unicorn root; six ounces each of black cohash, pleurisy root, and life root; twelve ounces of fenugreek seed; and, perhaps most crucial of all, 22 percent alcohol. But Necessity, not some agent of Satan, was its mother, and it rose from the "toil and trouble" of the economic crises of the mid-1870s.

Lydia Estes was a Quaker girl born in Lynn, Massachusetts on February 9, 1819. Given the sort of Friends upbringing that enabled her to see herself as an "equal but separate" partner to any man, deeply interested in women's suffrage and women's rights, she married a New Hampshire-born widower, Isaac Pinkham, when she was twenty-four and he was twenty-nine. He turned out to be, as the French might say, *d'affaires* and had plans for making a great fortune. Once or twice he nearly did, but ultimately his habit of overreaching, combining with the national depression, undid him, and in the end it was up to his wife and children to provide as well as "save" the bacon.

Mrs. Pinkham's job was typical of the middle-class woman of her time, and she performed "the work that is never done" with a sort of Franklinesque bent. One result of her Yankee mind, and perhaps her husband's problems, was a set of "Rules for Success in Business" which featured such aphorisms as "A sure sixpence is better than a doubtful shilling"—advice she was to follow no better in later years than Franklin followed his Poor Richardisms. But locally it was as a "good neighbor," not as an aphorist, she was best known. For though the Pinkhams could never afford servants, Lydia was always acting as midwife or visiting nurse down the road, baking cookies and pies, and putting up preserves for someone who was sick or baby-sitting for a friend. And it was such charity that eventually led to her fame.

She had developed, in the course of her do-good activities, a stock of home remedies. Some of the recipes had come down in her family, but most she got from her indefatigable reading in whatever medical books and pamphlets she was able to procure. Probably the most influential was *The American Dispensatory* by Dr. John King of Cincinnati. King was a prominent member of the American Eclectics, a group of doctors who relied heavily on the patriotic and therapeutic value of "our native plants," and a pioneer in the field of pharmacology. His *Dispensatory* was an extremely popular and widely used compendium of herbal lore (eighteen editions to be exact) and it contained in it the formula that became the basis of Mrs. Pinkham's famous elixer.

The "old squaw remedy," as Dr. King's mixture of true unicorn and pleurisy root had originally been labeled, was included for its efficacy in uterine matters, and it was in such matters that "good neighbor" Pinkham began to use it around Lynn. Because just about every detail of the female reproductive system and process was a source of chronic pain, indisposition, and embarrassment 130 years ago, Mrs. Pinkham's all-purpose remedy was more than welcomed. As later advertising was to put it, "success was immediate." Neighbor told neighbor about it and the Vegetable Compound quickly became the talk of first the town and then the surrounding territories. Perfect strangers began presenting themselves at the Pinkhams' door asking for the "cure," and letters began to pour in. Friend that she was, Lydia Pinkham just handed out a bottle of the brew and often gave a free meal and candy for the children to boot.

Isaac Pinkham was wiped out in the Panic of 1873. By this time the three boys of the family—Charles, Daniel, and Will—were grown, but not really started upon their careers, and the "baby," Aroline, was a high school girl. As a group they were aware of the fact that "mother's compound" was widely sought, and were beginning to toy with the idea that people might be willing pay to get it. Factors simply combined, with the result that in 1875 the desperate family set out to recoup their losses by selling Lydia E. Pinkham's Vegetable Compound from their home. The "children" (the three boys already had gotten themselves jobs) were to put food on the table, provide what capital was needed, and distribute handbills after hours. Mrs. Pinkham was to be treasurer and general manager—that is, write the handbills, the labels, and a little four-page "Guide for Women" which accompanied each bottle; make, bottle, and dispense the Compound; and run the home office (keep house). Isaac, sapped by his failures, had no real role and remained in the background throughout.

The venture went from modest success to a national and international phenomenon well within one decade. It is an Horatio Alger story of incredibly hard work, particularly on the part of Dan Pinkham; of pioneering in advertising, especially advertising aimed at women; and of national education in a tabooed area. The theme is always the same: "a positive cure for female complaints," "trust Lydia Pinkham, not the doctor who doesn't understand your problems," "it *is* possible to feel well," "Lydia Pinkham is the saviour of her sex." And it clicked with the aid of such sure-fire promotional gimmicks as "quick cure," "easy administration," "Nature's way," "men don't understand women," and a chance to take a nip of alcohol without appearing to drink.   Two other techniques were used relentlessly: testimonials and pictures. "The doctor gave me up, then I wrote Lydia Pinkham . . ."; "After giving up all hopes of ever feeling well, I tried a bottle . . ."; "I underwent the horrors of local treatment, then . . ." As Mrs. Pinkham's picture smiled out at these unfortunate females from bottle after bottle, poster after poster, and ad after ad in the local newspapers, her likeness became widely recognized, a cliche on its own, causing one editor to request that "she get a new one taken" with a different hair-do and without that never-ceasing smile.

Part of the success of the campaign centered on the fact that Lydia Pinkham's Vegetable Compound was "an old squaw remedy," the sort of thing people fresh from the country could understand and feel nostalgically safe with. America of the late nineteenth century was beginning to suffer the ailment we are still subject to today. Folks were leaving the old rural homes and coming into the cities to make their fortunes, towns were expanding, farms were being broken up, and the world was getting "fenced in." The impetus that enables a cracker-barrel comedian to seem wiser than a college professor, that enables developers to sell half-acre lots under names like Greene Countrie beside tarred roads called Possum Run, that encourages people to think water-witching works, that country flies are cleaner than city flies, or that honey and vinegar is a cure-all, bore Lydia Pinkham along. People who had grown up using boneset tea for colds, monk's hood for fever, witch hazel for aches and pains, wild indigo for eye-sores, white pine bark for sluggish kidneys, and fox-glove for heart trouble found the Vegetable Compound not only familiar, but a comfort in "foreign climes." And to be sure, many of those old folk remedies did some good. Willow-bark tea has salicylates in it and so offers some of the relief of aspirin, as does spirea. Fox-glove is a source of digitalis; nightshade and mandrake of atropine; China's *Ma Huang* of ephedrine; the bark of the evergreen cinchona of quinine—to start a long list. So it shouldn't have come as much of a surprise when it was discovered that Mrs. Pinkham's variation of Dr. King's "old squaw remedy" gave a woman a rough approximation of estrogen therapy and that it did supplement the sedative effects of its high alcoholic content with something more than psychosomatic succor.

The Lydia Pinkham advertising was also successful in establishing and maintaining the idea that Mrs. Pinkham was nothing more than the lady down the street who knew all about doctoring and curing in the old way. Basically, it was honest copy, for she always dispensed goody-type advice with her recipe, first by mouth, later by her little four-page "Guide for Women," and finally through a widely publicized and read *Handbook*. Her early contributions along these lines centered on comments concerning general hygiene, bathing, refraining from spitting, and sanitation. "Keep clean inside and out" she would say or write, and she continually advised people to "Ventilate!" She stressed good diet, the chance to be alone for at least an hour a day, and getting out of the house into the fresh air—things that "never occurred" to the housewives of a century ago. Most of her effort concentrated on the ignorance of both men and women concerning a woman's right to health. Today it is hard to take seriously the famous

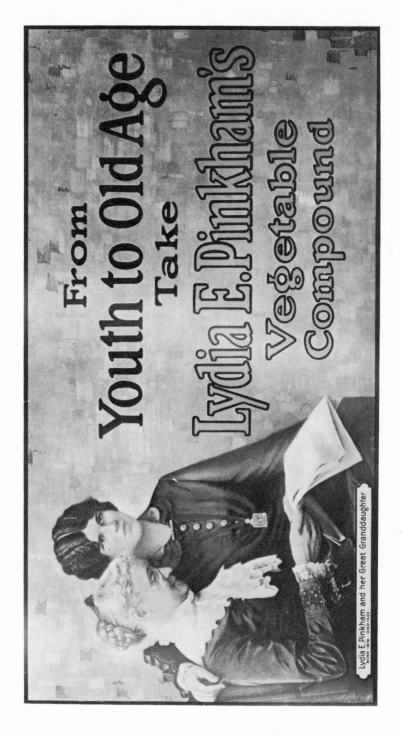

A 1930 ad for the Lydia E. Pinkham Medicine Co. showing Mrs. Pinkham with a great-granddaughter she never saw.

anecdote of Susan Anthony's cousin, the young lady who was to die some weeks after bearing her fourth child. During the interval between childbirth and her death, her husband approached her and said he had a headache. She ventured that she had a bad one herself. "Yes," he supposedly replied, "but I mean a real headache. Yours is just a natural consequence." This sort of belief that the daughters of Eve were cursed to aches, pains, and feeling poorly, combined with the staggering workload of the pre-washer/dryer housewife, the rigidly cumbersome clothes she had to wear, and the ordinary dangers of childbirth, made it quite true a woman's lot was neither a happy, nor a nappy, one. Lydia Pinkham just couldn't believe that women must suffer, that pain was normal, or that fragility was a characteristic of her sex.

Before long the copy was aimed not only at every part of the country, but at every stage of female existence as well. Starting with the young girl and her mother, it warned that "many a dutiful daughter pays in pain for her mother's ignorance," warning mothers to watch the young girl's health, to keep her from pining or reading morbid poetry ("no matter how pious"). Recognizing that engagement and marriage often acted as a cure-all on young female spirits, the copy also stressed that a letdown soon set in, that the young husband would be baffled by the return of his happy, blushing bride to "backache, bearing down, and displacements." Next the baby and the plea, "If only I could get my strength back!", followed by more babies, more backache, more weakness: "Crying children, tired mothers, nerves all unstrung" and the wail "How old I look and not yet thirty." Then there was the ogre menopause. Even the mourning widower and his search for a healthy replacement was not omitted. Of course the answer to each problem at every stage of this ever-renewing unhappiness was a shot or two of the Vegetable Compound which kept the daughter easy to live with; the young bride "ready to go" with her husband; the "dewy" mother beaming at her equally bright-eyed children; the middle years a pleasure; and was responsible for a climax of "Young at Sixty" instead of "Old at Thirty." Even the fashionably coiffured dowager was contrasted to the Whistler-type granny huddled rocking and toothless, with emphasis on the idea that "a delightful old lady—*in good health*" is a most "pleasant influence" in a home.

The vast success of these campaigns was reflected in the jokes and rhymes which began to circulate with the elixir.

> Young girl: "Momma, I dropped my bottle
> of Lydia Pinkham's on the floor
> and it broke!"
> Doctor: "Ah yes, my dear—a
> Compound fracture."

> * * *

> Boy, seeing Mrs. Pinkham's picture in an
> apothecary's window: "Mom, I want to see
> the play that Lydia Pinkham's coming to town
> in."

> * * *

> Elsie W. had no children,
> There was nothing in her blouse.
> So she took some Vegetable Compound;
> Now they milk her with the cows.

> * * *

> There's a baby in every bottle,
> So the old quotation ran.
> But Mrs. Pinkham has admitted
> You may also need a man.

There were also Lydia Pinkham songs, often about her well-known picture:

> Whate'er I do, where're I be,
> At home, abroad, on land or sea,
> Both day and night it follows me,
>   That face.

Another printed in *The Dartmouth,* a college publication, includes the lines:

There's a face that haunts me ever,
There are eyes mine always meet;
As I read the morning paper,
As I walk the crowded street.

Ah, she knows not how I suffer,
Hers is now a world-wide fame,
But 'til death that face shall greet me;
Lydia Pinkham is her name.

One result of Lydia Pinkham's correspondence with indisposed ladies about the land was that she began to serve as an early Dorothea Dix or Ann Landers, her files soon bulging with female complaints of a social and personal as well as a medical nature. "No confidence has ever been violated"; "Men never see your letters"—the advertising read, and the copyists seized on this by-product of the Compound to label Mrs. Pinkham as "the Mother to the Race."   Over and over, Mrs. Pinkham found herself appalled at the lack of knowledge most females had concerning their own bodies.   Somewhat in the spirit of the actor-officer in the old Army veneral disease film ("most men know more about their own cars than they do about their own bodies"), Lydia Pinkham decided that utter ignorance of sexual matters was just about universal among the young women of the late nineteenth century. And she knew, from her letters, that there was no one these blushing girls could turn to for advice or accurate information.   Male doctors were of no use because of the embarrassment caused by the questions.   Mothers, even after their own trials, were reluctant to talk to their daughters about a subject upon which they weren't very well informed anyhow.   Today we have forgotten the chamber of horrors in which the Victorian-Edwardian wedding night took place and the kinds of ignorance, fear, and taboos that forced people to put pantalettes on the legs of drawing-room furniture.

So Lydia Pinkham wrote a book explaining it all, making the volume a broad reply to her Compound-inspired correspondence. It was published as a simple contribution to the nation's health and welfare and was distributed without charge—each copy bearing the familiar photograph and the signature "Yours for Health." For years it was the only book of its kind available for free distribution and it wasn't supplanted until the Government began issuing its free pamphlets on pre-and post-natal care and child-rearing. The pages were unsentimental and described accurately such verboten topics as puberty, conception, birth and menopause. Mrs. Pinkham used scientific terms for the parts and functions of the body, not euphemisms, and the information could still serve a girl of today. When one realizes that less than 100 years ago, "consultants" like J. H. Kellogg of cereal-industry fame (in his *Ladies Guide In Health and Disease)* related novel reading to excitement, uterine congestion, and so uterine disease; that, outside the small confines of the medical world, almost no American had the slightest idea of the mechanics of fertilization or of ovulation; that many, many people did not connect menopause to the reproductive process at all; and that national ignorance was sufficient for young girls to worry about producing "bouncing baby boys" after "the first kiss," he can understand the impact, importance, and shock value that Lydia Pinkham's handbook had—particularly when it was accompanied by illustrations with titles like "The Female Pelvis and its Contents." The booklet went through millions of copies and it is probable that it had more influence on American mores than far more heralded works such as *McGuffey's Reader,* the *Boy Scout Handbook, Pilgrim's Progress* or *Uncle Tom's Cabin.*

Of course, Mrs. Pinkham was subject to the usual battery that greets the Dorothea Dixes and Ann Landers' of the world. Joke complaints came in, often obscene. A man would complain he had offered the Compound to a frail, sexless librarian only to be assaulted a few weeks later by the now "too healthy" female. Or a traveling salesman would object that he was being sued by a lady friend to whom he had offered a bottle with the spectacular result that she was rendered almost immediately pregnant. One man even wrote asking permission to christen his yacht the *Lydia E. Pinkham,* suggesting that the publicity would aid in advertising both "on sea and on land." And even though the Company was scrupulous in publicizing that after Mrs. Pinkham's death in 1883 letters were being answered by her daughter-in-law, and even though these notices were repeated year after year, many people cried "foul." In 1895, a Seattle newspaper stated that the Lydia Pinkham ads were a "bare-faced fraud," saying "this very nice old lady died upwards of ten years ago." Yet, they added, "respectable women" still write her letters and go into details of their "female irregularities with a shocking disregard to the proprieties." The paper went on to state that Lydia Pinkham had no children, left no recipes of her "valuable lotions," and claimed someone was "working the old lady's name for all there is in it." Rumors that no such person ever existed, that Lydia Pinkham was but a trade name, that "Miss Lydia" was both a quack and a man at that, abounded. One paper even inveighed against the Company: "Don't show yourself in the guise of an old female any longer, Mr. Lydia E. Pinkham."

But such difficulties were minor compared to the "growing pains" of the enterprise. The business, which had all the advantages of being a family endeavor, soon became subject to all the attendant complications. Six years after it began, Dan Pinkham, the brother whose energy and advanced ideas in advertising were responsible for the national success of the venture, died of consumption. His death, like his life, led the family business toward a true incorporation. Within days after the funeral, a reorganization was effected. Mrs. Pinkham herself stepped down, investing the actual ownership of the company in her surviving children, Charles, Will, and Aroline. That year the three organized a partnership called Lydia E. Pinkham's Sons & Co. It was decided that all profits would be divided equally and all accounts would be accurately kept. However, within two months Will also died of consumption and was followed to the grave by his wife within the year. So Charles and Will Gove (Aroline's lawyer husband) emerged as the controlling voices in the Company, and by September another reorganization had taken place.

It was decided to terminate the partnership and incorporate as the Lydia E. Pinkham Medicine Co., with the corporate structure set up in Maine to take advantage of favorable tax laws. Charles Pinkham was President and General Manager; Aroline was Treasurer, and Gove, Secretary. They constituted the entire Board of Directors. Mrs. Pinkham, already engrossed in the "spiritualism" through which she "communicated" with her dead sons, confined herself to correspondence and other writings. By May, 1883, she was dead. However, this new form of the Company, run by Charles and Will Gove, became a very profitable and successful venture, in spite of one big setback in their initial effort to expand into Canada and in spite of huge debts run up by overreaching in the advertising market. When Charles died in 1900, his obituary in the Chicago *Times-Herald* stated that "he was one of the most liberal advertisers in the world" and told how he had helped build "from an exceedingly small beginning the largest business in the proprietary medicine line in the United States." And because the company was so successful, the Goves, who immediately inherited control, found themselves in a legal fight with Charles' widow and his family, now led by the oldest son Arthur.

In brief, Arthur Pinkham began producing the exact same Compound as the Lydia E. Pinkham Medicine Co. sold, calling it Delmac Vegetable Compound (the name coined from the first letters of the names of Charles' children), and began plans for a huge initial advertising campaign. As Mrs. Pinkham's elixir, "the old squaw remedy," had never been patented, perhaps couldn't be patented, the Goves realized a compromise was called for, and one was quickly reached. The two companies merged into the Pinkham Medicine Company, and the venture, once again a happy family enterprise, continued to thrive. The foreign market was especially exploited during this time, and such labels as Le Rémède Vegetal de Lydia E. Pinkham, Lydia E. Pinkham's Fräutermittel, Lydia E. Pinkham's Ört-Medicin, El Compuesto Vegetal de Lydia E. Pinkham became commonplace in Europe, Canada, and the Latin lands. Even the Orient was invaded, and the Bing Hai Sze Tai Tsai Shen Sui (translated Smooth Sea's Pregnancy Womb Birth-giving Magical 100% Effective Water) was launched. When it was discovered that Oriental modesty prevented unmarried women from purchasing it, the name was changed to Bing Hai Sze Fu Koo Yao Sui (Smooth Sea's Women's Disease Medical Water). Later India, the Philippines, and Oceania fell. In 1944, an Army chaplain ashore on a South Sea Island photographed a native woman beside a hut surrounded by her children and most of her possessions, one of which was a bottle of the Vegetable Compound.

Will Gove died in 1920, and again trouble broke out. The ensuing corporate struggle is as complex and dull for the layman as the average law school seminar. Oddly, it boiled down to a "war of the sexes," carried on between "the Pinkhams" (that is, the old "Delmac" group led by Charles' son Arthur, who was President of the Company) and "the Goves" (led by the vigorous Lydia Pinkham Gove, Smith '07, who was assistant treasurer as well as advertising manager and purchasing agent and among whose other distinctions was the fact she had been the first woman to be flown across the Continent). The dispute originally concerned how much money was to go into advertising, but it degenerated into a family feud. Because each side controlled exactly half the stock, no upper hand could be gained. If the six directors met, the vote went 3-3. If either group stayed away, there was no quorum. The matter dragged to a climax in 1934 when Lydia Gove characteristically told Arthur Pinkham that she was going to run the Company and that "the Pinkhams" had better stop interfering with her or sell their interests. Her main argument pivoted on the fact that "her side" had loaned the company about a quarter of a million dollars in personal funds, and she even threatened to get herself appointed as receiver if the Pinkhams didn't capitulate.

The case was decided in 1937 in favor of "the boys," when the Massachusetts Supreme Court handed down a decision supporting the Pinkhams' petition for an injunction to prevent the Goves from interfering with the business. A dispatch two days later stressed the boy-girl side of the feud, saying that "Henceforth the Lydia E. Pinkham Medicine Company will be under male direction." Appeals were to no avail in Massachusetts and a subsequent "receivership petition" in Maine was also lost. Remarkably, the boys and the girls closed ranks after this, a credit to their belief in fair play, maturity, and humor (though not necessarily in that order).

But times were changing fast. Soon the old compound was to be undone by what Lydia Estes Pinkham had worked for all her life—an ever-increasing medical sophistication among the American people, especially concerning the female body and its inner purposes. Moreover, by the Second World War, far more effective "elixirs" were coming into wide use in the form of artificially manufactured estrogens and other hormones, and (as the cynics point out) open consumption of alcohol was increasingly accepted. Still, that "old squaw remedy" had proved an amazingly constant folk medicine. Originally modified by Mrs. Pinkham from Dr. King's formula, it was updated in 1914 by the addition of dandelion, yellow gentian, and a base of bitter Swiss cordial. About a year later, the alcoholic content was cut to below 15 percent. Still, Federal Food and Drug regulations never affected its contents, not even forcing a change in name, for vegetable compound is what it was and what the label said it was. In the early days of "food and drug exposure," during and right after the First World War, nothing much was directed against Lydia Pinkham's "sure cure," except that it "possessed no distinctive characteristics" and that it "did no one any particular good." The nearest thing to regulation came in 1925 when the Company was forced to change the wording on the bottle, and the nearest thing to a catastrophe occurred in 1938 when the Food and Drug people sent the Federal Trade Commission a report that the Compound was best as a mild stomachic tonic and as good for men as for women. But the Commission sort of "backed down" on this point, and the Company was allowed to keep advertising as before.

Then on November 20, 1973, the following poignant release appeared in the New York *Times:*

When the Lydia E. Pinkham Medicine Company closes its factory in Lynn, Mass., the last of her descendants still working for the corporation will be among those losing their jobs.

Charles Pinkham, the 57-year-old plant manager, and Herman Smith, the 61-year-old production supervisor—both great-grandsons of the woman who formed the company in 1875—were among the heirs who sold the concern to Cooper Laboratories around five years ago. Cooper plans to produce the Vegetable Compound . . . at another of its facilities. . . .

It had been a Quaker enterprise, and at least in the day of the "robber baron" lived up to the *Rules of Discipline and Advice* of the Society of Friends:

We affectionately desire that Friends may wait for Divine counsel in

all their engagements and not suffer their minds to be hurried away by
an inordinate desire for worldly riches; remembering the observation of
the Apostle in his day, so often sorrowfully verified in ours that, "They
that desire to be rich fall into a temptation and a snare and many foolish
and hurtful lusts."

For although the "elixir" led to riches and a few snares it began
in "good works" and for the most part the Company never lost
sight of its founder's transcendental goal.

Mrs. Pinkham's success story was involved in another transcendental goal, the overall emancipation of women, not just from
the prejudices about their bodies, but from the prejudices about
their minds. The Quakers were in the forefront of this reform,
too, for the Society of Friends regarded females as both the
spiritual and mental equals of their brothers, capable of being
"moved" to important action and words by God, worthy of being
given ministerial rank. If the Friends did not expect women to
enter business or the professions, their work, their roles, their
selves were deemed quite as important as anything masculine,
and their ladies grew up confident in themselves, intellectually
free to argue whatever case their "inner light" directed them to
argue. It is no accident that much of the nineteenth-century van-
guard of women's suffrage, women's independence, women's
rights—the Lucretia Motts and the Susan B. Anthonys—came
from the Quaker ranks. M. Carey Thomas, first Dean, then President, always guiding hand of Bryn Mawr College, was one of the
most determined.

There's an old saying about Bryn Mawr—that it is "a men's college for women," and since its founding it has always had the
reputation of bringing together the most intellectual, the most
unorthodox, and the least attractive group of college girls in the
nation. A Bryn Mawrtyr is traditionally a woman who scares
the "everyday young man," who scorns "normal" feminine goals
like motherhood and marriage, and who during the first half of
the twentieth century served as a neo-Gothic symbol for what
has become the "women's libber." To be sure, a college like Bryn
Mawr was inevitable in a democracy like America, as inevitable
as "women's lib" and the movement toward coeducation. But it
came early, and its founders were pioneers.

If the nature of the College had a specific moment of conception, that moment must have come during 1871 in Baltimore, Maryland, when the fourteen-year-old Minnie Thomas wrote in her diary that,

> If I ever live and grow up my *one* aim and concentrated purpose *shall be* and *is* to show that women *can learn, can reason, can compete* with man in the grand fields of literature and science and conjecture that open before the nineteenth century, that a woman can be a woman and a *true* one without having all her time engrossed by dress and society.

But the struggle was long, and before her concept came into being, Minnie Thomas had to labor her way to a doctorate in English literature through the kingdoms of Cornell, Johns Hopkins, Leipzig, and Zurich, had to help nurse the first genuinely scholarly college for "girls only"; and in close to forty years as its Dean and President had to keep up its chin of unashamed (in fact, militant) intellectualism.

Even before she stated her "concentrated purpose" in the diary of 1871, little Minnie Thomas showed her colors, never missing a chance to prove to the local boys that "anything you can do we can do better." Edith Finch, Bryn Mawr '22, author of the definitive biography *Carey Thomas of Bryn Mawr,* cites all sorts of grade school skirmishes involving pushing matches, water fights, and escapades in which the girls, led by Minnie, made sure they held their own against the boys. One anecdote tells of her attempts to catch, kill, and dissect a mouse in order to get its skeleton—an experiment she had characteristically read about in *The Boys' Play Book of Science.* After drowning the mouse in a pail of water, Minnie and her cousin Bessie King began to cut into it. But the mouse's fur was so soft they had trouble puncturing it, and their hands began to tremble and they began to feel sick. Carey concluded, however, that "all such feminine nonsense" had to cease, and so she recalls, "We simply made a hole in him and squeezed his insides out." Another which catches her spirit even better involves her desire to build a telegraph instrument with the same Bessie King similar to one that a college boy Willie Roberts had put together. When her mother heard about it, she told them: "You can't, you're only girls!" "When I heard that," Finch quotes Minnie as writing, "I ground my teeth and swore that no one should say that of us—as if we hadn't as much sense, invention, and perseverance as boys." It is also characteristic that whenever she wrote "boys and girls" in her diary, she crossed it out and changed it to "girls and boys."

Minnie was as voracious a reader and writer as she was sexist. Irritated onward by the belief of her family, teachers, and contemporaries that "women's brains weigh a few ounces less than men's," that there was "a sacred shrine of womanhood" centering about being a wife and mother, that "power, strength, force and intellect" belonged to men just as surely as "sweetness, beauty, and love" belonged to women, she strove to make her own mind the equal of that of her cousin Frank Smith, who, four years older, was preparing himself for entrance to boarding school and then college, goals that were "of course" for him, "out of the question" for her. She spent hours with Frank during her early teen-age years, discussing her readings, his courses, the problems he encountered when he entered Haverford College, and his transfer to Princeton where he felt the intellectual climate was better. Frank's goals, in a real sense, became her goals. She longed to be a doctor, to learn Latin, Greek, German, and French, to study metaphysics and higher math. She seemed fated to marry Frank Smith. Looking back on her youth years later, she wrote that they were probably in love during that time without knowing it. Had she, she might well have entered the "sacred shrine of womanhood" and become one more widely-read Quaker housewife, putting her brilliance into the education of her family, living out her intellectual dreams through one or the other of her children. But she didn't. Frank Smith died of typhoid fever in the summer of 1872, and though she was to consider and reject a proposal of marriage later on, fate had done much to free her toward an education of her own.

Edith Finch goes over the struggle rebuff by rebuff by triumph. It culminates in Switzerland, where Minnie was awarded the second Ph.D. ever earned by a woman, *summa cum laude,* an honor seldom bestowed on any student—much less one who had only her "silly little head" to prepare with. Carey Thomas, as

M. Carey Thomas, first woman president of Bryn Mawr.

she was calling herself by then, wrote her family that it was "the very nicest thing that ever has happened to me except having a nice home and such enlightened parents." Her accomplishment was widely hailed, and it made her a celebrity of sorts, one Philadelphia paper reporting that the examination had lasted "five weeks" and would be followed by "five years" of study in the British Museum. The timing was good, too. Bryn Mawr College, an experimental school that was to use Pallas Athene's Owl of Wisdom as its symbol, was about to receive its charter.

The legendary M. Carey Thomas begins to emerge with her role at the college. Bryn Mawr opened its doors in the fall of 1885 with the new Dr. Thomas as Dean and Professor of English Literature. She had been active in many of the preliminaries, and though she had wanted to be the first president, she was content to work under the more mature, if less spectacular, Dr. Rhoads. He let her, even helped her, make the college hers. And though it didn't happen without a struggle, it was quite natural that she became President when Rhoads stepped down. It was a position she held from 1894 to 1922, by which time both the college and her image were firmly based.

In actuality, the major characteristics of the real Carey Thomas were a zealot's energy, burning determination, extroversion, and a good brain, the whole tempered with generosity, intuition, the ability to laugh at herself, and a real willingness to take advice. The anecdotes that show her as she really was center on these qualities. Edith Finch recalls how, as a stout, lame woman in her sixties she found a church in Sussex locked on the day she had chosen to visit it. Undeterred, she simply tried the windows till she found one that could be forced, then sent her young woman companion through it to unlock the door from the inside. When the rood screen also proved to be locked, Carey Thomas found a space in the grill through which she could clamber after mounting a bench. While this ability to take command of circumstances enabled her to get her doctorate and enabled her to set and hold standards for the institution she was fostering, it also caused her to run roughshod over the various obstacles in her administrative way. As these obstacles were often the opinions of faculty, members of the Board of Trustees, or alumnae, she was continually "on the carpet." But she got in and out of trouble honestly and endearingly, often with a bit of unconscious humor or flair. Once a teacher came to her offices asking for a leave of absence in order to have a baby. "Nonsense!" Dr. Thomas replied. "Have it during summer vacation." Later she was discussing the matter with a friend. "I had to give her a leave of absence," she reflected, "because you know she couldn't have that baby in the summer. I forget, for the moment, the reason why."

There are a legion of anecdotes telling how she hired secretaries, "dorm mothers," even faculty who had no qualifications except the fact that they measured up to Dr. Thomas' intuition. It is no small matter that most of these appointments proved highly successful. An exception, however, was the most famous: Woodrow Wilson, hired this way by Dr. Rhoads and Carey Thomas together. Wilson was added to the Department of History and Political Science, although he had no advanced degree at the time and no experience as a teacher. From the start, he and Carey Thomas didn't get along. For one insurmountable thing, he didn't like aggressive, independent women, being "old school" Southern in this respect. Moreover, he found the atmosphere of Bryn Mawr both too parochial and too zealous, preferring a more outward-looking, relaxed campus. In three years he left, going on to other things.

One of the characteristics of the real Carey Thomas which was particularly annoying to Wilson was her singular inability to participate in or even tolerate "small talk" and "chit-chat." Although she could talk brightly and for hours about "shop," she hadn't the remotest idea of the skill Wilson felt was a *sine qua non* of an appealing female. Nonetheless, Carey Thomas was naturally wise and tolerant. A zealot devoted to the liberation of the thinking woman, she was not one to buck nature. Never a "unisexist," she approved good looks and even good grooming in a woman. It is typical of her that late in her lifetime of battling for female independence, she was able to remark that, *perhaps,* the idea that "there is no way a woman can use her splendid talents better than by being a wife and mother" *might* have a *grain* of truth about it.

To be sure, the legendary Carey Thomas developed and has flourished only within the confines of the Bryn Mawr College student body and Alumnae Association. But even at that, behind George Lyman Kittredge of Harvard and possibly Dean Christian Gauss (of Fitzgerald fame) at Princeton, she may be the American educator about whom the most tales are told "over the teacups." Inevitably, she became both creator of and Platonic Image to what has been termed "the counter-flapper," that excentric, independent, batty, but terribly brainy figure who was synonymous with the word "Bryn Mawr" in the early twentieth century—the slightly masculine Katharine Hepburn taking a shower nude in the fountain in the Cloisters of the College Library; the "mad, bad girl" of the Thurber *New Yorker* cartoon who is high-kicking at a bowler hat held by a man at a cocktail party ("She's all I know about Bryn Mawr and she's all I have to know."); the creature with microscopes for glasses who whispers to her date during the October hay-ride, "Did you find those trial scenes in *The Eumenides* as agonizing as I did?"

Not that there wasn't a good bit of all this in Minnie-Carey-Doctor Thomas. President Taft, father of Helen Taft Manning, a Professor of History and Dean of the College, was greeted by M. Carey Thomas, his daughter, and leaders of the student body each wearing full academic regalia. Vincente Ibáñez, author of *The Four Horsemen of the Apocalypse*, was met by four students mounted on horseback. And Elisabeth of Belgium was hailed by a large portion of the student body who stood on the library steps and cheered for her: "Rah, rah, rah, the Queen of the Belgians!" Moreover, Dr. Thomas had "a way with words" similar to those that movie columnists and sportswriters have ascribed to Sam Goldwyn and Yogi Berra. On one occasion she is supposed to have stated that "Thirty-three percent of the Bryn Mawr alumnae are married and fifty percent have children." On another, speaking of the Versailles plan to put Constantinople under the joint rule of Britain and the United States, she commented that it would be too bad to put that city under the rule of "too sanitary a nation." And entertaining William Butler Yeats at her home, The Deanery, she passed out the usual "wine" for the evening (grape juice). Then, turning to Yeats, she said, "You, Dr. Yeats, you may have claret!" To cheer up one ill companion, she purchased a small mummy case containing the embalmed body of an infant princess. She comforted another, who had just lost her father, by giving her a half-dozen pairs of white gloves which fit her own hands but not those of her friend. Then, one time, she actually threw a copy of Hutchinson's *This Freedom* into the waters of the Bosporus, feeling, quixotically, that its reactionary attitude toward women might confuse her local landlady should that good soul read it at a time when the Turks were making "such great strides" toward the enfranchisement of their women. The story quickly developed into one in which she was so irritated by the male Hutchinson's "chauvinistic" remarks that she hurled the book off the boat in high dudgeon, or better yet, read its worst portions while in the dining salon and, livid, called the steward over and had him pitch it out a porthole.

Today, a mere generation after her death, persons outside, and many persons within, the Bryn Mawr family know nothing about M. Carey Thomas. Like so many figures of local legend, her "heroics" have not gone abroad. In an era of compulsive coeducation, at a time when men as well as women study and take degrees at Bryn Mawr College, where a new library has not only replaced the old one in whose cloisters she is buried but has usurped the site of her campus home, one does realize that Minnie Thomas' "concentrated purpose" which seemed so remote in 1871 has become everyday. And because that purpose is everyday, her struggle toward it is simply ignored, if not utterly forgotten, as a matter of course. Its memory may soon be completely faded, for the Class of '22 (the last to know her as President) is already well beyond woman's "three score and ten." When she died on December 2, 1935, she had already had the experience of being refused admission to the Library during the May Day ceremonies by a guard who didn't know who she was and wouldn't let her in without a ticket—her very own library in which her ashes were to be buried.

Oh, now and then an alum still recalls how she was "that girl" who called "Who's there?" in answer to a knock at her dormitory door one night.

"It's me, M. Carey Thomas," came the voice of the President herself. "Let me in."

"The hell it's you," yelled the girl. "M. Carey Thomas would say, 'It is I'!" And a few freshmen are still told they can see the ghost of Dr. Thomas striding through the Cloisters of the Library during exam week or as the "extra chanter" in the Lantern Night procession. But it is likely her legend really succumbed seven years after her death when a World War II Victory ship was dedicated to her memory—christened for "the former President of Bryn Mawr College: Mrs. Martha C. Thomas."

* * *

There is, alas, a futility in the name of that Victory ship which every female must confront. Of course one can argue that the "ballads of dead ladies" just surveyed are "snows of yesteryear," dead legends from a night that was ended by the ample food supplies, machineries, and contraceptions of an industrial dawn. Tomorrow's ballads will be sung to different tunes. But I, for one, am wondering. Right now humankind huddles confused, not sure where he and she are to turn after their expulsion from the "doll's house." Will "they all" be the generations of M. Carey

Thomas? Can we believe that masculinity, even femininity, will dismiss its golden girls, its Roses; that there actually will be *pas de différence?* We don't, I keep remembering, split in half like amoebae.